D1357312

LUIGI PIRANDELLO

THE THEATRE OF PARADOX

Edited and Introduced by

JULIE DASHWOOD

Library of Congress Cataloging-in-Publication Data

Dashwood, Julie, editor
     Luigi Pirandello: The Theatre of Paradox

ISBN 0-7734-8746-8

Cataloguing information for this volume is available from The Library of Congress
Washington, D.C.

The Edwin Mellen Press
Box 450
Lewiston, New York
USA 14092-0450

The Edwin Mellen Press
Box 67
Queenston, Ontario
Canada LOS 1LO

The Edwin Mellen Press Ltd
Lampeter, Dyfed, Wales
UNITED KINGDOM SA48 7DY

Contents
Acknowledgements
Note on Abbreviations and Translations

Introduction

1

Acknowledgements

We wish to thank the following for permission to quote from already published works:

Biblioteca di Quaderni d'Italianistica, for the extract from *Tonight We Improvise and Leonora Addio!*, translated by J. Douglas Campbell and Leonard G. Sbrocchi, 1987, on pages 86-87.

John Calder and the Riverrun Press for the extract from the *Preface*, translated by Felicity Firth, to *Six Characters in Search of an Author*, edited by Robert Rietty, in *Luigi Pirandello. Collected Plays 2*, 1988, on page 258.

Cambridge University Press, for the extract from Vera Gottlieb, *Chekhov and the Vaudeville*, 1982, on page 115.

Edinburgh University Press, for the extracts from Olga Ragusa, *Luigi Pirandello: An Approach to his Theatre*, 1980, on pages 58 and 63.

Einaudi, for the extract from G. Nencioni, *Tra grammatica e retorica. Da Dante a Pirandello*, 1983, on page 212.

Faber, for the extract from K. Stanislavsky, *Stanislavsky on the Art of Stage*, translated by David Magarsnack, 1961, on page 59.

Felicity Firth, for the extracts from her translation of *I giganti della montagna* [*The Mountain Giants*] in *The Yearbook of the British Pirandello Society*, No. 10, 1990, on pages 52, 59 and 68-69.

Grafton, for the extract from Virginia Woolf, *Orlando*, 1985, on page 203.

Harrap, for the extract from J. A. Henderson, *The First Avant-Garde. 1887-1894. Sources of the Modern French Theatre*, 1971, on page 115.

Harwood Academic Publishers, for the extract from Susan Bassnett and Jennifer Lorch (editors), *Luigi Pirandello in the Theatre*, 1991, on page 283.

Macmillan Publishers, for the extract from Susan Bassnett McGuire, *Luigi Pirandello*, 1983, on page 55.

Northwestern University Press, for the extract from Eric Bentley, *The Pirandello Commentaries*, 1986, on pages 52-53.

Penguin Books, for the extract from F. Dostoyevsky, *Notes from Underground*, translated by J. Coulson, on page 117.

Romance Studies, for permission to reproduce the essay by Ann Hallamore Caesar, on pages 197-209.

The Scarecrow Press, for the extract from A. Richard Sogliuzzo, *Luigi Pirandello, Director: The Playwright in the Theatre*, 1982, on pages 58-59.

The Johns Hopkins University Press, for the extract from Tony Tanner, *Adultery and the Novel. Contract and Transgression*, 1979, quoted on pages 173-174.

UTET, for the extracts from Gaspare Giudice, *Luigi Pirandello*, 1963, on pages 56 and 159.

We also thank Arnaldo Mondadori, Milan, for the assurance that the works of Luigi Pirandello are at present in the public domain.

Every effort has been made to trace copyright holders. If any have been omitted, we would be pleased to include them in future editions of this volume.

We wish to express our warmest thanks to Richard Mobbs, of the Computer Centre at the University of Leicester, for his unstinting help in preparing camera-ready copy for this volume. The editor wishes to express her personal thanks to all the contributors, and especially to Laura Lepschy and Jennifer Lorch for their advice and support at all stages of this volume, to the Edwin Mellen Press, and to Alan Dashwood, whose contribution to her work and well-being has been, and remains, immeasurable.

A note on abbreviations

Unless otherwise indicated, the references to Pirandello's works in this book
are to the edition in six volumes published by Mondadori, Milan, in the series
'I classici contemporanei italiani' and directed by G. Ferrata. The following
abbreviations have been used:

NA, I,   *Novelle per un anno*, vol. I, 1957.

NA, II,   *Novelle per un anno*, vol. II, 1957.

TR,   *Tutti i romanzi*, 1966 (4th ed.).

MN, I,   *Maschere nude*, I, 1958.

MN, II,   *Maschere nude*, II, 1958.

SPSV,   *Saggi, poesie, scritti vari*, 1965 (2nd ed.)

A note on translations

Most of the translations of passages from Pirandello's works are by the editor
in collaboration with the individual contributor. Where other translations have
been used acknowledgement is made in the relevant chapter.

INTRODUCTION

The purpose of this book can be stated quite simply: it is to offer a series of essays which will enable readers, whether or not they be students of Italian or Drama, to broaden and deepen their knowledge of one of Europe's major writers. Great claims have been made for Pirandello's influence on the drama of the twentieth century. Robert Brustein, for example, in his book *The Theatre of Revolt*, lists twelve playwrights whose work, he says, was anticipated by that of Pirandello, and he concludes that: 'the extent of even this partial list of influences marks Pirandello as the most seminal dramatist of our time'.[1] James McFarlane re-states Brustein's evaluation, adding to that: 'it has taken much time to see just how deep and pervasive Pirandello's influence on twentieth-century drama has been, and indeed continues to be'.[2] Part of the difficulty inherent in assessing the extent of Pirandello's influence on subsequent writers stems without doubt from the fact that he is still, in the English-speaking world, an author associated with, at best, a handful of plays, including *Sei personaggi in cerca d'autore* [Six Characters in Search of an Author], *Enrico IV* [Henry IV] and, possibly *Vestire gli ignudi* [To Clothe the Naked] and *L'uomo, la bestia e la virtù* [Man, Beast and Virtue]. Outside Italy, and with the possible exception of France, his other plays are still rarely performed, and he is scarcely known at all as a writer of poetry, novels, short stories and essays. Drawing up a balance-sheet for our author for 1991 Eric Bentley writes that, while Pirandello is recognised as a seminal writer, he is 'ignored by the reading public'.[3] It is clear, then, that much remains to be done if we, outside Italy, are to arrive at a better-informed view of Pirandello and his work. The task certainly has its arduous side, as indeed does the search to understand much of the literature and art of Pirandello's times. There is, however, 'another Pirandello waiting for a new generation to go out and find him', as Susan Bassnett puts it,[4] and it is to this new generation, young or old, that we address these essays.

Sicily and the Nineteenth Century

We should not, however, lose sight of the fact that this seminal figure for twentieth-century theatre had his roots deep in the preceding century. Close to the beginning of his biography of Pirandello Gaspare Giudice, rightly, criticises those (the majority) who think of Pirandello exclusively in terms of the twentieth century. As Giudice reminds us at the turn of the century Pirandello was 33, almost halfway through his life, and the ensuing 15 years were spent in pre-First World War, Giolittian, Italy.[5] Of equal importance, as Giudice emphasises in his first chapter, is the fact that Pirandello was born not in mainland Italy but in Sicily, and only a few years after Sicily had become part of the newly-united Kingdom of Italy. In many ways, history and geography seem inextricable in Pirandello's formation, and it is to them that we should now, briefly, turn our attention.

Pirandello was born on 28 June 1867 just outside Agrigento (which at the time was called Girgenti) on the south coast of Sicily. Just over seven years previously, in April 1860, there had been popular uprisings in Palermo and elsewhere in Sicily against the ruling Bourbon monarchy. These were quickly suppressed, but as a result Giuseppe Garibaldi, the great popular hero of the Italian Risorgimento, was persuaded to sail to Sicily with the force he had gathered at Quarto, to the east of Genoa. He and his famous 'Thousand' landed unopposed at Marsala on the west coast of Sicily on 11 May 1860, and by the end of July 1860 he was in control of the whole of Sicily. He then crossed to mainland Italy and entered Naples on 7 September 1860. The king of Naples and Sicily at the time was Francesco II, whose family, the Bourbons, had been restored to the throne of the Kingdom of the Two Sicilies, as it then became known, by the Congress of Vienna in 1814-1815. As a result of Garibaldi's expedition Francesco II and his family withdrew to Gaeta in the North of their kingdom. A plebiscite was held on 28 October 1860 during which the people of Sicily and of the mainland part of the Bourbon kingdom voted overwhelmingly for annexation by the kingdom of Piedmont-Sardinia and its king Vittorio Emanuele II. The Bourbon troops surrendered at Capua on 2 November, and Francesco II took refuge in Rome, which was not to become a part of the kingdom of Italy until 1870. Vittorio Emmanuele II was declared king of a united Italy in March 1861.

On both sides of Pirandello's family there were supporters of Garibaldi. His father, Stefano, the descendant of immigrants to Sicily from Liguria, fought against the Bourbon troops when Garibaldi reached Palermo in 1860. He then followed Garibaldi through Sicily and across to the mainland, fighting both at Reggio and on the Volturno. Two years later he joined Garibaldi's ill-fated attempt to seize Rome for the kingdom of Italy, which was stopped by the army of the kingdom of Italy itself at Aspromonte in Calabria. At this point Stefano Pirandello decided to avoid capture and to flee for home.[6] On his return to Sicily he was sent to manage some sulphur mines which his family had rented near Agrigento, and there, in November 1863, he married Caterina Ricci Gramitto.

The Ricci Gramitto family had been involved for much longer, and much more closely, in the struggle against the Bourbon monarchy. Caterina's father, Giovanni, was a lawyer from Agrigento whose political credo was both anti-Bourbon and separatist. He was involved in the uprisings in Palermo in 1848 and became a Minister in the provisional government set up in Palermo in the same year by Ruggiero Settimo. With his family, including Caterina, he went into exile on Malta after the failure of the 1848 revolution, and there he died after making his wife and children swear that they would fight for the liberation of Sicily from the Bourbons.[7] He greatly influenced his children who, after the annexation of Sicily to Italy, saw mainly the harm and wrongs done to their island by successive Italian governments. Giudice tells us that Giovanni's wife, Anna Bartoli, and their children were among the few in Agrigento who actively supported Garibaldi. When one of these children, Innocenzo, later fought against Garibaldi's army at Aspromonte in 1862 his mother banished him for years from the family. The marriage between Caterina and Stefano Pirandello was, says Giudice, a patriotic one, born of the fervour of the times.[8]

Pirandello, however, belongs to a different, and unheroic, age. When he writes about the Risorgimento it is in order to voice the profound sense of disillusionment in Sicily which followed on from the previous aspirations and idealism. Donna Caterina Auriti, in the novel *I vecchi e i giovani* [The Old and the Young] (1911), speaks for many of Pirandello's characters when she hurls abuse at corrupt governments in Rome, and bitterly tells her son that Sicily is now treated as a conquered land and its people as barbarians. For his own part Pirandello experienced and described the contradictions and conflicts of the age of transition through which he lived. To use the title of one of his volumes of poems, he felt he was 'fuori di chiave', that is, out of tune, discordant, talking wildly and saying what was inopportune.

Pirandello left Sicily when he was 20. After a brief period at the University of Palermo, he moved on to La Sapienza University in Rome, and then, after a quarrel with his Professor of Latin, Onorato Occioni, who was also the Rector of the University, he was encouraged to study in Germany, at the University of Bonn, by another of his professors, Ernesto Monaci. There he graduated on 21 March 1891 with a doctoral thesis on the dialect of Agrigento, after which he went back to Sicily only to return to Rome later in the same year. His twelve plays in Sicilian dialect, as well as the subject of his doctoral thesis, are nevertheless clear proof of his lasting Sicilian identity. Moreover, his fiction is peopled by Sicilians, especially by poor Sicilian peasants. The Pirandello family owned and managed sulphur mines in Sicily, and although Pirandello's father did not always manage his financial affairs well he was mostly able to provide his wife and children with a reasonable degree of middle-class comfort. Until 1903, when Stefano Pirandello lost all his capital, as well as his daughter-in-law's dowry, his son could rely on him for financial support. In contrast, the general economic decline in Sicily in the nineteenth century, which was accelerated after the unification of Italy by the heavy taxation imposed on the island, led millions of Sicilians to emigrate, while cholera outbreaks, including one at the time of Pirandello's birth, were frequent. The sheer poverty and hardship of the lives of the Sicilian peasants left a lasting impression on Pirandello, as did the characteristics of the Sicilians. Indeed, Giudice argues that the reticence, secrecy, allusiveness and explosiveness of the Sicilians are captured in Pirandello's very style.[9]

Dominating ideas in Pirandello's works, such as strongly anarchic and individualistic tendencies which are curbed and repressed by rigid social norms, a strict concept of individual and family honour and the vital importance of land, property and possessions for the construction of identity can all be traced back to his Sicilian roots. In the play *Il berretto a sonagli* [Cap and Bells] (1918) Ciampa's rigid insistence on the maintenance of his honour clashes with Beatrice's anarchic desire to free herself from society's restraints and to shout out to all that her husband and Ciampa's wife are having an affair. The outcome is that she is forced to play, or become, the madwoman and sent to a mental home, while Ciampa himself appears to disintegrate at the end of the play. If appearances are not maintained, even at the cost of concealing private suffering, chaos and madness ensue. Pirandello, who was born just outside Agrigento at a place significantly called Càvusu (Chaos) referred to himself as the son of chaos, and the threat of chaos and anarchy hangs over all his works.

The First World War

In 1891 Pirandello settled in Rome. He frequented the same literary circles as some of his fellow-Sicilians, but maintained a certain aloofness from them and spent his time reading and writing, especially poetry, short stories and reviews. In January 1894, at the instigation of his father, he married Antonietta

Portulano, the daughter of his father's business associate. Their three children, Stefano, Lietta and Fausto, were born, respectively, in 1895, 1897 and 1899. In 1897 Pirandello obtained a teaching post at the Magistero, a training college in Rome for women. He seems, initially, to have been happy in his marriage, but in 1903 disaster struck. Pirandello's father had invested Antonietta's dowry, and his own capital, in a sulphur mine. When this became flooded all the money was lost. Pirandello returned home one afternoon to discover that Antonietta, who had received the bad news in a letter from Agrigento, was semi-paralysed by it. He suddenly had to face both the crisis of Antonietta's illness and serious financial need. His salary from the Magistero was meagre, and he had to supplement it by giving German and Italian lessons. He had also to try to make more money from his writing, and he wrote his novel *Il fu Mattia Pascal* [The Late Mattia Pascal] (1904) at night, while watching over his wife. The pressing need for money to support his family meant that Pirandello had to continue to teach, a job he greatly disliked, until 1922.

The following years were very difficult. Antonietta slowly recovered from the paralysis, but she began increasingly to show signs of paranoia. From 1909 onwards quarrels, separations and reconciliations followed on from each other. Antonietta became obsessively jealous of Pirandello's students at the Magistero. Her persecution mania became so serious during the war years that she came to suspect her daughter, Lietta, of trying to poison her, and even that Pirandello and Lietta were having an incestuous relationship. Lietta attempted suicide, and Pirandello was forced to send his daughter to live with an aunt in Florence. When his son Stefano returned from the war the family agreed that Antonietta should be institutionalised, and at the beginning of 1919 she was committed to a nursing home in Rome, the Villa Giuseppina, where she remained until her death thirty years later. Giudice says that she is the model for the repressed and hysterical wife in Pirandello's short story *La realtà del sogno* [The Reality of the Dream] (1914), whose jealous and tyrannical father had inculcated into her a profound terror of men.[10] What he does not say is that the husband in the story acts in complete accordance with the Sicilian code, which Pirandello shared, of keeping up appearances. The wife has an erotic dream and then, the following day, lives out her dream in front of her husband and the male friend who had appeared in her dream. She writhes on the floor in an onset of hysteria and madness but, chillingly, before he helps his wife the husband escorts his friend to the door and apologises for her behaviour. Only then does he rush back to deal with what he obviously regards as a problem which, as far as possible, should be hidden from public, or male public, view. It is impossible to know how far this fictional account corresponds to any event in Antonietta's, or Pirandello's, life. But the madman in Pirandello's works is accorded the status of the wise fool, while the madwoman has to be put away, or kept out of sight.

A different picture can be found in the book which Antonietta's granddaughter based on the letters between her mother, grandmother and grandfather. She says that she found in them clear proof that her mother, Lietta, hoped to bring Antonietta out of the Villa Giuseppina, and came to think that Pirandello's father, Calogero Portulano (Antonietta's father), Pirandello himself and her own father, Manuel might have been in part responsible for the tragedy in the lives of both Antonietta and Lietta. She goes on to say that Pirandello was a writer who fed on his own torments, and those of others, in order to create his fictional characters, and that this was at the cost of the women in his family.[11] Whatever the case, it is clear that Pirandello experienced madness, and the disparity between public manners and private suffering, at first hand.

The war years caused him great suffering in other ways. His elder son, Stefano, went to fight in the Italian army as a volunteer, and his younger son, Fausto, was called up as soon as he was of age. Both sons contracted tuberculosis, and Stefano was taken prisoner by the Austrians in 1915. Although Pirandello tried to have him released, he remained in prison until the end of the war. The tragic experiences of this period led Pirandello to a sense of personal and generational crisis which is the leitmotiv of his writings, in this period and beyond. It is a crisis that can be seen at all levels in his favourite novella *Berecche e la guerra* [Berecche and the War], written and published in stages during the war years but not given its final form until 1934.[12]

Berecche, the father-figure in the story, has like Pirandello been educated in what are called the German disciplines of History and Philology. His admiration for Germany is boundless, and he has created for himself a 'German' identity which is heroic, masculine and patriarchal. He rigorously and methodically imposes his 'German-ness' on his family, giving his children germanic names, for example, and forcing them to live on the edge of Rome where the setting is almost a parody of a nordic construct of Italy. This is just one of the many simulacra in a story where attempts to legitimate identity collapse under the weight of the historical circumstances of the war years. Italy had joined the Triple Alliance with Germany and Austro-Hungary in 1882, but declared her neutrality when war broke out claiming that the pact was only a defensive one. There followed, in Italy, a nine-month campaign for intervention on the side of the Triple Entente, comprising Britain, France and Russia. The interventionists, whose leaders included Benito Mussolini and the writer and sometime politician Gabriele D'Annunzio, carried the day. Italy changed alliances and declared war first on Austria in 1915 and then on Germany in 1916. Berecche had loudly proclaimed the need to fight on the side of Germany, but now that Germany is the enemy his dilemma becomes unbearable. His son, also Fausto, goes off heroically to fight on the side of the Entente, and as Berecche is too old to follow him he is forced into non-participation, into impotence. Pirandello found himself in an analogous situation.

The interventionist current which sweeps Fausto into the war has very precise implications for Pirandello in another way. He greatly disliked D'Annunzio, but D'Annunzio's interventionist rhetoric, which in the story has a powerful appeal for Fausto, was intended to revive the patriotic fervour of the Risorgimento, and of the garibaldine tradition in particular. Implicit in the text is the sense of a double usurpation: of the authority of fathers by their sons, and also of the tradition which was Pirandello's own, here used to send those much-loved sons to a likely death. Pirandello uses the metaphor of the 'theatre of war' in *Berecche e la guerra*, and perhaps even from this brief analysis of the story we can begin to see why he later said that he perceived the need for theatre rather than narrative during the war, and why his theatre is one of conflict, crisis and paradox. Too young to have participated in the Risorgimento, too old to fight in the war, and with the world 'in movement' around him he came to think that theatre was the only possible form for the age.

Fascism

Pirandello joined the Fascist party in September 1924, in circumstances which continue to cause great problems for his biographers, critics, readers and directors. By this time, after the success of *Sei personaggi in cerca d'autore* (1921) and *Enrico IV* (1922) he had gained an international reputation as a playwright. When he first met Mussolini in October 1923 his plays had been performed from London and New York to Paris and Prague, and certainly Mussolini was eager to enrol him as a supporter of the Fascist regime. On his side, Pirandello was flattered by the attention shown to him by the Duce, and spoke of him in very positive, if pirandellian, terms. In an interview of 1924 Pirandello declared that he was apolitical, but then in the same interview went on to criticise democracy.[13] Mussolini's regime was then in its infancy, and had not yet begun to introduce the repressive measures which followed later in the 1920s, but this is not the point at issue. The inescapable fact is that Pirandello became a member of the Fascist party after a Socialist Member of Parliament, Giacomo Matteotti, had criticised the Fascist regime and had then been murdered by right-wing extremists. After the murder of Matteotti there was a great outcry in Italy, which Pirandello must have been aware of. Nevertheless he became a Fascist because of the difficulties faced by the party as a result of the murder of Matteotti, as is made clear by the letter he sent to Mussolini asking to become a party member. In conversation and in interviews in 1924 he made this position even clearer.[14] His action was immediately seized on for propaganda purposes by Fascist newspapers.

Attempts to explain his decision remain highly speculative. Pirandello did not have a coherent political position, but as we have seen he witnessed the betrayal of the ideals of the Risorgimento, for Sicily in particular. He was also keenly aware of the corruption and scandals which marked the pre-war Liberal regime in Italy, and he experienced directly the conflicting and contradictory ideologies in Italy during the first World War. The failure of the pre-war ruling classes may well have induced him to share the illusion of other Italian intellectuals of his time that 'Fascism would provide a solution to the various problems which agitated the contemporary mind'.[15]

After showing some sympathy for early Socialism, Pirandello became anti-socialist and anti-democratic. Mattia Pascal is a spokesman in this instance when he says that democracy, and government by the majority, is the real source of present evils, as one man in government knows that he has to please the many, but democrats in the same position think only of pleasing themselves, so that they are tyrants masquerading as democrats. What Pirandello, like his character Lando Laurentano in *I vecchi e i giovani*, possibly wanted was not the dictatorship of the proletariat but cooperation between the different social classes, and in this he has been seen as a forerunner of the Fascist Corporate State.[16]

These explanations certainly help to explain the attraction of Fascism for Pirandello, as does his pleasure at finally, in his mid-fifties, obtaining recognition abroad and at home. But what interests us in particular is his desire to persuade Mussolini of the need for a national, state-funded theatre, or to put it in more abstract terms to 'achieve a reconciliation or synthesis' between Fascism and culture.[17] The problem is that Pirandello sought financial support from the regime, and declared his allegiance to Mussolini, in the worst possible circumstances, and his gesture has dogged his reputation ever since. Although he rapidly became disillusioned with the Fascist government he remained in the Fascist Party all his life, at times acting as its ambassador, and he became a member of the Fascist Academy in 1929, when Mussolini finally succeeded in setting it up.

He never achieved a synthesis with the Fascist regime, and attempts to establish links between some of his later plays and Fascist ideology are questionable. It may be possible to argue that *Lazzaro* [Lazarus] (1928) encapsulates to some extent Mussolini's desire to 'ruralise' Italy, but it is difficult to see in Sara, the mother in the play of two families, one legitimate and the other illegitimate, the ideal type of Fascist motherhood. Others of the later plays seem to contain a critique of what the regime was trying to achieve, and to signal that reconciliation between culture and Fascism was impossible. So in *I giganti della montagna* [The Mountain Giants], a play Pirandello never finished, the gulf between the marginalised representatives of culture and the violent and unjust holders of political and economic power cannot be bridged. The dispositions Pirandello made for his funeral clearly show his distance by then from the government. Far from asking for state obsequies he wanted death to be passed over in silence, and his funeral to be of the humblest kind. He asked to be cremated and for his ashes to be scattered, and failing this, he requested that his funeral urn should be taken to Sicily and interred in the place where he was born.

The Theatre [18]

There were few playwrights of note in Italy during the nineteenth century, and working conditions for theatrical companies, particularly after the unification of Italy, were poor. The royal houses of Turin, Milan, Parma and Naples had each subsidised a company which had the right to perform in their theatres, but when Vittorio Emanuele II of Savoy became king of Italy in 1861 the other royal houses disappeared. The Italian State decided that education and the army were the best means of uniting the country, so theatre was left to its own devices, and although the newly-established municipalities renovated some of the old opera-houses, or built new ones, they considered that giving financial support to theatrical companies was not their responsibility. The government itself continued with the tradition of the House of Savoy of offering the prize to the winning playwright in national competitions, but would go no further than that. Otherwise, it made its presence felt by imposing taxes particularly in relation to copyright, but apparently these were easily avoided. The companies which had not had the privilege (called 'il privilegio') of playing in the royal theatres remained much as they were before unification, that is, privately-run and itinerant, with the difference that there were now far more companies competing to rent theatres for short seasons.

One result of the economic difficulties experienced by the companies was the emergence of the star actor, or *mattatore,* who was seen as essential in order to attract the rather sparse theatre-going public of the time and so to ensure box-office success. [19] Some of the star actors of the mid to late nineteenth century, such as Adelaide Ristori, Ernesto Rossi, Tommaso Salvini and, later, Eleonora Duse reached international celebrity, and toured extensively abroad. Because of them theatre acquired a new respectability in Italy, and sometimes they had an influence which went well beyond the stage. Apocryphal stories abound. It was said, for example, that Adelaide Ristori was able to persuade the Queen of Spain to reprieve a prisoner who had been condemned to death, and that in Brazil Ernesto Rossi freed a child from slavery. But the star actors were few in number, and most Italian actors were simply on stage to support the star, while outside the theatre they often led lives of poverty. Even the top companies were usually small, and consisted of a producer ('capocomico'),a leading man ('primo attore'), a leading lady ('prima attrice'), a comic actor ('brillante'), a character actor ('caratterista'), a mother ('madre'), a male juvenile lead ('primo attore giovane'), a female juvenile lead ('prima attrice giovane'), a second actress ('seconda donna'), an actor able to take on various minor roles ('promiscuo') and a number of bit-part players ('generici'). [20] It was a hierarchical structure which militated against good ensemble playing, and the status of the actors depended on that of the roles they played. Given the itinerant nature of the companies scenery, and, except for the wealthy, costumes and props had to be kept to a minimum. The performance schedule, however, was punishing, leaving little time for rehearsal and making great demands on the learning powers of the leading actors. Parts had to be memorised quickly, and not all actors were conscientious in learning their lines. As a result, the prompter came to be an important figure, and not only when actors forgot their lines. The prompter's voice could be heard throughout the performance, as he would speak all the lines in a tone audible to both actors and audience and so fill any unscheduled pause in the action of the play. Knowing this, we have a different slant on the figure of the prompter in *Sei personaggi in cerca d'autore*. When he is told to write down the exchanges between the Characters he performs a different, less intrusive and, for Pirandello, more useful task than his usual one.

But the fact that the prompter spoke all the lines does not imply great respect for the dramatic text in nineteenth-century theatre. On the contrary, the text was seen as a vehicle for performance, and amendments and cuts were frequently made, while the leading actors felt free to vary the tone of their acting to the point of radically altering the genre they were playing. So when the three great star actors of the time - Ristori, Rossi and Salvini - came together in Florence for a performance of Silvio Pellico's *Francesca da Rimini* in 1865, Salvini made of Francesca's husband not a murdering monster but an affectionate man, deeply wronged and worthy of compassion. Actors would also move quite gratuitously from tragedy to comedy within a single play, and Pirandello criticised these practices. For him the dramatic text was sacrosanct. But one wonders if he did not, in part at least, draw on these acting techniques when creating a character who slips in and out of his roles, such as Enrico IV.

Pirandello had begun to write for the theatre when he was quite young, and although little of these youthful attempts remains letters and photographs show his early interest in theatre. He was fiercely critical of the theatre and the dramatists of his times. He insisted throughout his career on the primacy of the dramatic text and the need for authorial control, perhaps understandably given the lack of respect we have seen shown towards the text by certain actors. While he was doubtful that a performance could ever be a faithful translation onto the stage of the author's text, Pirandello thought that it was the task of the actor to respect that text to the full when giving life to a character. One can understand his fury, therefore, when the actress Irma Gramatica shifted the focus of his play *Se non così* [If Not Like This] [21] for its first performance in Milan in April 1915. In the play a middle-class woman uses moral blackmail to force her husband's lover to hand over their illegitimate son to her. For Pirandello the play revolved around the drama of the infertile wife, but Irma Gramatica declared her intention to play the part of the lover, who had more dramatic and affecting scenes. This actress had a powerful stage presence, and the character of the lover stole the show. [22]

Other sources of dissatisfaction were the theatrical genres and repertoire which dominated the Italian stage. Pirandello criticised the poor writing and bad acting which he thought characterised naturalistic theatre, and he also attacked the prevalence of translations of French plays, mostly farces or well-made plays, in the Italian repertoire. He had little in common with the mostly fragmentary and iconoclastic theatre of the futurists. His greatest wrath was, however, reserved for Gabriele D'Annunzio, a man close to him in age but very different as a playwright. D'Annunzio became interested in theatre when he met the actress Eleonora Duse in 1896, and with her he sketched out plans for a new theatre and its future home.[23] D'Annunzio's models were to be Greek classical theatre and Renaissance experiments with musical drama, the theory and practice of Wagner and the ideas of Nietzsche. The new theatre was to be an open-air amphitheatre on the shore of Lake Albano where there would be productions of classical tragedies and of D'Annunzio's own plays. These plans were never realised, as like D'Annunzio's desire for a total theatre fusing words, movement, spectacle, music and dance they proved too demanding, economically as well as artistically. Conceptually the two playwrights could not have been further apart. D'Annunzio wanted a mass, open-air theatre constructed on a huge scale, while Pirandello's greatest plays are physically and psychologically 'inner', probing into the human psyche. Professional rivalry, too, had its part, as before Pirandello won success as a playwright the most popular Italian play was D'Annunzio's *La figlia di Iorio* [Iorio's Daughter] (1904), but although Pirandello produced this play in 1934 he remained firmly anti-dannunzian throughout his career.

By the time Pirandello began to write intensively for the theatre during and after the first World War some of the problems facing Italian theatre were beginning to be resolved. The system of star actors was in decline, and the voice of the prompter was no longer an inescapable aspect of performance. But he thought more was required than the gradual disappearance of some negative factors. He came to the conclusion that the only lasting solution to the problems lay in the creation of a state-subsidised theatre so that theatrical companies had some financial security, proper time for rehearsal and the opportunity to devise a well-planned repertoire. This was why he continued, at least officially, to support Mussolini.

Success as a playwright came to Pirandello when he was in his mid-fifties, and as well as writing plays in rapid succession he also completed his last novel, *Uno, nessuno e centomila* [One, No-one and a Hundred Thousand] (1925). His reputation spread with equal rapidity and he was finally able to realise his desire to establish a Teatro d'Arte [Art Theatre], which opened on 2 April 1925. As well as writing plays for the company, and for its leading actress, Marta Abba, in particular, Pirandello also became a director, and haunted the Teatro Odescalchi in Rome where the company was housed. The years of the Teatro d'Arte were fulfilling ones for Pirandello, and he was delighted by the successful tours which took the company as far as South America. However, the government withdrew its subsidy to the company in 1928, and because of the financial problems which ensued it had to close. After the collapse of his dream Pirandello decided to leave Italy, and for the next five years he lived in Germany and France, working for the cinema as well as the theatre. He returned to Italy in 1933, but even the award of the Nobel Prize for Literature in 1934 did little to dispel his bitterness at what for him was the insufficient support and recognition he now received in Italy. He died on 10 December 1936 after leaving instructions, as we have seen, that he should have a pauper's funeral.

The Essays

The revival of interest in Pirandello's theatre came in the 1950s and 1960s when he was viewed as a precursor of Existentialism and the Theatre of the Absurd. However, with few exceptions his plays and his other writings continued to be little-known. Only over the last 10 to 15 years has there been a gradual reassessment of his contribution to the theatre and he is now seen not just as an experimental playwright or a pre-existentialist philosophical writer but as a man of the theatre.[24] His work has also been analysed from the point of view of recent developments in the textual analysis of gender relations.[25] Finally, we now have an extensive, and much-needed, account of his involvement with cinema.[26] But much remains to be done to make texts, performances and sheer information available in English. In order to provide some guidance for the reader, the essays in this volume have been grouped very loosely under the four headings of issues of theory, issues of genre, issues of gender and issues of language and theatre, although the essays themselves were conceived autonomously.

1. Issues of Theory

When discussing Pirandello's theoretical writings it is still customary to concentrate on the early essays and articles, and on *L'Umorismo* [Humorism] (1908) in particular, extrapolating certain ideas from them and isolating them from the later writings on theatre. In the first essay in this volume Éanna Ó Ceallacháin redresses the balance and examines the full range of Pirandello's ideas on theatre, relating them to the general aesthetic concerns which form the background to his writings on theatre. He moves from the time when Pirandello, then in his early thirties, showed great suspicion of theatre to the later years when he became the defender of theatre as a sacred heritage. Ó Ceallacháin's detailed analysis shows that Pirandello is preoccupied with the process of literary creation and the centrality of the character to the creative process, and that he is acutely aware of the incompatibilities between art and life. Under the impact of changing personal circumstances, cultural trends and historical developments, though, his approaches vary, and inherent in these changes are notions of contrast and contradiction, leading to the 'doubling' of every idea in the appearance of its opposite. Complementing the first essay, Mary Casey takes a comparative approach to issues of theory in Pirandello, arguing that Pirandello's near-obsession with role play and self-invention validates comparisons with Stanislavsky. In examining the extent to which he is both a playwright for a Stanislavsky-trained actor and one who poses problems for such an actor, we move to the point of view of the actor and the director. Mary Casey reminds us that Pirandello's theories on acting are most clearly articulated in his plays, and shows how his critique of acting becomes a critique of director's theatre in *Questa sera si recita a soggetto* [Tonight We Improvise] (1929). But, she concludes, in spite of all his experience in the theatre in the 1920s, Pirandello's theatre remains an 'author's theatre' while Stanislavsky's is an 'actor's theatre'.

2. Issues of Genre

Art, wrote Pirandello, should not be based on a formula, a system, a pretence or a pre-established method.[27] In the second group of essays, John Barnes gives us the first complete account of Pirandello's fiction as evidence of his interest in theatre and cinema, and concludes that he was forever probing his themes in different ways and continually experimenting with new artistic forms. All the present essays, in their different ways, exemplify what John Barnes says. Barnes points out that, while few of Pirandello's fictional writings contain a great variety of references to theatre, the forms chosen are all unique. So Pirandello wrote one cinema novel, one theatre novel, one short story set in the theatre, another focusing on a playwright and his play, one where Sicilian puppet theatre is prominent and one coloured by opera, and this suggests a continuous process of experimentation with genre which can be found throughout Pirandello's writings. Pirandello began to write one-act plays at a time when this genre was acquiring autonomy and respectability, when it was, in fact, becoming a genre. The second essay in this group examines the context within which Pirandello began to write for the theatre, seeing his earliest completed one-acts as stagings of 'psychic murder'. Pirandello derived many of his plays from his own earlier works, and ten of his one-acts were based on his short stories, so he was a transformer of genres as well as an experimenter with individual genres. Two of his transformations are discussed in detail in this essay, and we see that they have very different results. The first remains within the area of naturalism, while the second defamiliarizes some of the most banal of everyday events. The third essay concerns Pirandello's use, and questioning, of historical drama, a genre very popular at the time. Pirandello parodies the forms and conventions of his time, in particular the preference for the static and the detailed search for minutely accurate historical reconstruction. In so doing he also questions and parodies mimetic art, and his play *Enrico IV* becomes an exploration not of the external world but of the creative mind at work. But Pirandello's ceaseless experimentation did not stop there. Fulvia Airoldi Namer's essay examines Pirandello's 'myth' plays which were written (the exception is *I giganti della montagna,* which was never completed) in the late 1920s. She examines the meaning of the term 'myth' as used by Pirandello and discusses the vexed question of the chronology of the myths, then gives a detailed analysis of the search for an inner truth which leads Pirandello to create some of his greatest roles for women. His inability to finish *I giganti della montagna,* though, is seen as the extreme outcome in his writings of the recurring, and irreconcileable, conflict between life and art.

3. Issues of Gender

As we have said, there are some excellent roles for women in Pirandello's theatre waiting to be explored. In *Vestire gli ignudi* mention is made of Pirandello's earlier novel, *L'Esclusa* [The Excluded Woman] (1901). These two works, the novel and the play, and their respective female protagonists, Marta Ajala and Ersilia Drei, are discussed in the first of the essays in the section on issues of gender. Felicity Firth shows that Pirandello had a predilection for adultery, and for female adultery in particular. *L'Esclusa* is a disorienting novel which subverts the genre of adultery. The major features of realism, such as causality, verisimilitude, motivation and plentiful background detail are all parodied in a transitional novel which is an epitaph to the realist mode. For Felicity Firth *L'Esclusa*, like *Il fu Mattia Pascal*, is an existential metaphor about the nature of awareness, identity and freedom, and she goes even further, saying that they are the same novel. As well as a valuable contribution to our understanding of these novels this interpretation also helps to substantiate the argument advanced in the second half of this essay. Ersilia Drei is dispossessed from the beginning of *Vestire gli ignudi*, and she is judged and condemned by masculine law. Surrounded by vampiric characters who see her only as an extension of themselves she cannot have or does not want the identities which are associated with her. Pirandello's male characters find themselves in the most irreparably absurd situations, but they are never so dispossessed or exposed to the same voyeuristic gaze as is Ersilia. Ann Hallamore Caesar extends the debate on the woman question in the 1920s to a discussion of plays by Bontempelli and Wedekind, as well as Pirandello's *Come tu mi vuoi* [As You Desire Me] (1929). Female identity becomes concentrated on surface, and by extension costume, in part because of the impact of cinema. The plays in question rely on the visual representation of the woman protagonist for their effect, and there is a shift away from attention to the spoken word. The shift, though, is not purely technical, but rather carries an ideological price for women. She argues that Pirandello's work should prompt further exploration of the complex interaction between culture and technology.

4. Issues of Language and Theatre

Pirandello's theatre requires a particularly acute attention to dialogue. Laura Lepschy analyses the syntactical patterns of *Bellavita* (1928) and *Tutto per bene* [All for the Best] (1920) to show the link between the dialogue form and certain themes in these plays. She shows that through the use of repetitions, exclamations, interrogations and suspensions the pace of the plays becomes emotional and excited, and that syntax and dialogue reveal the shifts within the characters themselves and indicate the different outcomes of the plot for the characters. It is an analysis which should be extended to Pirandello's theatre in general. A study of the texts from this point of view would surely aid delivery and performance, and enable us better to understand Pirandello's creation of a new language for the theatre. *Sei personaggi in cerca d'autore* was originally conceived as a novel, but, Corrado Donati argues, the state of conflict between the characters makes dialogic formulation of the projected novel impossible. The play is, therefore, a theatrical exploitation of verbal and instinctual chaos at the expense of the story, and the only possible form for this chaos is dramatic. Theatre, and all its signifying practices, are put on trial, as Pirandello seeks a new language of the theatre which can encompass the drama of rejection, the absence of the author and the absence of the audience. It is with the notion of language in this wider sense in mind that we can approach Jennifer Lorch's essay on *Questa sera si recita a soggetto*. She argues that an understanding of the play is enhanced if we know the contexts within which it was written and produced, which are: the 'talkies' and Pirandello's response to them; Pirandello's knowledge of the mechanics of theatre resulting from his attendance at rehearsals and even more his years as a director; and the impact on him of German theatre and theories of directing. The play, she says, contains highly enjoyable visual extravaganzas such as a procession, a cabaret and an airfield, but fundamentally it requires ensemble playing at its best, as only through collaboration can the actors evoke the presence of the characters and invest the story with its power and illusion.

Pirandello is a writer of paradox in an age of paradox and transition marked by the loss of certainty and the increasing pace of technological advancement. His plays also increasingly show a profound knowledge of the theatre, its capacities and its potential. He should be widely read and even more widely performed, and we hope these essays will stimulate more new readings and more performances.

[1] Robert Brustein, 'Luigi Pirandello' in *The Theatre of Revolt*, London, Methuen, 1965, p. 316.

[2] James McFarlane, 'Neo-modernist Drama: Yeats and Pirandello' in *Modernism. A Guide to European Literature. 1890-1930*. Edited by Malcolm Bradbury and James McFarlane, London, Penguin, 1976 (1991 reprint) p. 569.

[3] Eric Bentley, 'Foreword' to *A Companion to Pirandello Studies*, edited by John Louis DiGaetani, New York, Westport, Connecticut, London, Greenwood Press, 1991, xv.

[4] Susan Bassnett, 'Female Masks: Luigi Pirandello's Plays for Women' in *Twentieth-Century European Drama*, edited by Brian Docherty, London, Macmillan, 1994, p. 23.

[5] Gaspare Giudice, *Luigi Pirandello*, Turin, UTET, 1963, p. 2.

[6] Gaspare Giudice, *Luigi Pirandello*, cit., p. 18.

[7] Pirandello wrote of these events in 1915 in a short story, *Colloquii coi personaggi*, which he did not include in his collected short stories. It can now be found in Luigi Pirandello, *Novelle per un anno,* ed. Mario Costanzo, vol. III, Milan, Mondadori, series 'I Meridiani', 1990, pp. 1138-1153.

[8] Gaspare Giudice, *Luigi Pirandello*, cit., p. 11.

[9] Giudice, *Luigi Pirandello*, cit., p. 87.

[10] Giudice, *Luigi Pirandello*, cit., p. 247.

[11] Maria Luisa Aguirre D'Amico, *Vivere con Pirandello*, Milan, Mondadori, 1989, p. 13.

[12] To my knowledge this novella has never been translated into English.

[13] Giudice, *Luigi Pirandello*, cit., p. 422.

[14] Giudice, *Luigi Pirandello*, cit., p. 423.

[15] Adrian Lyttelton, *The Seizure of Power. Fascism in Italy 1919-1929,* London, Weidenfeld and Nicolson, 1987 (2nd ed.), p. 378.

22

[16] See Gian Franco Venè, 'Pirandello e il fascismo' in AA. VV., *Pirandello e la politica*, Milan, Mursia, 1992, p. 172.

[17] Lyttelton, *The Seizure of Power*, cit., p. 378.

[18] See especially Roberto Alonge, *Teatro e spettacolo nel secondo Ottocento*, Bari, Laterza, 1993 (2nd ed.) There is now an excellent account in English of the Italian theatre context within which Pirandello worked in *Luigi Pirandello in the Theatre*, edited by Susan Bassnett and Jennifer Lorch, Switzerland etc., Harwood Academic Publishers, 1993, esp. pp. 5-10. Much of this section of the Introduction is based on information given in these two sources.

[19] On the star actor see Jennifer Lorch, 'The Rise of the *Mattatore* in Late-Nineteenth Century Italian Theatre', in J. R. Dashwood and J. E. Everson (eds), *Writers and Performers in Italian Drama from the Time of Dante to Pirandello*, Lewiston, Queenston, Lampeter, The Edwin Mellen Press, 1991, pp. 115-128.

[20] See Susan Bassnett and Jennifer Lorch (eds), *Luigi Pirandello in the Theatre*, cit., pp. 6-7.

[21] The play was first called *Il nido* [The Nest] when written in 1895 and then *Il nibbio* [The Kite]. Its definitive title is *La ragione degli altri* [Other People's Reason].

[22] Giudice, *Luigi Pirandello*, cit., pp. 307-308.

[23] These ideas, and the affair between D'Annunzio and Eleonora Duse, are described in D'Annunzio's novel *Il fuoco* [The Fire] (1900).

[24] See especially A. Richard Sogliuzzo, *Luigi Pirandello, Director: the Playwright in the Theatre*, New Jersey and London, Scarecrow Press, 1982; Michele Cometa, *Il teatro di Pirandello in Germania*, Palermo, Novecento, 1986; Alessandro d'Amico and Alessandro Tinterri, *Pirandello capocomico. La Compagnia del Teatro d'Arte di Roma, 1925-1928*, Palermo, Sellerio, 1987; Felicity Firth, *Pirandello in Performance*, Cambridge and Alexandria, VA, Chadwyck-Healey, 1990; John Louis DiGaetani (ed.), *A Companion to Pirandello Studies*, New York, Westport, London, Greenwood Press, 1991; Susan Bassnett and Jennifer Lorch (eds), *Pirandello in the Theatre*, cit., 1993.

[25] See Maggie Günsberg, *Patriarchal Representations. Gender and Discourse in Pirandello's Theatre*, Oxford/Providence, Berg, 1994.

[26] Francesco Càllari, *Pirandello e il cinema*, Venice, Marsilio, 1991.

[27] See his essay of 1908 *Soggettivismo e oggettivismo nell'arte narrativa*, in *SPSV*, Milan, Mondadori, 2nd. ed., 1965, p. 186.

CONTRADICTIONS AND THE DOUBLING OF IDEAS:
PIRANDELLO'S WRITINGS ON THEATRE AND THE ESSAY
L'UMORISMO.

In 1908 Pirandello, then a 41-year-old, moderately successful short story writer and novelist, expressed in no uncertain terms his views on the supremacy of the written text over dramatic performance:

> L'attore insomma dà una consistenza artefatta, in un ambiente posticcio, illusorio, a persone e ad azioni che hanno già avuto una espressione di vita superiore alle contingenze materiali e che vivono già nell'idealità essenziale caratteristica della poesia, cioè in una realtà superiore. [*Illustratori, attori e traduttori, SPSV*, 218].
> [In other words, the actor gives a false consistency, in an artificial, illusory environment, to people and actions that have already received an expression of life superior to material contingencies and that already live in the essential ideality characteristic of poetry, that is, in a superior kind of reality. [Illustrators, Actors and Translators] [1]

By 1936, however, he had, as an internationally renowned playwright, apparently abandoned any such notion of the essential superiority of the text in favour of a much more open and complex position:

> Perché l'opera d'arte, in teatro, non è più il lavoro di uno scrittore, che si può sempre del resto in altro modo salvaguardare, ma un atto di vita da creare, momento per momento, sulla scena, col concorso del pubblico, che deve bearsene. [2]
> [Because the work of art, in the theatre, is no longer the work of a writer, which moreover can always be safeguarded in a different way,

but an act of life to be created, moment by moment, on the stage, with the concurrence of the audience, which must be delighted by it.]

This essay will examine the full range of Pirandello's ideas on theatre, as expressed, at times in contradictory fashion, in various theoretical and occasional writings over the last forty or so years of his life. It will also explore how these ideas relate to and reflect other more general aesthetic concerns which form the background to his writings on the theatre as such, and which are expressed in particular in the essay *L'umorismo*.

1. An intellectual schizophrenia?

Pirandello's attitude to the theatre as an art form, as expressed both in his theoretical writings and in his dramatic production itself, is problematic. There are intimate links and echoes, both in broad lines and in detail, between the ideas on theatre expressed in the essays and the themes and techniques of the plays. But contradictions also abound within the theoretical writings, within the plays themselves, and between the two bodies of work. The essays of the early years of the century form an important conceptual background to issues dealt with in the plays of the early 1920s. But the relationship can never be easy between a theory of drama that denies the possibility of theatrical performance as art and plays that proclaim the right of the dramatist's creation to 'live' on stage. In turn the figure of the radical, iconoclastic theatrical practitioner of the 1920s seems to sit ill at ease with that of the staunch defender of theatre as a 'patrimonio sacro e monumentale' [sacred and monumental heritage] of the mid 1930s ['Discorso al convegno "Volta" ', *SPSV*, 1041]. The interaction of these various elements of Pirandello's thought and creative activity has been seen as constituting 'un rapporto di attrazione-ripulsione' between the writer and the theatre, and indeed one critic goes so far as to call it 'una schizofrenia, una dilacerazione indubbia fra le cose che teorizza e le cose che fa'.[3]

Whether we accept such a radical notion as that of an intellectual schizophrenia depends to some extent on how we view the diachronic development of Pirandello's thought. Is there, as some critics maintain, a fundamental evolution of ideas from the time of *L'azione parlata* [Spoken Action] (1899) to the end of his life? Was there indeed an intellectual 'conversion' along the way, in the transformation of the narrative author, at best suspicious of the theatre, into the champion of the stage as a privileged artistic space?[4] Or can we discern an underlying coherence and continuity of ideas in Pirandello's writings? Does the repeated 'condanna radicale del teatro' perhaps represent, as Vicentini suggests, 'l'ossatura e il motivo profondo' of Pirandello's theatrical activity?[5] The answer I will propose here is that there is undoubtedly a continuity of underlying aesthetic and philosophical concerns in Pirandello's theoretical and creative work: a preoccupation with the process of literary creation; an acute awareness of incompatibilities between art and life; in particular a concern with the *personaggio* [character], whose birth is the basis for any dramatic work and whose privileged status transcends the material contingencies in which the mere person is immersed. These concerns are, however, necessarily manifested in different approaches to the reality of the theatre under the impact of changing personal circumstances, cultural trends and historical developments. But also, underpinning these changes in attitude in response to different problems, there is the perennial presence of inherent notions of contrast and contradiction, indicators of a profoundly dialectical approach to the problem. Arising out of this, a phenomenon of duality, of the 'doubling' of every idea in the appearance of its opposite, can be seen as a unifying conceptual element in the theoretical writings as a whole.

2. *L'azione parlata*

In *L'azione parlata* Pirandello's main concerns are, firstly, the relationship between the writer and the dramatic text and secondly the particular difficulties of creating 'living' characters for the stage. The question of performance, so important in subsequent essays, is not considered, probably because at this stage Pirandello is still writing as an outsider to the theatre (although he had written several plays during the 1890s, none of these had yet

been performed).[6] In the article, his attitude to contemporary theatrical
practice is none too favourable. The objects of his disdain are several: on the
one hand D'Annunzio, whose characters are submerged under the weight of his
rhetorical style, and on the other the contemporary theatrical mainstream, the
so-called 'professionisti del teatro' for whom theatre is not a literary art but
'quasi mestiere', and the stuff of whose plays is 'la sciatteria del cosí detto stile
conversativo alla francese' [SPSV, 1017] [theatre professionals [...] almost a
trade [...] the slovenliness of the so-called French conversational style].
Neither the one nor the other, as Pirandello sees it, is producing good theatrical
writing. If D'Annunzio writes 'too beautifully', the average professional
playwright simply writes badly, indeed 'malissimo' [very badly]. The principal
defect however, in both cases, is not one of exterior form, but rather an
intrinsic flaw in the writing process. That is, the initial conception of the work
as 'un dato fatto [...] una data situazione' [SPSV, 1016] [a given fact [...] a
given situation]; an abstract idea onto which are then grafted mechanically
various characters according to theatrical convention and the particular talents
of whatever actors may be available. [7] This process, writes Pirandello, should
be reversed: the characters must come first, born 'alive' and autonomous at the
moment of artistic creation. Citing (not for the last time) Heine's ballad
'Geoffroy Rudèl und Melisande von Tripoli', in which the figures of a tapestry
come to life in the moonlight, he tells us that this is how dramatic characters
should emerge from the page : 'per prodigio d'arte, dovrebbero uscire, staccarsi
vivi, semoventi ...' [SPSV, 1015] [through the prodigy of art, they should come
out, step out alive in their own right]. Thus:

> Non il dramma fa le persone; ma queste, il dramma. E prima d'ogni
> altro dunque bisogna aver le persone: vive, libere, operanti. Con esse
> e in esse nascerà l'idea del dramma, il primo germe dove staran
> racchiusi il destino e la forma; [SPSV, 1016].
> [The play does not make people; people make the play. And therefore
> one must have the people before anything else, living, free and active.
> In them and through them will come the idea of the play, the first
> germ in which their destiny and form will be contained]

Here with hindsight we can see the first 'germ' of the idea of *personaggio* which will come to fruition in *Sei personaggi in cerca d'autore*. [8] This centrality of the character to the creative process is a recurring theme in the theoretical writings.

If this prodigy of artistic creation is to be realized formally, however, it will require a stylistic effort apparently beyond the powers of those whom Pirandello sees writing for the contemporary stage. Apart from the abolition of 'ogni sostegno descrittivo o narrativo' [*SPSV*, 1015] [every descriptive or narrative prop], true dramatic style must strive to achieve the unique, necessary form for each living situation, 'l'espressione immediata, connaturata con l'azione' [*SPSV*, 1015-1016] [the immediate expression at one with the action]. This can only happen when a qualitative leap has taken place involving the complete identification of the author with his characters, '... quando l'autore si sia veramente immedesimato con la sua creatura fino a sentirla com'essa si sente, a volerla com'essa si vuole' [*SPSV*, 1016] [...when the author is fully at one with his creation so as to feel what it feels, to want it to be as it wants itself to be]. Here another key term, *immedesimarsi* [to be at one with] makes its appearance. A dramatic work conceived in this way will have no style other than the many styles of its individual characters, each one created and expressed in all of its many-faceted reality.

3. Illustratori, attori e traduttori

In *Illustratori, attori e traduttori* [Illustrators, Actors and Translators] (1908) Pirandello returns to the problems of the theatre, but in a broader context, that of the aesthetic problem of the transformation of a work of art from one form to another, whether through illustration, translation or dramatic performance. Here the issues dealt with in *L'azione parlata* are taken as the basis for the discussion of dramatic art, to the extent that Pirandello begins this discussion by quoting and paraphrasing from the earlier essay the passages on the prodigy of the birth of the living character and the process of *immedesimazione* of the author with his material. [9] The focus soon shifts however to the next step in the dramatic process, the transformation of the text in performance. Here Pirandello gives us the first and fullest elaboration of his radical doubts as to the very possibility of the faithful representation on stage of the dramatic text, as he questions the feasibility of theatre itself as an artistic activity.

For Pirandello the formal execution of a work of art should spring forth in a vital organic movement intimately bound up with its very conception. In this he disputes Croce's contention 'che il rapporto tra il fatto estetico, ossia la visione artistica, e il fatto fisico, ossia l'istrumento che serve d'ajuto per la riproduzione, sia puramente estrinseco...' [*SPSV*, 210] [that the relationship between the aesthetic, that is the artistic vision, and the physical, that is the instrument which serves as aid to the reproduction, is purely extrinsic]. There is, rather, an intrinsic relationship between the artist's vision and its formal expression: 'L'esecuzione insomma è la concezione stessa, viva in atto' [*SPSV*, 211] [The execution is therefore the conception itself, alive in action]. But in dramatic art, the formal execution of the original is subject inevitably to the intervention of an external force: the actor,

> Sempre, purtroppo, tra l'autore drammatico e la sua creatura, nella materialità della rappresentazione, s'introduce necessariamente un terzo elemento imprescindibile: l'attore.
> Questa, com'è noto, è per l'arte drammatica una soggezione inovviabile [*SPSV*, 215]
> [Unfortunately there always has to be a third, unavoidable element that intrudes between the dramatic author and his creation in the material being of the performance: the actor.
> As is well known, this is inevitably a limitation for dramatic art].

So Pirandello sees the near impossibility of a faithful interpretation as the inevitable and frustrating lot of the dramatist, as the bipolar relationship between the writer and his character in the text is superseded by the more complex triangular relationship between the writer, the text and the actor. We should note that in 1908 Pirandello is still writing not from personal experience of the theatre but from the strictly theoretical viewpoint of the essayist, whose creative output has been chiefly in the lyrical and narrative fields. He is clearly speculating when he writes of the 'ingrata sorpresa che [...] deve provar senza dubbio un autore drammatico nel veder rappresentato dagli attori in teatro il suo dramma' [*SPSV*, 215] [distasteful surprise that [...] a dramatic author must doubtless feel on seeing his play acted out by actors in the theatre].

The presence of the actor as the necessary third element in dramatic performance involves for Pirandello a doubling of the creative process itself. And this in turn means a doubling of the process of *immedesimazione* with the character.

> Come l'autore, per fare opera viva, deve immedesimarsi con la sua creatura, fino a sentirla com'essa sente sé stessa, a volerla com'essa vuole sé stessa: cosí, e non altrimenti, se fosse possibile, dovrebbe fare l'attore. [*SPSV*, 215]
> [Just as the author must merge with his character in order to make it live, to the point of feeling as it feels, wanting it to be as it wants to be itself, so also, and to no lesser degree, if that can be accomplished, should the actor].

Here is where problems begin to arise. There are of course practical problems involving the physical appearance of the actor who cannot fully become the 'incarnation' of the character. No matter how expertly the make-up is applied, we still merely have an adaptation, a mask (here a major motif of the great plays of the '20s is prefigured). But there is a more fundamental problem, namely that the actor's conception of the character, if he truly attempts to identify with it as he should, cannot coincide exactly with the author's original conception. The actor must feel the author's 'creatura', 'come essa sente sé stessa', making it his own to the extent that, were the author to intervene with some objection during rehearsals, the actor would feel this as a violation no less than does the author on seeing the 'translation' of his original conception into the material reality of the stage.

> Perché l'attore, se non vuole (né può volerlo) che le parole scritte del dramma gli escano dalla bocca come da un portavoce o da un fonografo, bisogna che riconcepisca il personaggio, lo concepisca cioè

a sua volta per conto suo; bisogna che l'immagine già espressa torni ad organarsi in lui e tenda a divenire il movimento che la effettui e la renda reale su la scena. [*SPSV*, 216]
[Because unless the actor wants the written words of the play to come from his mouth artificially, as through a mouthpiece or a phonograph (and he cannot possibly want that to happen), then he has to reconceive the character, that is, conceive it in turn himself; the image that has already been expressed must be taken back and restructured inside him so that it can become the movement which will carry it out and make it real on the stage].

Pirandello has arrived at a paradoxical conclusion: any self-respecting actor cannot simply aspire to reproducing mechanically the words of the script; the actor must recreate the character if it is to live. But the character then can only live on the stage by becoming another.

In this process of becoming another, of 'translation' from the text to the stage, there is always says Pirandello a diminution, a falling off. Here he uses the theatre as the main illustration of a more general aesthetic point regarding the relationship between art and life. While material reality limits and restricts men and their actions, art frees them from contingencies as the artist idealizes and concentrates life. So the artistic creation, in particular the *personaggio*, is with respect to the material world 'meno reale e tuttavia piú vero' [*SPSV*, 219] [less real and yet more true] (these words are famously echoed by the father in *Sei personaggi*). There is, moreover, a hierarchical relationship between these terms *realtà* and *verità* for Pirandello, the latter being superior. For, he tells us, in giving material reality to the writer's vision, in rendering it *more real* and *less true*, the actor is merely giving 'materialità fittizia' to a creation which of itself exists on a higher plane of original expression, 'nell'idealità essenziale caratteristica della poesia, cioè in una realtà superiore' [*SPSV*, 218] [fictitious matereality [...] in the essential ideality characteristic of poetry, that is, in a superior kind of reality].

Given the total identification of the work of art with its formal execution, the rejection of dramatic art as an inferior and flawed genre is a seemingly inevitable conclusion of the essay. And yet in the concluding section there is, one feels, a reluctance to condemn so unequivocally an art form whose dilemmas have clearly exercised the author's mind a great deal. Are there not those cases where the translation outshines the original and, similarly, where the excellence of an actor's performance can enhance a flawed play? There is, it seems, an opening here, a space where the actor can give true life on stage to what effectively becomes his own creation. Also there are the great dramatic characters (such as Shakespeare's) whose own individuality and life is so powerful that it outshines the meanness of inadequate interpreters, and yet who do, albeit rarely, find the actors worthy of 'filling' them.

So Pirandello returns at the end of this aesthetic enquiry to the idea of the free, living *personaggio* as the basis of dramatic art. But he also insists on the fundamental dichotomy between the play and its representation on stage. For this latter to come to original artistic life it would have to become a free space for the actor's own free creativity, and we would ultimately have a return to the improvisation of the *commedia dell'arte*, dismissed as inevitably trivial since it does not allow the process of idealizing concentration essential to 'superior' art. Nevertheless, the idea of improvisation touched on here will become one of the avenues of thematic and technical innovation explored in the 'theatre trilogy', and eventually indeed Pirandello will cite the *commedia dell'arte* as the historical source of vitality and originality in the Italian theatre.

4. The writings of 1918 - 1925

The theoretical positions of *L'azione parlata* and *Illustratori, attori e traduttori* are echoed and repeated in later years, even after Pirandello had become actively involved in writing for the theatre. The production of *Così è (se vi pare)* [Right You Are (If You Think So)] in 1917 marks the beginning of a long period of successful dramatic activity. Nevertheless, in 'Teatro e letteratura' (1918) we find several passages from the 1908 essay repeated verbatim: there is a reiteration of the superior reality of art and the impossibility of the perfect recreation of the author's vision on stage. Also, as in 1899, he attacks the theatre professionals, more interested in theatre as a business than as an art. And he underlines again the centrality of the character in dramatic writing.

Yet there are indications of Pirandello's changing relationship with the theatre. What are we to make of the following affirmation?

> E se i personaggi parleranno ciascuno in questo lor proprio modo [...] la commedia sarà scritta bene, e una commedia scritta bene, se anche ben concepita e ben condotta, è opera d'arte letteraria come un bel romanzo o una bella novella o una bella lirica [*SPSV*, 1020].
> [And if all the characters speak in their own special way [...] then the play will be well written and a well-written play, particularly if well-shaped and well-acted, is a literary work just as much as a good novel, or a good story or a good lyric].

This is the voice of Pirandello the playwright defending literary standards in the theatre against purveyors of popular 'pulp' drama. The polemicist's battleground has shifted here from that of aesthetic debate to that of theatrical practice. He has not renounced his earlier views; indeed, he has just reiterated some of them. But he can, it seems, put them to one side, if only momentarily, in order to take part in a separate debate on issues which have now become important in his own cultural life, where an accommodation of sorts with theatre has undoubtedly taken place.

The affirmation that theatre is indeed literature is made here in response to those professionals who would devalue and trivialize it. Pirandello stands against them, concluding: 'Ma per noi il teatro vuol esser un'altra cosa' [*SPSV*, 1024] [But for us theatre aspires to be something else]. The 'us' here can probably best be identified with the practitioners of the new theatre of the grotesque, such as Chiarelli and Rosso di San Secondo. [10] The latter's *Marionette, che passione!* [Marionettes, What Passion!] was reviewed in this same year by Pirandello, who stressed its value as a literary text [*SPSV*, 1007]. Pirandello is no longer an outsider, but rather sees himself as belonging to a literary community for whose members theatre is a natural vehicle.

A number of writings of the following years confirm this view. In 1920 we find Pirandello writing specifically on the subject of the *teatro del grottesco* in *Immagine del grottesco* [Image of the Grotesque] and *Ironia* [Irony]. In these articles we see him carefully distancing himself from the imitators of the original grotesque manner, whose 'stravaganza' [excess] has become a little too widespread and so risks becoming as much a cliché as the theatrical conventions it mocked. [11] Again, in *Teatro nuovo e teatro vecchio* [New and Old Theatre] (1922), it is clear from the title that Pirandello is engaged in a discussion within the field of theatre rather than on the validity of theatre itself. Furthermore, this time he assumes a polemical position against the professionals of pure literary criticism who would dismiss the possibility of theatre being considered as a potential source of that innovation or originality which is a necessary (though not sufficient) condition for the creation of true art. The bulk of the essay considers general aesthetic questions on what constitutes or gives rise to originality in artistic activity. Truly new or original art will endure while the merely novel will grow old. The *novità* of any truly creative spirit lies in giving unique formal expression to problems of universal significance and permanence [*SPSV*, 235-237]. [12] Work, in whatever genre, that is truly 'new' in this sense (that is, not merely dealing modishly with contemporary issues) will never become 'old', will always remain vital and significant, as for example the works of Dante or Goldoni [*SPSV*, 238-242]. It would appear, then, that in this essay we have a full-scale validation of the theatre, which may, like any other genre, throw up both original creations and imitations, but whose capacity to produce works of enduring value in any era is affirmed.

Does this represent a profound change of heart, then, from the anti-theatre positions of the earlier essays? The answer can only be no, in the light of an article, 'En confidence' [In Confidence], published in Paris in 1925, and decribed by Vicentini as 'indubbiamente la più inquietante delle testimonianze pirandelliane d'argomento teatrale' [undoubtedly the most disquieting of Pirandello's writings on the theatre]. [13] What is striking about this piece (quoted here in English translation) is the frankness with which the author spells out the contradictions within his own positions on theatre. Having quoted *Illustratori, attori e traduttori* on the impossibility of adequately rendering the play in the inferior reality of the stage, he declares: 'I would not change one comma in that conclusion'. [14] Going on to face the fact that he has become compromised with this 'inferior' art form to the extent of becoming a director, he concludes that 'neither logic nor imagination can furnish me any longer with even the smallest excuse'. What does emerge, however, is the extent to which historical events acted as a catalyst for Pirandello and, he says, for his generation, in bringing about the 'theatre revival'. It was, it seems, the first World War that finally made the narrative form unworkable for him. In a world 'in movement' he felt the need for a new immediacy of expression. With his ideas 'reaching out towards action', he found that 'words could no longer stay written on paper'. This, then, was how his 'passion' for theatre took over. [15]

It is interesting that Pirandello sees his experience as part of a collective one 'undergone by all those writers who are working at the present time to create a new Italian theatre'. He seems to see himself as a spokesman for the new theatre, lamenting the hostility of public reaction in Italy to what he calls 'our attempts', and acting (given the occasion of this piece) as a sort of ambassador for Italian theatre abroad. He declares himself to be 'totally involved in this movement' whose works 'pose questions on the boundaries of realism'. [16] In this period, then, with Pirandello reaching the height of his powers and success as a dramatist, theatre has become the primary vehicle for the expression of his artistic vision, and he defends the themes and practice of contemporary drama while openly stating the paradox of the irreconcilable conflict between this position and his reiterated belief in the inferiority of theatre as art.

5. In defence of theatre, 1929 - 1936

A few years later the ground on which Pirandello expresses his views on theatre shifts yet again. The new element that intrudes into the world he now occupies (however uneasy that occupation may be from a theoretical point of view) appears in the title of his 1929 article 'Se il film parlante abolirà il teatro' [Will the Talkies Do Away with Theatre?]. This article marks the beginning of a new and final phase in Pirandello's theoretical statements on theatre, a phase in which the overwhelming impression is that of the theatre under threat, not because of any inherent aesthetical problems, but because of the practical difficulties of increased competition for audiences and the ever-increasing need for public funding.

The article begins by returning to a familiar problem, that of the necessity for life to consist in various forms (as discussed for example in *L'umorismo* and in the Preface to *Sei personaggi*). The point made here is that certain forms of life are natural and insuppressible and that one of these is theatre, whose existence as 'un'espressione naturale della vita' [*SPSV*, 1031] [a natural expression of life] cannot be called into question. But such a radical affirmation of the theatre's right to exist in fact conceals a new insecurity in the face of competition from the mass-entertainment industry of the talking pictures. To speak of the death of the theatre, proclaims Pirandello, is heresy, and he puts forward a number of specious arguments to show that the cinema cannot supplant it (for example, that mere 'images', on speaking, will appear ridiculous and 'unnatural'). His rather hopeful conclusion is that the serious competitive threat to theatre represented by silent films ('una minaccia che, specialmente in questi ultimi tempi, s'era fatta molto grave'; [a threat which, especially in recent times, had become very serious] will, with the arrival of the talkies, disappear [*SPSV*, 1034].

This was wishful thinking, and Pirandello implicitly recognized the fact five years later in his 'Discorso al Convegno "Volta" sul teatro drammatico' [Address to the Volta Conference on Dramatic Theatre]. [17] This piece elevates theatre to the status of an immortal institution: 'Il Teatro non può morire' [*SPSV*, 1037] [The Theatre cannot die]. And yet it is mostly concerned with defending the theatre's position in contemporary society. In this, and given the prestigious setting of the international congress to which it was first delivered, the Address has an undeniably political function. Pirandello performs the balancing act of proclaiming the political autonomy of art while making a case for its subsidization by the state: if art is to obey its own laws, the mysterious laws of spontaneous and natural birth, it cannot be called on to support one cause or another; therefore any subsidy given to art must be 'disinterested'. But the theatre must be defended [*SPSV*, 1038-1039].

In fact this speech must be seen in the broader context of Pirandello's difficult relationship with the fascist regime in these years. In particular we should bear in mind his ongoing hope that Mussolini could be persuaded to support a State Theatre. [18] So as he puts forward his ideas for restrictions on cinema showings and the subsidization of new 'mass' theatres, there is an attempt to use the politically acceptable language of populism and mass culture in order to attract state aid for his proposals:

> Ma si dovrebbe poi provvedere alla costruzione dei teatri nuovi, cosí come si costruiscono i nuovi stadii per le gare sportive, giacché ancora al teatro si fa respirare l'aria soffocante delle vecchie sedi non piú confacenti alle nuove esigenze, non solo dell'arte stessa, ma anche e soprattutto dell'economia e del costume.
> ... e forse con ciò sarebbe risolto anche, nello spirito, l'auspicato teatro di masse. Sale appropriatamente architettate, capaci d'accogliere tanto pubblico da pagare largamente le spese dello spettacolo, tenendo il prezzo dei posti pari a quello dei cinematografi, e i posti senz'altra distinzione tra loro che quella inovviabile della maggiore e minore distanza dalla scena. [*SPSV*, 1040-1041].
> [But we should also plan to build new theatres, just as new stadiums are being built for sporting events, since in the theatre we are still breathing the musty air of old places that are no longer suited to modern needs, not only the needs of art but also, and principally, the needs of economics and custom.
> ...and perhaps in this way the question of the hoped-for mass theatre will also be solved in spirit. What are needed are purpose-built halls, capable of holding enough people to more than cover the costs of performances, whilst keeping seat prices level with those of the cinema, and with seating arranged in such a way that there is no other distinction between them than the unavoidable one of greater or lesser distance from the stage].

But the ensuing discussion of the new possibilities for spectacular stage effects brings us back to the theoretical problem of the text and its relationship to performance. Here we find the only clear pronouncement in these writings on the controversial role of the director, treated so ambiguously in *Questa sera si recita a soggetto* [Tonight We Improvise]. Pirandello now unequivocally gives the director a subordinate role, as 'creatore responsabile soltanto dello spettacolo' [*SPSV*, 1041] [responsible only for creating the performance], who must not be allowed to interfere with the autonomous life of the work of art, 'quella vita, intendo, inviolabile perché coerente in ogni punto a sé stessa che l'opera d'arte vuole avere per sé e che perciò non dovrebbe essere ad arbitrio del regista alterare né tanto meno manomettere' [*SPSV*, 1041] [that life, I mean, that is inviolable because it is in every way coherent throughout that the work of art wants for itself, and that therefore should not be left to the judgment of the director to alter and even less to adapt in any way]. [19]

We seem to be back once again to the position of *Illustratori, attori e traduttori*: the work of art, the text, is sacred. But immediately the text's sacrality is subsumed into the overarching sacrality of the great enduring institution of the Theatre. This piece ends with the apotheosis of the theatre, a 'patrimonio sacro e monumentale' [sacred and monumental heritage] handed down from the ancient Greeks, with the high moral function of calling human actions to a 'giudizio pubblico' [public judgment], a public institution which is also, however, 'la suprema e piú matura espressione dell'arte' [the highest and most mature expression of art] [*SPSV*, 1041-1042]. What is striking is the rapidity with which Pirandello moves here, in the space of one page, from a consideration of the problematic relationship between text, director and performance to a rhetorical exaltation of theatre itself. This is symptomatic not only of the conceptual tensions now inherent in his attitude to dramatic art but also of the uneasy coexistence in this piece of the literary theorist and the campaigning propagandist.

This coexistence continues to some extent in the *Introduzione al teatro italiano* [Introduction to Italian Theatre] (1936). Here Pirandello reiterates the

concept of theatre as a 'forma della vita', going so far this time as to see its
origins in the collective experience of ancient religious rites. Dismissing any
talk of the decadence of contemporary theatre, he maintains that any 'true'
theatre will always have that 'moral' value referred to in the previous piece
(from which he quotes directly). The tone is celebratory as he goes on to argue
the historical primacy of Italian theatre, indulging along the way in some
nationalist and pro-regime rhetoric ('la nostra grandissima nazione' [our very
great nation], 'la sacrosanta rinnovazione del costume apportata dal Fascismo'
[the sacrosanct renewal of customs brought about by Fascism]. [20]

The bulk of the essay, however, constitutes a serious historical analysis of
the development of Italian and European theatre from the middle ages
onwards. We may note in particular the emphasis placed on the 'humanity' of
dramatic characters, on vitality and spontaneity as against the rigidity of form,
virtues which came to the fore in the *commedia dell'arte*. The latter, writes
Pirandello, could never have been born of the pure improvisation of actors
themselves, but was rather created by certain 'uomini di teatro' [men of the
theatre], authors turned actors who could give the necessary direction to
otherwise formless improvisation. The result, however, was a loss of all
artistic ambition, consumed by the passion for spectacle, for 'puro movimento'
[pure movement]. Nevertheless, the *commedia dell'arte*, with its lesson of
vitality, was a seminal experience for European theatre.

The emphasis on vitality as a core value in theatre leads on to a
conclusion which, in the light of Pirandello's repeated assertions over three
decades of the primacy of the text, is quite surprising:

> Il Teatro non è archeologia. Il non rimettere le mani nelle opere
> antiche, per aggiornarle e renderle adatte a nuovo spettacolo, significa
> incuria, non già scrupolo degno di rispetto. Il Teatro *vuole* questi
> rimaneggiamenti, e se n'è giovato incessantemente, in tutte le epoche
> ch'era più vivo.
> Il testo resta integro per chi se lo vorrà rileggere in casa, per sua
> cultura; chi vorrà divertircisi, andrà a teatro, dove gli sarà ripresentato
> mondo di tutte le parti vizze, rinnovato nelle espressioni non più
> correnti, riadattato ai gusti dell'oggi. [21]

[The Theatre is not archaeology. The refusal to work on old plays in order to modernise them and make them suitable for today's theatre shows apathy, not a scruple worthy of respect. The Theatre *wants* these adaptations, and has continually benefited from them in all the ages when it was most alive.

The text remains unchanged for those who want to re-read it at home, for their own interest; those who want to be entertained by it will go to the theatre where it will be re-presented cleansed of all its faded parts, its old-fashioned expressions brought up to date, readapted for today's tastes].

This full legitimization of stage production is undeniably new and cannot be reconciled with the strict limitations placed on the director's role in the 1935 speech. The next paragraph (which I have quoted in the introduction to this essay) gives a new vision of the theatrical *production* as an organic, vital work of art, whose text should indeed be appropriately preserved, but whose creation, whose form, is in its performance: 'un atto di vita da creare, momento per momento, sulla scena'[22] [an act of life to be created, moment by moment, on the stage]. It is perhaps at last an attempted resolution of the paradox underlying all the writings we have examined so far. These all revolved around various conflicts involving a constant set of elements: art; life; form; creation; text; performance. This is the single most concise theoretical formulation of the coexistence of these elements in a living 'symbiosis'.[23]

But the emergence of such a reconciliation or symbiosis should not, and in fact does not, surprise us in the light of Pirandello's practice as a dramatist over the preceding twenty years. He had never been afraid to incorporate contradictions in his artistic vision. On the contrary, contradictions and dualities formed a vital structural and thematic element in his greatest plays. The concluding paragraph of the 1936 essay dwells on this very aspect of the new Italian theatre, whose field of exploration lies in:

l'espressione diretta e libera dei reali sentimenti presenti e in contrasto nell'anima d'ogni uomo, senza paura di tutte le contraddizioni di questo sentimento e di quelle della fantasia e della volontà, che fino ad allora erano state scrupolosamente eliminate come inassimilabili alla compattezza morale e anche estetica del personaggio.[24]

[the direct and free expression of the real and contrasting feelings present in the soul of every man, without fear of all the contradictions inherent in this feeling or of those of the imagination and the will, which until then had been scrupulously eliminated as running counter to the moral and also the aesthetic unity of the character].

Contradictions in the soul; cracks in the character's 'compattezza': these thematic elements reflect the same aesthetic concerns which inform the different theoretical approaches to theatrical reality encountered in the essays. For a further insight into these underlying concerns we will turn to the longest and best-known of Pirandello's essays, *L'umorismo* [Humorism] (1908).

6. *L'umorismo*

As far back as 1893, in *Arte e coscienza d'oggi*, Pirandello took the trouble to outline the basic foundation of a 'humorist's' vision, namely the presence of a contrast between illusion and reality: 'Malinconico posto però questo che la scienza ha assegnato all'uomo nella natura, in confronto almeno a quello ch'egli s'immaginava in altri tempi di tenervi. Un poeta umorista potrebbe trovare in ciò motivo a qualche suo canto' [*SPSV*, 895] [This is a melancholy place, however, that science has assigned to man in nature, at least by comparison with the one he thought he held in previous times. A humorist poet could find in this the subject for some of his verses]. *L'umorismo* is principally concerned with defining and describing in detail Pirandello's concept of humour as a literary phenomenon.

The essay is divided into two substantial parts, each sub-divided into shorter sections. Part I is a wide-ranging and erudite consideration of the word *umorismo* itself and the history of the phenomenon it describes. The density of its historical, philosophical and above all literary references reflects its original purpose: that of an academic treatise intended to further the author's career at the Istituto Superiore di Magistero in Rome. The term *umorismo* is carefully distinguished from others such as comedy, satire, caricature and, more subtly, irony. Pirandello argues that it is not an exclusively modern phenomenon, but is found in isolated cases throughout literary history and in all literatures. In the course of his argument he provides ample illustrations, including memorable discussions of the works of Ariosto, Cervantes and Manzoni (and in the second edition of 1920 he includes several broadsides against Croce, whose criticism of the original essay had antagonized him greatly). In Part II he goes on to define the essence of *umorismo* and to describe in detail the processes involved in the creation of a humoristic work. This second part is often taken as a general statement of Pirandello's own poetics.

L'umorismo then is a very different type of essay to those we have previously examined. Above all, it does not directly address the specific problems of the dramatic genre. Nevertheless the essay as a whole considers a broad range of general aesthetic issues which underpin and prefigure many of the problems we have seen considered in the writings on the theatre. By viewing those problems in the wider context of *L'umorismo*, we can discern more easily lines of continuity running through Pirandello's theoretical writings. Thus we find here recurrences of themes such as the need for *immedesimazione* between author and character, or the problematic dichotomy between art and life [*SPSV*, 55; 81]. These are fundamental concepts that we have already seen developed and applied to the special problems of the stage. Here we can see that they are strands of a general thematic thread running throughout the theoretical writings.

But the main concern of *L'umorismo* lies elsewhere: in the definition of the peculiar artistic vision of the humorist and the description of the creative process involved in realizing that vision. In any humoristic situation, we are told, there is present, as a matter of course, a contradiction. The simple awareness of that contradiction (or *avvertimento del contrario*) gives rise to the merely comic. It is through the special activity of reflection in the conception of the work of art that there arises the more profound *feeling* of contradiction or *sentimento del contrario*. In what is probably the most frequently-quoted passage in the essay, Pirandello exemplifies this process in the description of 'una vecchia signora' [an old lady], whose excessive application of make-up and inappropriately youthful dress make her appear ridiculous (the initial *avvertimento).* It is only on reflection that the personal anguish behind this display, the pathetic self-deceit it entails, come to the fore, and:

> ecco che io non posso piú riderne come prima, perché appunto la riflessione, lavorando in me, mi ha fatto andar oltre a quel primo avvertimento, o piuttosto, piú addentro: da quel primo *avvertimento del contrario* mi ha fatto passare a questo *sentimento del contrario.* Ed è tutto qui la differenza tra il comico e l'umoristico. [*SPSV*, 127] [and now I can no longer laugh, precisely because reflection, working in me, has made me go beyond that first awareness, or rather further within it: It has made me go from that first *awareness of contradiction* to this *feeling of contradiction.* And all the difference between the comic and the humoristic lies here].

The process of *immedesimazione* of the author with his creation, necessary in all writing, has a special characteristic in the humourist in that it involves a 'doubling' of the spirit, a full belief both in the character's illusions and in the reality with which they collide. This distinguishes *umorismo,* with its *essential* contradictions, from irony, where contradicions are merely *apparent.* Thus if a sense of 'sdegno' [disdain] or 'dispetto' [contempt] provokes as its opposite 'compatimento' [compassion] or 'pietà' [pity], the humorist will be equally sincere in both emotions: 'Ogni sentimento, ogni pensiero, ogni moto che sorga nell'umorista si sdoppia subito nel suo contrario ...' [*SPSV*, 139] [Every feeling, every thought, every impulse which arises in the humourist immediately finds its double in its own opposite].

The thrust of humoristic writing is *scomporre* [to bring disorder], unlike art governed by rhetoric which is 'composizione esteriore' [*SPSV*, 49] [external composition]. Humoristic reflection breaks down the many edifices constructed by our illusions, such as the masks and the lies on which social interaction depends, the vain forms in which we try to fix the ever-changing flux of reality [*SPSV*, 146-154].

Art is itself one of these constructions, and in the concluding section VI of Part II Pirandello notes that the humourist is as much opposed to the falsifications inherent in artistic idealization as he is to those found in everyday life. Thus Pirandello explains the apparent 'scompostezza' [disorder] typical of humoristic writing:

> *L'arte in genere astrae e concentra*, coglie, cioè e rappresenta cosí degli individui come delle cose, *l'idealità essenziale e caratteristica*. Ora pare all'umorista che tutto ciò *semplifichi* troppo la natura e tenda a rendere troppo ragionevole o almeno troppo coerente la vita. [*SPSV*, 157].
> [*Art in general abstracts and concentrates*, that is, it gathers and represents the *essential and characteristic ideality* both of people and of things. Now to the humorist it seems that all this *simplifies* nature too much and tends to make life too reasonable or at least too coherent].

The epic or dramatic writer strives to *compose* a coherent character, but:

> l'umorista fa proprio l'inverso: egli *scompone* il carattere nei suoi elementi; e mentre quegli cura di coglierlo coerente in ogni atto, questi si diverte a rappresentarlo nelle sue incongruenze. [...]
> *Nella realtà vera le azioni che mettono in rilievo un carattere si stagliano su un fondo di vicende ordinarie, di particolari comuni.* Ebbene, gli scrittori in genere non se n'avvalgono, o poco se ne curano, come se queste vicende, questi particolari *non abbiano alcun valore e siano inutili e trascurabili.* Ne fa tesoro invece l'umorista. [*SPSV*, 158-159]
> [the humorist does the complete opposite: he *destructures* the character into its elements; and while the former [the epic and dramatic writer] is intent on capturing the coherence of the character in all its acts, the latter [the humorist] finds pleasure in representing it in all its inconsistencies ...
> *In reality the actions which throw a character into relief stand out against a background of ordinary events, of everyday details.* Well, writers in general do not make use of them, or pay little attention to them, as though these events and details *are of no value and are useless and unimportant.* The humorist, instead, avails himself fully of them].

The italics throughout are mine. I have quoted these passages because of the peculiar way in which they relate to an idea we have already seen in *Illustratori, attori e traduttori*, where we find almost word for word some of the phrases underlined here. In that passage (dating from the same year as *l'umorismo* and repeated in *Teatro e letteratura*) Pirandello argues for the superiority of the artistic creation over material reality precisely in so far as art idealizes and simplifies life. So we read in *Illustratori, attori e traduttori*:

> *Nella realtà le azioni che mettono in rilievo un carattere si stagliano su un fondo di contingenze senza valore, di particolari comuni.* [...]
> L'arte invece libera le cose, gli uomini e le loro azioni di queste contingenze senza valore, di questi particolari comuni, di questi volgari ostacoli o minute miserie; in un certo senso li *astrae*; [...] In questo senso appunto *l'artista idealizza.* Non già che egli rappresenti tipi o dipinga idee; *semplifica e concentra.* [...]
> Ora che fa l'attore? Fa proprio il contrario di ciò che ha fatto il poeta. Rende, cioè, piú reale e tuttavia men vero il personaggio creato dal poeta [...] L'attore insomma dà una consistenza artefatta, in un ambiente posticcio, illusorio, a persone e ad azioni che hanno già avuto una espressione di vita superiore alle contingenze materiali e che vivono già *nell'idealità essenziale caratteristica della poesia*, cioè in una realtà superiore. [*SPSV*, 217-218]
> [*In reality the actions which throw a character into relief stand out against a background of useless contingencies, of everyday details* [..]
> Art, instead, frees things, people and their actions from these trivial matters, these everday details, these vulgar obstacles or trifling misfortunes; in a certain sense it *abstracts* them; [...] In precisely this sense, *the artist idealizes.* It is not that he represents types or depicts ideas; *he simplifies and concentrates.*[...]
> Now, what does the actor do? He does the exact opposite of what the author has done. That is, he makes the character created by the author more real and yet less true [...] . In other words the actor gives a false consistency, in an artificial, illusory environment, to people and actions that have already received an expression of life superior to material contingencies and that already live *in the essential ideality characteristic of poetry*, that is, in a superior kind of reality].

As we can see from the presence of almost identical terms and phrases, but with quite different functions, the terms and values of the argument have been reversed between the two essays. What were 'useless contingencies' to be simplified and made coherent by the hypothetical dramatist in *Illustratori, attori e traduttori* are for the humoristic writer the very stuff of his art. The activity of the actor (we are told in *Illustratori*) in returning the character to the world of 'contingencies' represents a diminution, a falsification of the poet's vision. In *L'umorismo*, however, that art which idealizes and concentrates life is itself seen to involve a falsification. Described as 'art in general', it may indeed include the work of the 'dramatic writer' and is clearly distinguished from the humorist's art. We can conclude then that the literary art referred to in *Illustratori, attori e traduttori* is not *umorismo*, and that the humorist's art is in some respects more akin to that of the actor than to that of the playwright.

This should lead us on the one hand to guard against the easily-made assumption that the concepts expressed in *L'umorismo* represent a comprehensive statement of Pirandello's poetics, that in describing the process of humoristic creation he is prescribing generalized aesthetic norms, for himself or others. We should not forget that the essay does not pretend to be such a statement of poetics, but, explicitly, a description in historical and abstract terms of a particular literary phenomenon. And yet, on the other hand, it is clear that Pirandello has a great deal of sympathy for the type of artistic sensibility he describes here. It is undeniable that many of the ideas we find in *L'umorismo*, particularly in Part II, have the strongest of thematic resonances throughout his creative works (one need only think of the many instances of the conflict between mask and reality, or the doomed attempts to construct the abstraction of Truth from the flux of life). Perhaps, then, we can see in this affirmation of the legitimacy of *scompostezza* in art, of the admissibility of an art which eschews idealizing abstractions, a key to the intellectual mechanism which would allow Pirandello to embrace the theatre while maintaining his abstract objections to it as an art form. Theatre conceived as *umorismo* would not after all need to aspire to the 'idealità essenziale caratteristica della poesia'. On the contrary, it ought to subvert any such idealizing aspirations, thus rendering irrelevant the objections to dramatic art contained in *Illustratori, attori e traduttori*.

But above all, this further example of contradiction within Pirandello's theoretical writings must surely lead us to abandon the search for any unequivocal stance on his part regarding the question of theatre. In this respect

L'umorismo gives us a valuable insight into his intellectual make-up. There emerges a portrait of a writer and thinker for whom the constant breaking down of concepts, the undermining of abstract ideals and formulae, is an important element in creative activity. *Forma-vita; illusione-realtà; comporre-scomporre*: no sooner is a concept enunciated than its opposite appears as if to mock it, 'come l'ombra segue il corpo' *[SPSV*, 160] [as the shadow follows the body]. It is a conceptual dualism, a dialectic without synthesis, which gives rise, in the humorist's procedures described by Pirandello, to 'un fenomeno di sdoppiamento nell'atto della concezione' *[SPSV*, 134] [a phenomenon of doubling in the act of conception]. [25]

It is clear, I think, from our examination of the texts that there are analogous dualisms contained in the writings specifically concerning the theatre. One obvious division in the theatre essays is a chronological one: between those that pre-date Pirandello's theatrical activity and those that are informed by it. But, as we have seen, this watershed is more apparent than real, with conflicting positions being held simultaneously by the writer in both phases of his career. And yet, throughout, the underlying concerns of the essays are the same: the process of artistic creation; the nature and status of the created work; the relationship of art to life. These are areas in which, from the beginning, Pirandello cannot provide unequivocal truths. Theoretical conclusions are challenged by reality, by practice, out of which opposing truths are born. Irreconcilable positions co-exist openly, and the contingencies of history, with all their 'incongruenze', impinge more than once on the realm of pure ideas. Rather than seeing a dichotomy between theory and practice, we should perhaps discern a constant 'sdoppiamento', a forthright accommodation of contradictions both within and between theory and practice, constituting a rich structural and thematic matrix for Pirandello's creative production.

ÉANNA P. Ó CEALLACHÁIN

[1] The translations of the passages from the essays *Illustratori, attori e traduttori*, the *Discorso al Convegno "Volta" sul teatro drammatico*, *L'azione parlata*, *Teatro e letteratura* and *Se il film parlante abolirà il teatro* are largely based on those in the volume *Luigi Pirandello in the Theatre*, edited by Susan Bassnett and Jennifer Lorch, Switzerland etc., Harwood, 1993. The essays are here translated as: *Illustrators, Actors and Translators*, (pp, 23-34); *Address to the Volta Conference on Dramatic Theatre*, (pp. 172-176); *Spoken Action*, (pp. 20-23); *Theatre and Literature*, (pp. 47-51); *Will the Talkies Do Away with Theatre?*, (pp. 153-157).

[2] 'Introduzione al teatro italiano' in *Storia del teatro italiano*, edited by Silvio D'Amico, Milan, Bompiani, 1936, p. 26.

[3] In turn, a 'relationship of attraction and repulsion', Mario Baratto, 'Gli "Scritti teatrali" di Pirandello' in *Pirandello e il teatro*, Palermo, Palumbo, 1985, p. 38; 'a schizophrenia, a real laceration between his theories and what he does'; Roberto Alonge, 'Pirandello, l'attore, il regista' in *Pirandello e il teatro del suo tempo*, edited by Stefano Milioto, Palermo, Palumbo, 1983, p. 157.

[4] Dante Della Terza, for example, writes of Pirandello's 'belated conversion to the theatre' in 'On Pirandello's Humorism', in *Luigi Pirandello*, ed. H. Bloom, New York, Chelsea Hine, 1989, p. 38. Jennifer Lorch describes the 'development' of Pirandello's position, facilitated by his practical involvement in theatre: see 'Testo e teatro: la teoria e la pratica di Luigi Pirandello', in *Pirandello e il teatro del suo tempo*, cit., pp. 287-295.

[5] In turn, the 'radical condemnation of theatre' and 'the structure and underlying theme'; Claudio Vicentini, 'Il problema del teatro nell'opera di Pirandello', in *Pirandello e il teatro del suo tempo*, cit., p. 9.

[6] See Claudio Vicentini, 'Il problema del teatro nell'opera di Pirandello', cit, p. 7.

[7] A very useful source of information on the theatrical companies of the time with their stock roles and star system is Jennifer Lorch, 'Setting the Scene: Theater in Italy before Pirandello', in *A Companion to Pirandello Studies*, edited by J. DiGaetani, New York, Westport, London, Greenwood Press, 1991, pp. 125-143.

[8] See Roberto Alonge, 'Pirandello, l'attore, il regista', cit., p. 145.

[9] Jennifer Lorch calls Pirandello a 'scissors and paste' writer because of his constant recycling of ideas, phrases, and indeed whole passages in his essays; 'Testo e teatro: la teoria e la pratica di Luigi Pirandello', cit., p. 292, note 1.

[10] See Jana O'Keefe Bazzoni, 'The Reluctant Pilgrim: Pirandello's Journey toward the Modern Stage', in *A Companion to Pirandello Studies*, cit., p. 51.

[11] See especially the closing paragraphs of these two articles: *SPSV*, 1026 and 1029.

[12] The question of the 'fixing' of life's problems in incorruptible form reminds us that we are in the period of *Sei personaggi in cerca d'autore*. In the Preface to the play the Mother's anguished cry is described as 'imbalsamato vivo nella sua forma immarcescibile' [*MN*, I, 65] [embalmed alive in its incorruptible form]. In the 1922 essay, referring to the 'problems' represented in a finished work of art, Pirandello writes: 'La forma perfetta [...] li ha fissati per sempre, li ha raccolti in sé, lei che è immarcescibile, quasi imbalsamati vivi [*SPSV*, 236] [The perfect form [...] has fixed them for ever, has gathered them into itself, which is incorruptible, almost as if embalmed alive].

[13] Claudio Vicentini, 'Il problema del teatro nell'opera di Pirandello', cit., p. 8. The article 'En confidence', published in *Le Temps*, 29 July 1925, can be read in Susan Bassnett's English translation under the title 'Interview with Luigi Pirandello', *The Yearbook of the British Pirandello Society*, 1984, pp. 48-55. The article reappeared in a shortened and modified Italian version in *L'illustrazione del popolo*, 4 June 1935. See Sarah Zappulla Muscarà, 'Archetipi e rari del Pirandello saggista', in *Pirandello saggista*, Palermo, Palumbo, 1982, p. 385. This Italian version, 'La diminuzione dei nostri grandi attori dipende dalla supremazia del regista?', is reprinted in *Pirandello saggista*, pp. 417-419.

[14] *The Yearbook of the British Pirandello Society*, 1984, p. 49.

[15] Ibid. pp. 51-52.

[16] Ibid. pp. 52-54.

[17] Given in 1934, published in 1935 [*SPSV*, 1036].

[18] See Gaspare Giudice, *Luigi Pirandello*, Turin, UTET, 1963, chapter 7.

[19] The question of the director's role is touched on again in 1935 in 'La diminuzione dei nostri grandi attori dipende dalla supremazia del regista?' (see note 13 above). This article confirms the limitations placed on the function of the director and emphasises the far greater importance of the actor's own contribution.

[20] *Introduzione al teatro italiano*, cit., pp. 5-9.

[21] Ibid., pp. 25-26.

[22] Ibid., pp. 26.

[23] See Jennifer Lorch, 'Testo e teatro: la teoria e la pratica di Luigi Pirandello', cit., p. 285.

[24] *Introduzione al teatro italiano*, cit. p. 27.

[25] Ulrich Schulz-Buschhaus dwells on the anti-synthetic character of *L'umorismo* in '*L'umorismo*: l'anti-retorica e l'anti-sintesi di un secondo realismo', in *Pirandello saggista*, cit., pp. 77-86 (see especially pp. 81-82).

BUILDING A CHARACTER: PIRANDELLO AND STANISLAVSKY

Dico che siete sciocchi! Dovevate sapervelo fare per voi stessi,
l'inganno; non per rappresentarlo davanti a me, davanti a chi viene
qua in visita di tanto in tanto; ma cosí, per come siete naturalmente,
tutti i giorni, davanti a nessuno
> a Bertoldo, prendendolo per le braccia

per te, capisci, che in questa tua finzione ci potevi mangiare, dormire,
e grattarti anche una spalla, se ti sentivi un prurito;
> rivolgendosi anche agli altri

sentendovi vivi, vivi veramente nella storia del mille e cento, qua alla
Corte del vostro Imperatore Enrico IV! [*MN*, I, 377]

[I say you're fools! You should have been able to act out the illusion
for yourselves; not just for me and for occasional visitors; but like
this, as you are naturally, every day, with no-one watching
> to Bertoldo, taking him by the arm

for yourself, you see, because in this fiction of yours you could eat,
and sleep, and even scratch your shoulder if you felt an itch;
> turning also to the others

feeling yourselves alive, truly living in the history of the eleventh
century, here at the Court of your Emperor Henry IV!]

In this speech to his secret counsellors Enrico IV, the eponymous protagonist

of one of Pirandello's most famous plays, articulates his theory of 'living' a

part.

The idea of 'living' an identity or mask informs much of Pirandello's

thinking and all of his theatre. He uses the term 'costruirsi' [to construct

oneself] to explain the process by which man constructs the illusion of a

coherent and unified identity in an attempt to hide the inconsistencies and

uncertainties which lie beneath the surface. Pirandello explains the process

thus:

Ci vediamo noi nella nostra vera e schietta realtà, quali siamo, o non piuttosto quali vorremmo essere? Per uno spontaneo artificio interiore, frutto di segrete tendenze o d'incosciente imitazione, non ci crediamo noi in buona fede diversi da quel che sostanzialmente siamo? E pensiamo, operiamo, viviamo secondo questa interpretazione fittizia e pur sincera di noi stessi. [*SPSV*, 146]
[Do we really see ourselves in our true and genuine reality, as we are, or don't we rather see ourselves as we would wish to be? Through a spontaneous inner artifice, the fruit of secret tendencies or of unconscious imitation, do we not in good faith believe we are different from what we substantially are? And we think, work and live according to this fictitious yet sincere interpretation of ourselves.]

Pirandello's near-obsession with role play and self-invention, both on and off stage, makes him an ideal candidate for comparison with Konstantin Stanislavsky (1863-1938), the famous Russian actor/director who spent most of his working life devising a system of actor training and whose concept of 'building a character' bears an almost uncanny resemblance to Pirandello's concept of 'costruirsi'.

It should be pointed out at the outset that many of the analogies between the two theories are sometimes more apparent than real. Stanislavsky's method is 'actor-based' and is, ultimately, a technical system. He distrusts 'intuition', 'instinct' and 'inspiration', or at least the meanings that those words acquire in the mouths of incompetent and careless directors and teachers, and seeks instead to 'build his character' by utilising an acquired technique which is divided into two main parts:

(1) The inner and outer work of the actor on himself

(2) The inner and outer work of the actor on the part. [1]

Having acquired the necessary competence by a series of physical and vocal exercises, the actor then turns to the part and with the help of 'psycho-technique' (self-analytical exercises, imagination, emotional memory etc.) is enabled to achieve a 'feeling for truth' and to reach below the surface reality of the character and discover the inner quality.

It would be easy to suggest that the 'feeling for truth', which allows the actor to probe beneath the surface qualities of the character, is analogous with the humorist's ability to move from the 'avvertimento del contrario' [awareness of the opposite] to the 'sentimento del contrario' [feeling of the opposite]. However, Pirandello never suggests that this 'feeling' is other than an inherent quality which could not be acquired by technical means.

Pirandello's system was playwright-based (and, by extension, character-based). He did not concern himself wih the technicalities of the actors' craft (he was not, after all, a teacher); and the fusion of actor and character which he demanded was to be achieved, if at all, in an almost mystical fashion. The intense preparation functions almost as a purifying process which will render the recipient 'worthy' to effect the necessary 'transubstantiation'. What both men had in abundance was a fanatical devotion to their respective art, an almost super-human capacity for hard work and an expectation that their colleagues and subordinates shared these qualities.

It is often considered that Pirandello's plays are particularly suitable for 'method actors'. Robert Brustein states in an interview that Pirandello is 'a playwright for a Stanislavsky-trained actor. But he is a playwright for a Stanislavsky-trained actor who can also improvise, and of course Stanislavsky put a great deal of emphasis upon improvisation.' [2] But in fact Pirandello poses many problems for the Stanislavsky-trained actor. Rather than presenting a character whose perona emerges through an accumulation of presented information, Pirandello generally presents a coherent, complete character at the outset, and then proceeds to break him down, shredding his identity and leaving him trembling on the brink of the black abyss which the mask was designed to hide. He is similarly sparing of supplying motivation for the character's action. To cite an example, Eric Bentley suggests that:

> The part of Ponza presents the Stanislavsky-trained actor with an interesting problem - what to do about the motivation of a character whose motivation is a mystery. I suppose such an actor can invent motives [...] but a pre-Stanislavskian actor, for whom such questions

did not arise, would be in a simpler position: he need not ask why
Ponza is nearly fainting, he can just take Pirandello's word for it. [3]

A brief examination of Pirandello at work, both as director and as playwright,
is perhaps the best way to demonstrate the similarities and differences between
the two men.

1. The Director

In 1908, when Pirandello wrote his first and most comprehensive essay on
acting, *Illustratori, attori e traduttori* [Illustrators, Actors and Translators] he
had not yet acquired first-hand experience of either acting or directing.
Consequently, unrestricted and unenlightened by practical knowledge, the
theory he offered was idealistic, playwright-centered and somewhat sterile.
The basic premise of the essay is the impossibility of recapturing the perfection
of the original work of art in another form:

> Non sarà piú la stessa. Sarà magari un'immagine approssimativa, piú
> o meno somigliante; ma la stessa, no. Quel dato personaggio su la
> scena dirà le stesse parole del dramma scritto, ma non sarà mai quello
> del poeta, perché l'attore l'ha ricreato in sé, e sua è l'espressione
> quand'anche non siano sue le parole; sua la voce, suo il corpo, suo il
> gesto. [*SPSV*, 216]
> [[The image] will no longer be the same. It will perhaps be an
> approximate image that is more or less similar; but not the same.
> That given character on the stage will say the same words as those in
> the written play, but will never be that of the author because the actor
> has recreated it within himself, and the expression is his even though
> the words are not; his the voice, his the body, his the gestures.]

Notwithstanding the intervening years of practical theatrical experience, and
the admiration and respect which Pirandello came to feel for the acting
profession, he continues to articulate what is fundamentally the same view as
late as 1930 when, in *Questa sera si recita a soggetto* [Tonight We Improvise],
the director, Hinkfuss, states:

L'unica sarebbe se l'opera potesse rappresentarsi da sé, non piú con gli attori, ma coi suoi stessi personaggi che, per prodigio, assumessero corpo e voce. In tal caso sí, direttamente potrebbe essere giudicata a teatro. Ma è mai possibile un tal prodigio? [*MN*, I, 231]
[The only solution would be if the work of art could perform itself, no longer with actors but with its own characters who, by some prodigy, took on a body and a voice. In such an instance it could indeed be judged directly in the theatre. But is such a prodigy ever possible?]

Despite, or perhaps because of, this pessimistic attitude, Pirandello continued to write on the subject of actors and acting in order to formulate a theory which would meet the stringent requirements of his theatre. Gradually Pirandello's antipathy for actors lessened. He became:

...increasingly fascinated by the theatre, directing his own plays and those of other leading European playwrights; ultimately realising that the spontaneity and unpredictability of the performance was not a compromise of the text but its essence. [4]

From 1916 onwards the author became more and more involved in the practicalities of theatre production, but it was in the Teatro d'Arte [Art Theatre], of which he was co-founder and director, that he gained most of his experience as a working director. Gaspare Giudice, Pirandello's biographer, states that although Pirandello did not found a 'school' of acting in the accepted sense, his influence on Italian theatrical practice was significant and lasting. [5] Frustrated by the traditional 'hit and miss' approach of Italian theatrical companies, whose reputation hinged on improvisation, wit, charm and occasional flashes of brilliance, Pirandello turned to European schools, particularly those of Germany and Russia, whose approach was based on painstaking preparation, exhaustive study and analysis.

While he did not entirely reject the idiosyncratic but often effective methods of traditional Italian acting, Pirandello introduced many innovations as yet unknown on the Italian stage. According to Guido Salvini he began work at the Teatro d'Arte by giving his actors a lesson on the modern Russian theatre [6], and Dario Niccodemi relates how Pirandello insisted on an unprecedented commitment from his company, quoting him as saying:

> When I direct, the actors must study their parts and learn them by heart. They must study carefully, at home, on their own, in silence and meditation. And when they come on stage, they must not be actors any longer, they must be the characters in the play they are acting. That way they will have a reality in their own right that is absolute, not relative: it won't be the false truth of stage but the positive undeniable truth of life. [7]

It would, however, be a gross over-simplification to suggest that the obvious esteem in which Pirandello held Stanislavsky and the Russian school caused him to embrace the Russian's system in its entirety. Rather, he adapted those elements of Stanislavsky's technique which corresponded with his own theories. His frequently repeated exhortation that the actor should 'immerse himself' in the part certainly recalls Stanislavsky's teaching. According to Stanislavsky it was essential to reach the moment of 'identification' with the character, a point which must be reached by any means, rational or irrational, in order to achieve that 'circle of attention' in which nothing extraneous could interfere. [8]

But numerous accounts attest to the fact that Pirandello could apparently arrive at this point himself, spontaneously, without any apparent effort, while reading, directing or even viewing plays. Moreover he had 'neither the time, inclination, nor experience necessary to devise a system of exercises to train actors to become more natural on stage.' [9] He would read a scene, playing all the characters with such conviction that he imbued his company with a similar passionate intensity. This approach, although effective, would certainly not coincide with that of Stanislavsky, who lamented failr frequently that he had to treat his actors like mannequins and behave like a despot towards them. [10]

While it is true to say that no-one has claimed that Pirandello ever failed to 'go beyond external invention', it is equally valid to suggest that the sheer force of his personality had a greater effect on the company than 'careful study, silence and meditation'. Giudice relates that:

> Pirandello non condizionava lentamente e gradualmente gli attori; aveva poco tempo per farlo e il suo temperamento d'altra parte non era paziente oltre una limitata misura. Preferiva il metodo della suggestione diretta e veloce. Guido Salvini dice infatti che Pirandello faceva 'violenza' alla volontà degli attori e che le prove non erano lunghe, ma molto intense. [...] Pirandello non era un uomo normale. [11]

> [Pirandello did not condition the actors slowly and gradually; he had little time to do so and moreover he was not, by temperament, patient to more than a limited extent. He preferred the method of direct, rapid suggestion. In fact Guido Salvini says that Pirandello did 'violence' to the will of the actors and that rehearsals were not long, but very intense. [...] Pirandello was not a normal man.]

In *Illustratori, attori e traduttori* Pirandello said that the actor should 'spogliarsi del tutto della propria individualità per entrare in quella del personaggio ch'egli deve rappresentare' [*SPSV*, 215] [strip himself completely of his own individuality in order to enter into that of the character he has to impersonate]. He elaborates on and somewhat modifies the theory, however, in his essay on Eleanora Duse, when he stresses that her:

> 'lifelong ambition of dissolving herself into her roles was not to be construed as a superficial and mechanical notion of a total abandoning of ones own personality. Rather it was a judicious process of selection rejecting those aspects of her personality which conflicted with the character she was interpreting'. [12]

In other words Pirandello would appear to agree with Stanislavsky, whose Director said to actors:

> *Never lose yourself on the stage. Always act in your own person, as an artist. You can never get away from yourself. The moment you lose yourself on the stage marks the departure from truly living your part and the beginning of exaggerated false acting.* [Italics in text] [13]

Stanislavsky elaborates on his belief when he explains that an actor plays
himself but in different combinations and permutations of problems and given
circumstances, which he himself conceives for his part and melts in the furnace
of his own emotional memory. [14]

The laborious process by which Stanislavsky 'builds a character' would
clearly not appeal to a man as impatient as Pirandello, whose method was far
more direct and instinctive. Nor did Pirandello subscribe to the theory that
'emotional memory', that is, the memory that resides in the actor's feeling, was
necessary for the recreation of emotion on stage. Memory and emotional
experience, along with the other mutable aspects of human life, were
considered, in fact, counter-productive, as he says in *Illustratori, attori e
traduttori:*

> Nella realtà le azioni che mettono in rilievo un carattere si stagliano
> su un fondo di contingenze senza valore, di particolari comuni. [...]
> L'arte invece libera le cose, gli uomini e le loro azioni di queste
> contingenze senza valore [...]; in un certo senso li astrae; cioè rigetta,
> senza neppur badarvi, tutto ciò che contraria la concezione dell'artista
> e aggruppa invece tutto ciò che, in accordo con essa, le dà piú forza e
> piú ricchezza. [*SPSV*, 217]
> [In reality the actions which throw a character into relief stand out
> against a background of useless contingencies, of everyday details.
> [...] Art, instead, frees things, people and their actions from these
> useless contingencies [...]; in a certain sense it abstracts them; that is,
> it rejects out of hand all that stands in the way of the artist's
> conception, and instead brings together all that, in accord with it,
> gives it greater strength and richness.]

In spite of his unorthodox and taxing methods, under his tutelage
Pirandello's actors came to admire and respect him. Even well-established and
gifted actors like Ruggero Ruggeri and Lamberto Picasso benefited from his
advice and guidance, and won lavish praise at home and abroad for their
'superb playing', 'great acting' and 'masterful technique'. But no-one is more
worthy of the designation 'Pirandellian actor' than Marta Abba, a young actress
from Milan whom Pirandello employed in 1925 after reading an article by
Marco Praga, who wrote:

Marta Abba shows herself born for the stage and immediately ready to test herself in a major role, and that is why I call her to the attention of producers and directors who are looking for a leading lady, free of spurious blandishments and conventions and equally free of ornate or loutish traditionalisms. [15]

In Abba Pirandello found his ideal interpreter. According to what she herself said she was 'untrained', but she was possessed of that mixture of 'passion' and 'reflection' so necessary for the understanding of a Pirandellian character. Olga Ragusa writes that: 'More than anyone else she succeeded in achieving Pirandello's wish for complete identification between actor and role'. [16] It is, however, fair to suggest that Abba's method consisted in great natural ability coupled with a passionate subjugation to Pirandello's will (she consistently referred to him as 'Maestro') and, by extension, to the character. Giudice writes that: '*Per compiacere di più al Maestro*, arrivava ad attaccare alla porta del suo camerino, anzichè il proprio nome, quello del personaggio di turno'. [17] [*To please the Maestro more*, she even used to put on her dressing room door not her own name but that of the character she was playing] [my italics].

To the end of his career Pirandello held to the belief that the source of the character's reality lay in the text, and that the playwright held the key, and for this reason urged his actors to be strictly faithful to the printed word. He proved to be surprisingly patient during rehearsals, explaining what he wanted and guiding and encouraging his company. He said to Léopold Lacour in 1925;

Let me explain myself: don't begin the rehearsals until each actor has gone through the personal work of exploring in depth the character he is to perform. I assist this work with a personal conference in which I explain the spirit of the play and the spirit of his role. And when all these artists have assimilated these two levels of the acting process, when they have, I say, accomplished according to their own ability by themselves this necessary miracle of spiritual transubstantiation, I bring them together convinced that they will interact, utilizing the correct movements and vocal inflections. [18]

However, while Stanislavsky also advised, and in fact insisted on, close attention to the written text, he had a somewhat cavalier attitude to its importance, and in particular to the importance of the author. He pointed out that the playwright does not provide the actor with everything he has to know: it is, in fact, the actor himself who has to enhance and expand his part from the guidelines sketched out by the author. In this he is in direct opposition to Pirandello, who states categorically that the actor must not change the character but the character the actor.

The similarities between the theories of Pirandello and those of Stanislavsky are indeed striking, sometimes even extending to the use of analogous images to elucidate a point. Pirandello writes, in *Illustratori, attori e traduttori*:

> Perché l'attore, se non vuole (né può volerlo) che le parole scritte del dramma gli escano dalla bocca come da un portavoce o da un fonografo, bisogna che riconcepisca il personaggio, lo concepisca cioè a sua volta per conto suo. [*SPSV*, 216]
> [Because unless the actor wants the written words of the play to come from his mouth as through a mouthpiece or a phonograph (and he cannot want that to happen), he has to reconceive the character, that is, conceive it in turn himself, on his own account].

Stanislavsky on the same subject states:

> If an actor utters a word or does something on the stage in a mechanical way, without knowing who he is, where he comes from, why he is where he is, what he wants, where he will go and what he will do there, he is acting without imagination, and that fraction of time he spends on stage, whether long or short, is not truth, so far as he is concerned, for he has been acting without imagination, has been acting like an automaton. Not a single step must be taken on the stage mechanically and without some inner justification for it, that is without the work of the imagination. [19]

Fundamentally, however, because of their vastly differing starting points, the analogies between the two methods are more apparent than real. Both men hold the view that the cornerstone of the actor's performance is hard work and passionate dedication, but the methods which Stanislavsky employs - the reliance on 'emotional memory', improvisation and technical exercises - are a far cry from those of Pirandello. Pirandello's dream of turning intellect into passion required more than technique, it required a miracle, vouchsafed only to those who made a passionate act of faith in the author himself.

2. *The Writer.*

It is in the plays themselves that Pirandello's theories on acting are most clearly articulated, and characteristically his attitude is once more fundamentally negative. In *Sei personaggi in cerca d'autore* [Six Characters in Search of an Author], *Ciascuno al suo* [Each in His Own Way], *Questa sera si recita a soggetto* [Tonight We Improvise], *Trovarsi* [To Find Oneself] and the unfinished *I giganti della montagna* [The Mountain Giants] he explores the problems of the actor or, to be more accurate, he points out the inadequacies of actors and of the acting profession in general.

In *Sei personaggi in cerca d'autore* the inability of the characters to realize, or even to comprehend, the tragedy of the characters is obviously more than a mere broadside against the traditional theatrical companies. Nevertheless, Pirandello avails himself of every possible opportunity to emphasize their negative aspects. In the opening scene he establishes the scant competence of the company: the Leading Lady is late (a misdemeanour of which Stanislavsky was exceptionally critical, incidentally); the actors make no attempt to 'prepare' (another Stanislavskian principle) and the Producer demonstrates his total inability to comprehend the play in rehearsal, and his contempt for it.

After glossing over some technicalities with the Prompter and Stage Manager, he gives his one and only piece of 'directorial' advice:

> Mi raccomando, si metta di tre quarti, perché se no, tra le astruserie del dialogo e lei che non si farà sentire, addio ogni cosa!
> *Battendo di nuovo le mani:*

Attenzione, attenzione! Attacchiamo! [*MN*, I, 75-76]
[If I were you I would turn three quarters on, because if you don't,
what with the obscure dialogue and the fact that you can't be heard we
can say good night to it!
clapping his hands again:
Come on, let's start!] [20]

On to this scene come the characters, who force the actors to confront their

own inadequacies; but this proves to be a futile exercise. The actors may be

sincere, but they are incapable of understanding, let alone achieving, the

'fusion of actor and character' required by Pirandello (and Stanislavsky). The

Father says: 'Non sono forse abituati lor signori a vedere balzar vivi quassù,

uno di fronte all'altro, i personaggi creati da un autore?' [*MN*, I, 80] [Aren't you

used to seeing the characters created by an author dance into life here on the

stage? Face to face with each other?] [21] But the actors remain incredulous, as

is further emphasized by the Producer when he exclaims, with exasperation

(and unintentional irony):

> '... ma qua, caro signore, non recitano i personaggi. Qua recitano gli
> attori. I personaggi stanno lí nel copione
> *indicherà la buca del Suggeritore*
> - quando c'è un copione! [*MN*, I, 102]
> [...but characters don't act here. Actors act here. Characters stay
> there in the script
> *He points to the Prompter's box*
> - when there is a script.] [22]

When the characters attempt to enact the tragedy of the characters, their

incompetence is even more apparent. Although Pirandello insists that there

should be no air of parody about the performance of the actors, he nevertheless

constrains them to act in a stilted and mannered fashion. They imitate what

they have just seen, employing outmoded gestures and poses, but they make no

attempt whatsoever to 'feel'. According to Stanislavsky the theatre has

invented a whole assortment of signs, expressions of human passions, poses

and mechanical tricks which are always at the service of an actor when he feels

utterly helpless on the stage, and stands there with an empty soul. [23] The company, though, is preoccupied with tired conventions, and has no hope at all of moving from 'awareness' to 'feeling'. These are not, and can never be, Pirandellian actors; thus the characters are doomed to continue in their search for a medium which will give 'life' to their 'art'.

If Stanislavsky would have found nothing to criticise in the treatment of actors in *Sei personaggi*, he might well have had reservations about Pirandello's attitude in *Questa sera si recita a soggetto*. Written in 1930, after Pirandello had enjoyed a long and fruitful relationship with the actors of the Teatro d'Arte, *Questa sera* shows the actor in a different light, at least initially. It is Hinkfuss who bears the brunt of the author's criticism. Hinkfuss, a director who espouses all the techniques and tricks of the 'modern' theatre (many of which he could have learned from Stanislavsky), wishes to 'improvise' a play with an impossibly complicated outline. The actors are at first willing, indeed eager, to escape the tyranny of the printed script. They improvise their roles with enthusiasm - too much enthusiasm as it transpires - and anarchy soon prevails. No actor is willing to subjugate himself for the good of the play, and without the guiding hand of the author the dangers of excessive and uncontrolled improvisation are soon apparent, so that before long the actors demand a script with lines, parts and stage-directions. These are not the actors of *Sei personaggi*; they have become, in fact, Pirandellian actors. As the Leading Actor says, when he plays Rico Verri: 'per aver pronte le parole che debbono nascere, nascere dal personaggio che rappresento' he must 'vivere il personaggio di *Rico Verri*, essere *Rico Verri*' [*MN*, I, 238] [in order to have ready the words which must be born, born from the character I play [he must] live the character of *Rico Verri*, be *Rico Verri*]. Hinkfuss alone remains unchanged, making grandiose statements on the requirements of theatre.

In *Ciascuno al suo* and *Trovarsi* the portrait of the actor is almost completely positive. *Ciascuno al suo* is almost a reversal of the process examined in *Sei personaggi*. In it, a member of the audience interrupts the proceedings on stage to complain that an actress playing a character (which the member of the audience considers herself to be) has violated her privacy by being too 'life-like', too real. The actress in *Trovarsi*, a part which was written for Marta Abba, is so expert at emptying herself and dedicating all of her intellect and passion to her work that she is incapable of 'living' except as a character. Despite his gradually acquired enthusiasm for actors, however, it would be untrue to suggest that Pirandello ever departed from his stance of author supremacy. Even when the play calls for 'improvisation' most, if not all, 'business' and lines are written, leaving the actor virtually no freedom. Similarly, Pirandello's detailed and sometimes esoteric stage directions leave little scope for the actor's 'imagination'.

It is, in fact, Pirandello the playwright who 'builds the character'. The actors, at first considered a 'necessary evil', later became 'intermediaries' between the poet and his audience, almost as a priest functions as a intermediary between God and the faithful. The inner life of the work is made manifest by the actors who, by their efforts, have become worthy to act as its vehicles. To conclude, as Pirandello himself wrote:

> The thought and the hidden sentiment that guide the action and dictate the words in every work of mine are discovered not so much at its reading as at its performance, when act and word appear alive in that inner life enclosed within the thought of hidden sentiment, for my plays are constructed not externally from the outside, but from the inside. And thus 'inside' is discovered only at the footlights. [24]

MARY CASEY

[1] K. Stanislavsky, *An Actor Prepares*, trans. E. R. Hapgood, London, Eyre Methuen, 1981 (1994 reprint), esp. pp. 33-53.

[2] In *A Companion to Pirandello Studies*, ed. John Louis DiGaetani, New York etc., Greenwood Press, p. 302.

[3] Eric Bentley, *The Pirandello Commentaries*, Evanston, Illinois, Northwestern University Press, 1986, p. 30.

[4] A. Richard Sogliuzzo, *Luigi Pirandello Director: The Playwright in the Theatre*, Meluchen, New Jersey, Scarecrow Press, 1982, p. 29.

[5] Gaspare Giudice, *Luigi Pirandello*, Turin, UTET, 1963, p. 471.

[6] Gaspare Giudice, *Luigi Pirandello*, cit., p. 473.

[7] Quoted in Susan Bassnett McGuire, *Luigi Pirandello*, London, Macmillan, 1983, p. 21.

[8] Gaspare Giudice, *Luigi Pirandello*, cit., p. 473.

[9] A. Richard Sogliuzzo, *Luigi Pirandello Director*, cit., p. 39.

[10] See K. Stanislavsky, *My Life in Art*, trans J. J. Robbins, London, Geoffrey Bles, n.d., esp. pp. 229, 247, 308.

[11] Gaspare Giudice, *Luigi Pirandello*, cit., p. 477.

[12] Quoted in A. Richard Sogliuzzo, *Luigi Pirandello Director*, cit., p. 26.

[13] K. Stanislavsky, *An Actor Prepares*, cit., p. 177.

[14] K. Stanislavsky, *Stanislavsky on the Art of Stage*, trans. and introd. David Magarsnack, London, Faber, 1961, p. 54 .

[15] Quoted in Olga Ragusa, *Pirandello: An Approach to His Theatre*, Edinburgh, Edinburgh University Press, 1980, p. 174.

[16] Olga Ragusa, *Pirandello: An Approach to His Theatre*, cit., p. 175.

[17] Gaspare Giudice, *Luigi Pirandello*, cit., p. 470.

[18] Quoted in A. Richard Sogliuzzo, *Luigi Pirandello Director*, cit., p. 55.

[19] K. Stanislavsky, *Stanislavsky on the Art of the Stage*, cit., p. 39.

[20] Luigi Pirandello, *Six Characters in Search of an Author*, translated by Mary Casey (unpublished); performed in Dublin, 12-20 April 1994.

[21] Luigi Pirandello, *Six Characters*, trans. Mary Casey, cit.

[22] Luigi Pirandello, *Six Characters*, trans Mary Casey, cit.

[23] K. Stanislavsky, *An Actor Prepares*, cit., p. 52.

[24] Letter from Pirandello to Talli, quoted in Olga Ragusa, *Pirandello: An Approach to His Theatre*, cit., p. 107.

PIRANDELLO'S FICTION AS EVIDENCE OF HIS INTEREST IN THEATRE AND CINEMA

On 29 August 1894 the weekly *La domenica italiana* published a short story by Pirandello entitled *Le tre carissime* [*NA*, II, 832-40] [The Three Very Dear Ladies]. [1] The young ladies of the title are the Marúccoli sisters, who, although impoverished, make every effort to play their full part in Rome's upper middle-class society: 'Quelle tre che incontravate da per tutto: a ogni concerto, puntualissime; a ogni prima rappresentazione al *Valle* o al *Costanzi*, sempre in un palchetto di prima fila [...]' [*NA*, II, 1342] [Those three you used to meet everywhere: very punctual at every concert; at every première always in a little box in the front row at the *Valle* or the *Costanzi*]. [2] In this story, then, theatre is seen as a social institution and from the point of view of the theatre-goer. Such a view of theatre is consolidated later in the story, when the sisters are marvellously dressed, 'pronte per recarsi a qualche radunanza in casa di famiglie amiche o a teatro' [*NA*, II, 1346] [ready to go to a gathering in the house of a family with whom they were on friendly terms or to the theatre]; and when they are again pictured in their well-placed box: 'Quando in teatro vedevamo qualcuna di loro piú del solito raggiante [...]' [*NA*, II, 1347] [When in the theatre we saw one of them more radiant than usual [...]]. But this is not the only way in which theatre features in *Le tre carissime*, since this story also contains a theatrical simile which refers to a signal hinting at future developments; the narrator says this signal 'mi è rimasto impresso come in un dramma una frase che lasci intraveder la catastrofe' [*NA*, II, 1347] [has stayed in my mind like a phrase in a play which allows a glimpse of the dénouement]. Furthermore, one of the sisters takes it into her head to become an actress and rehearses plays with her long-suffering mother. Several lines of one of these rehearsals are included verbatim in the story, typographically presented in the form of a play-text. [3]

Few of Pirandello's fictional writings contain such a variety of references to theatre as *Le tre carissime*, but several of the other early short stories serve to extend that variety. Occasionally, for instance, the word *commedia* is used as a metaphor for insincere or over-elaborate behaviour, as it is in *Le dodici lettere* [The Twelve Letters], first published in 1897 ('rappresentando la commedia della gelosia' [*NA*, III, 1014] [acting the comedy of jealousy]) and *Dono della Vergine Maria* [Gift of the Virgin Mary] (1899). In this story, in the opinion of the anticlerical Don Bartolo Scimpri, 'Era tempo di finir la sciocca commedia dei Santi, delle processioni, delle immagini dipinte e scolpite nelle chiese' [*NA*, I, 1408] [It was time to end the foolish comedy of Saints, of processions, of painted and sculpted images in the churches]. The verb *rappresentare* (to act, to perform), in the theatrical sense, is used metaphorically with other direct objects besides *commedia*. In *La signorina* (1894) we read, 'La scena del giorno precedente gli si rappresentava alla mente' [*NA*, III, 847] [Yesterday's scene was acted out in his mind]; while the narrator of *La ricca* [The Rich Woman] (1892) says of Giulia Montana, 'Certe volte, pareva veramente ch'ella si fosse imposta *una parte*, e che la rappresentasse sempre, in casa e fuori' [*NA*, III, 799; Pirandello's italics] [Sometimes it really seemed that she had deliberately taken on *a part*, and that she always acted it, at home and elsewhere]. Sometimes fictional characters are metaphorically seen as actors, either in a serious drama, as in *Visitare gl'infermi* [Visiting the Sick] (1896), where they are 'gli attori muti di quella lugubre scena' [*NA*, II, 719] [the silent actors in that mournful scene], or with the emphasis on simulation, as when in *Le dodici lettere* Tito Rivoli remarks of the insincere Adele Montagnani, 'Che commediante!' [*NA*, III, 1014] [What an actress!]. Nor is play-text typography used only in *Le tre carissime*, or only fragmentarily: the four *Dialoghi tra il Gran Me e il piccolo me* [Dialogues between the Big Me and the little me], first published, respectively, in 1895, 1897, 1897 and 1906, are cast from beginning to end in the form of a play-text, complete with rudimentary stage directions [*NA*, III, 963-985].

Since none of Pirandello's plays was publicly performed until he was forty-three, it is sometimes thought that he became interested in theatre comparatively late in life. The contrary, however, is easily demonstrated. Gaspare Giudice's biography of Pirandello includes two photographs of him improvising comedies with friends on the terrace of his lodgings in Rome in the late 1880s. [4] We know of seventeen or eighteen plays that he wrote before 1900 - the earliest around 1878 - though most of them are lost (*La signorina* was a three-act play before it was published as a short story). [5] As early as the late 1880s, in Rome, he was in contact with professional theatre companies about the possible production of at least two of them, and in one case almost achieved a stage début. [6] It is thus not surprising that his earliest fictional writings include sporadic signs of an interest in theatre. It is true that, after early disappointments, Pirandello steered clear of theatre for many years - and this stance too is occasionally reflected in his fiction. [7] In *La scelta* [The Choice] (1898), which is presumably autobiographical (Giudice calls it a biographical memoir) [8], the first-person narrator characterizes himself only as a writer of novels and short stories ('ci vado per scegliervi gli eroi e le eroine de' miei romanzi e delle mie novelle') [*NA*, III, 1036] [I go there to choose the heroes and heroines of my novels and short stories]. This apparent *lack* of interest in theatre is maintained as late as 1915, in the first of the two *Colloquii coi personaggi* [Interviews with Characters], where a notice on the door of the first-person narrator's study is addressed to characters 'che hanno fatto domanda e presentato titoli per essere ammessi in qualche romanzo o novella' [*NA*, III, 1138] [who have applied and submitted qualifications for admission into a novel or short story]. [9] But in reality Pirandello's extensive early interest in theatre could not simply be erased.

Even so, it would be easy to over-estimate the evidence of Pirandello's interest in theatre afforded by his short stories and novels. Indeed, it could perhaps be observed that for a writer so deeply interested in the stage his fictional writings contain remarkably few explicit signs of that interest; and it is possible to read hundreds of pages of his short stories, in the order in which the author himself arranged them, without coming across any such signs at all. In only eleven of the 239 short stories is the theatre even fleetingly mentioned as a social institution or as a place where a character goes as a spectator. [10] In only seven is there any mention of theatre as a profession, and none of these includes anything of theatrical interest, unless it be *Tirocinio* [Apprenticeship] (1905; the source of the three-act play *Il piacere dell'onestà* [The Pleasure of Honesty]), which contains two remarks about the general immorality of theatre professionals [*NA*, III, 137-138]. [11] Moreover imitation of the style of the play-text becomes less frequent after 1900. *Un'altra allodola* [Another Skylark] (1902) contains a whole paragraph with no verbs which is a perfect stage direction [*NA*, III, 95]. *Mondo di carta* [Paper World] (1909) includes a near-perfect stage direction of a different kind - italic script in parenthesis in the middle of a speech [*NA*, I, 1025]. The novel *Il fu Mattia Pascal* [The Late Mattia Pascal] (1904; rewritten 1918) features a snatch of dialogue set out according to play-text conventions [*TR*, I, 426-427]. [12] *La morte addosso* (originally *Caffè notturno* [All-night Café]) (1918) consists of nothing but dialogue, though it does not adopt play-text layout [*NA*, II, 55-63].

Very often there is no way of knowing whether Pirandello is thinking of plays (*teatro di prosa*) or opera (*teatro lirico*); the Italian word *teatro* refers equally to both, whereas to an anglophone 'theatre' tends to suggest only the former. Occasionally, however, it is clear that Pirandello has operatic theatre in mind. Both *Lumie di Sicilia* (1900) and *Tirocinio*, for instance, have a prominent female character who is (or has been) a professional opera singer. But the story which is most fully steeped in opera is *'Leonora, addio!'* (1910) [*NA*, III, 374-383]. The protagonist, Mommina La Croce, is one of four Sicilian sisters who regularly go to the theatre and at home, with their mother at the piano, sing through 'tutti i "pezzi d'opera" che avevano sentito nell'ultima stagione' [*NA*, III, 374-375] [all the "best bits of opera" they had heard in the last season] - both the women's parts and the men's parts, in costumes representing both sexes, with simulated moustaches where appropriate (Mommina, for instance, sings the part of Siebel in Gounod's *Faust*). Mommina thus grows up with 'la passione dei melodrammi' [*NA*, III, 377] [a passion for melodramas] and finds Rico Verri irresistible after he fights three duels for her - Raul di Nangis, Ernani and Don Alvaro rolled into one! [13]

After their marriage, however, Verri proves to be ferociously jealous of his wife (in this he is based on Pirandello's in-laws). [14] He allows no outsiders to enter the house and keeps Mommina constantly at home under lock and key, with grave consequences for her health and her morale. The one aspect of Mommina that Verri cannot control is her memories, which include other young men and opera. Eventually, some years after the birth of her two daughters, while her husband is out (as usual), Mommina stumbles on the idea of enlivening her dismal existence by sharing her passion for *teatro lirico* with her daughters:

> Prese a descrivere affollatamente il teatro, gli spettacoli che vi si davano, la ribalta, l'orchestra, gli scenarii, poi a narrare l'argomento dell'opera e a dire dei varii personaggi, com'erano vestiti, e in fine, tra lo stupore delle piccine che la guardavano, sedute sul letto, con tanto d'occhi e temevano che fosse impazzita, si mise a cantare con strani gesti questa e quell'aria e i duetti e i cori, a rappresentar la parte dei varii personaggi, tutta *La forza del destino* [*NA*, III, 381].
> [She started to describe all in a rush the theatre, the productions that were put on, the footlights, the orchestra, the sets, then to relate the story of the opera and to talk about the various characters, and how they were dressed, and finally, to the amazement of the little girls who were sitting on the bed watching her, wide-eyed and fearful that she had gone mad, she started to sing with strange gestures this aria and that and the duets and the choruses, to act the part of the various characters, the whole of *The Force of Destiny*.]

The next day she performs the whole of *Les Huguenots* for them, and the day after that, *Il trovatore* (from which the story's title is a quotation); but Verri returns home near the end of this performance, and at that moment Mommina suddenly dies, presumably of a heart attack. The text is punctuated by six quotations (or misquotations), of between one and five lines, from five different operas - which apart from anything else demonstrates the author's familiarity with the operatic tradition.

Pirandello was born and brought up in Sicily, and one of the distinctive features of Sicilian culture is its puppet theatre, with its plots and characters drawn from sources such as the *commedia dell'arte* and especially an Italian adaptation (where the Roland of the *Chanson de Roland* had become the Orlando of Ariosto's *Orlando furioso*) of the epic cycles of medieval France. [15] Then as now, the puppets were also sold to the general public. Pirandello was fully exposed to this area of Sicilian culture. In the presumably autobiographical *La scelta* the narrator as a child is taken to a fair and allowed to choose one of 'le marionette, ch'eran la mia passione' [the marionettes, which were my passion]. Orlando, Rinaldo da Montalbano, Astolfo and Gano are mentioned by name; and the theatrical context of these puppets is alluded to when the stallholder remarks, ' [...] ci vuole il tristo e il buono, il paladino fedele e Gano il traditore, se no la rappresentazione non si può fare ...' [*NA*, III, 1035-1036] [you need the evil one and the good one, the faithful paladin and the traitor Gano, otherwise the performance can't go ahead ...]. [16]

A short story in which Pirandello deals affectionately with the Sicilian puppets is *La paura del sonno* [Fear of Sleep] [*NA*, III, 53-69] (1900; rewritten 1902). The protagonists are Don Saverio Càrzara, a professional puppet-maker known as the 'Mago delle fiere' [Wizard of the Fairs], and his wife Fana. Many unfinished puppets, hanging on wires stretched across a room in the Càrzaras' home, are witnesses to the couple's existence, and are personified to the point of having emotional responses and the power of speech (in Sicilian dialect). This 'popolo vario di burattini e marionette' [*NA*, III, 54] (that is, respectively, both glove-puppets and marionettes), of which each section is characterized by one or more of its most salient features, includes Pulcinellas with their jackets and little caps, 'i piccoli Pasquini, dalle folte sopracciglia dipinte e il codino arguto sulla nuca' [little Pasquinos, with thick painted eyebrows and thin pigtails on their necks] as well as 'la smorfia furbesca del sorriso che scontorce loro la bocca' [the cunning grimace of the smile which twists their faces], Florindos and Lindoros with their little wigs, Charlemagnes with their royal mantles, Ferraú di Spagna and the paladins of France, 'chiusi nelle loro armature di latta o di cartone indorato' [enclosed in their suits of armour of tin or gilded cardboard], judges with their caps and robes, little clowns with their vests and small peasants with their little breeches, not to mention the little caps and many-coloured little coats waiting to clothe unspecified figures [NA, III, 53-54 and 58]. At one point Don Saverio picks up a puppet, says to his wife, 'Ti rappresento una parte seria: della rotta di Roncisvalle...' [NA, III, 67] [I'll act a serious part for you: of the defeat at Roncevaux], and operates the puppet, declaiming the appropriate lines. [17]

Sometimes Sicilian puppet theatre was also used to perform plays intended for human actors; [18] and this is the context of a far-reaching speculation by Anselmo Paleari in Il fu Mattia Pascal (though this passage is set in Rome, where Sicilian puppet theatres also existed):

> La tragedia d'Oreste in un teatrino di marionette! [...] D'après Sophocle, dice il manifestino. Sarà l'Elettra. Ora senta un po' che bizzarria mi viene in mente! Se, nel momento culminante, proprio quando la marionetta che rappresenta Oreste è per vendicare la morte del padre sopra Egisto e la madre, si facesse uno strappo nel cielo di carta del teatrino, che avverrebbe? [...] Oreste rimarrebbe terribilmente sconcertato da quel buco nel cielo. [...] Sentirebbe ancora gl'impulsi della vendetta, vorrebbe seguirli con smaniosa passione, ma gli occhi, sul punto, gli andrebbero lí, a quello strappo, donde ora ogni sorta di mali influssi penetrerebbero nella scena, e si sentirebbe cader le braccia. Oreste, insomma, diventerebbe Amleto. Tutta la differenza [...] fra la tragedia antica e la moderna consiste in ciò [...]: in un buco nel cielo di carta. [TR, I, 467-468].
> [The tragedy of Orestes in a puppet theatre! [...] Based on Sophocles, says the poster. It'll be Electra. Now just listen what strange idea comes to my mind! If, at the crucial moment, when the marionette representing Orestes is about to take revenge on Aegisthus and his mother for the death of his father, a tear was made in the puppet theatre's paper sky, what would happen? [...] Orestes would be

terribly disconcerted by that hole in the sky. [...] He would still feel a great impulse towards revenge, and would want passionately to follow that impulse, but at the vital moment his eyes would turn to that tear, from which all kinds of evil influences would now penetrate onto the stage, and he would feel his arms fall to his side. Orestes, in short, would become Hamlet. The whole difference [...] between ancient tragedy and modern tragedy lies here [...]; in a hole in the paper sky.]

Although Paleari is a character of doubtful authority in the economy of *Il fu Mattia Pascal*, [19] he is here making a serious if somewhat obvious point about modern tragedy (he uses the adjective 'modern' in its broadest sense, thus classing Shakespeare as a modern tragedian). Since the difference between ancient tragedy and modern tragedy is epitomized in 'un buco nel cielo di carta', we should note that *cielo* means both 'sky' and 'heaven': if heaven is punctured, and indeed deflated, this may mean, as Laura Richards suggests, a 'loss of faith in divine providence, of belief that the world is controlled and ordered by a superior Will'. [20] Even without a specifically religious interpretation, it points to a distinction between art which is governed by a coherent set of conventions and art which is open to the problematic nature of life. In Sophocles' *Electra*, Orestes can act with self-assurance because the logic of his actions is dictated by a stable ideology, whereas the tear in the paper sky would be a sign of instability: it would force Orestes into an act of metaphysical reflection which is alien to his nature, and this in turn would lead him to discover all the tensions and contradictions of which life consists. As a result he would be paralysed by uncertainty, like Hamlet; the hero would become an anti-hero.

It might be thought that in making this point Pirandello would have been better advised not to introduce the complication of marionettes, but to focus instead either on Orestes himself or on a human actor playing the part of Orestes. But it turns out that the distinction between ancient and modern tragedy is not the only point at issue. A few lines later the protagonist reflects:

Beate le marionette, [...] su le cui teste di legno il finto cielo si conserva senza strappi! Non perplessità angosciose, né ritegni, né intoppi, né ombre, né pietà: nulla! E possono attendere bravamente e

prender gusto alla loro commedia e amare e tener se stesse in
considerazione e in pregio, senza soffrir mai vertigini o capogiri,
poiché per la loro statura e per le loro azioni quel cielo è un tetto
proporzionato. [TR, I, 468]
[Blessed are the marionettes, [...] over whose wooden heads the make
believe sky has no tears in it! No anguished bewilderment, no
restraints or obstacles or shadows or pity: nothing! And they can wait
sturdily and enjoy their comedy and love and hold themselves in
consideration and esteem, without ever feeling dizzy or light-headed,
since that sky is a roof in proportion with their height and actions.]

Here a second distinction is being made, between marionettes and human
beings. Whereas the marionette never has to face the situation where
metaphysical speculation deprives it of the stable reality of which it is a part,
human beings might well find themselves in that situation. In the 'Avvertenza
sugli scrupoli della fantasia' [Consideration on the Scruples of the
Imagination], which Pirandello appended to *Il fu Mattia Pascal* in 1921, this
idea is taken up and developed. The moment at which the marionette notices
the tear in the paper sky is a metaphorical representation of the moment when
a person becomes aware of the distance between an aspect of reality and the
illusory version of that aspect of reality according to which - together with
other illusions - he has hitherto lived his life. A standard Pirandellian example
of such a moment is Vitangelo Moscarda's discovery that his nose is crooked at
the beginning of *Uno, nessuno e centomila* [One, No-one and a Hundred
Thousand] (1925-26). And the remainder of Vitangelo's story - a story of acute
self-doubt, possible insanity and alienation from life itself - dramatizes one set
of natural consequences of such a discovery. The alternative is to continue
living as before, but in the knowledge that one is living out a set of illusions,
which is hardly bearable [*TR*, I, 582-583]. These considerations, then, bring us
to the heart of Pirandello's *umorismo* [humorism]. Pirandello is using the
marionette as an image of everyday behaviour governed by a complex system
of illusion-based constructs and conventions - the behaviour which he
elsewhere labels 'form' as opposed to 'life', [21] and to which he also applies the
related image of the mask.

In the second of the two passages from *Il fu Mattia Pascal* quoted above, the puppet serves as metaphor for the human condition as Pirandello sees it; and the same metaphor is used elsewhere in his fiction, though - oddly, perhaps - only in the novels, never in the short stories, and not always with reference to something as comprehensive as 'the human condition'. In *Il turno* [The Turn] (1902) Pepè Alletto performs so ineffectually in his duel with Luca Borrani that one of his seconds says he was 'come un pupazzo da teatrino' [*TR*, I, 245] [like a puppet in a puppet theatre]. More seriously, Vitangelo Moscarda in *Uno, nessuno e centomila* repeatedly refers to the version of himself that inhabits his wife's consciousness as a marionette, with 'quella comoda consistenza di marionetta che lui [Moscarda's father-in-law] da un canto e la figlia dall'altro, e dal canto loro tutti i socii della banca gli avevano dato' [*TR*, II, 858, 859, 867] [that convenient, puppet-like coherence which he [Moscarda's father-in-law] on his part and his daughter on hers, and on theirs all the partners in the bank had given him]. These people see him as a puppet in as much as they do not imagine him to be capable of metaphysical reflection or unconventional action.

The theatrical image of the mask also occurs occasionally. In *La veglia* [Keeping Watch] (1904; the source of *Come prima, meglio di prima* [As Before, Better Than Before]) Marco Mauri exhorts Silvio Gelli to lay aside what he sees as his hypocrisy by telling him to take off his mask [*NA*, II, 155]. Fabrizio, the first-person narrator of *La trappola* [The Trap] (1912; rewritten 1915), who anticipates Vitangelo Moscarda in his urge to escape the single identity, says: 'Truccarmi, come un attore di teatro? Ne ho avuto qualche volta la tentazione. Ma poi ho pensato che, sotto la maschera, il mio corpo rimaneva sempre quello ... e invecchiava!' [*NA*, I, 777] [Disguise myself, like a theatre actor? I've sometimes been tempted. But then I thought that, beneath the mask, my body stayed the same ... and grew older!] The mask has a more visual function in *Quaderni di Serafino Gubbio operatore* (originally published as *Si gira...* in 1915) [Notebooks of Serafino Gubbio Cinematograph Operator, originally published in 1915 as Shoot!). [22] Here Simone Pau is described as having 'l'enorme bocca tumida aperta, come quella di un'antica maschera comica' [an enormous fleshy open mouth, like that of an ancient comic mask]; in the same novel, though, Carlo Ferro calls human beings 'mascherati' who, 'appena insieme, l'uno di fronte all'altro, diventiamo tutti tanti pagliacci' [*TR*, II, 525, 617] [masked [who] as soon as we are together, facing each other, we all become so many clowns].

Theatrical imagery more generally quite often suggests that Pirandello tended to see life itself as theatre, particularly where such imagery either focuses on single aspects of theatre activity or is used in a self-conscious manner. An example of a self-conscious simile would be this one from *La levata del sole* [The Rising of the Sun] (1901, rewritten 1926): 'Anche la natura, come un qualunque teatro, dava i suoi spettacoli a ore fisse' [*NA*, II, 898] [Nature too, like any theatre, would put on its shows at fixed times]; or the rather more specific comparison in *Il vitalizio* [The Life Annuity] (1901, rewritten 1919) where the protagonist gazes at 'Girgenti che sedeva alta sul colle con le vecchie case dorate dal sole, come in uno scenario' [*NA*, II, 842] [Girgenti sitting high up on its hill with its old houses gilded by the sun, like a stage set]. For a self-conscious metaphor we might turn to *Frammento di cronaca di Marco Leccio* [Fragment of the Chronicle of Marco Leccio] (1919), where we read, 'Fra quattro ore sarà chiuso un quadro di questa scena' [*NA*, III, 1201] [In four hours' time a tableau of this scene will have closed].

References to figurative actors are relatively frequent, as in this metaphor from *Il fu Mattia Pascal*: 'Mi vidi, in quell'istante, attore d'una tragedia che piú buffa non si sarebbe potuta immaginare' [*TR*, I, 360] [I saw myself, in that instant, as the actor in a tragedy than which nothing more comic could be imagined]. There is also the simile in *Pallino e Mimí* [Pallino and Mimí] (1905) which has Basilio Gori looking up 'come per godere, lui attore, dello spettacolo di tanti spettatori' [*NA*, I, 295] [as though he, the actor, were enjoying the spectacle of so many spectators]; or the sentence in *Acqua e lí* [Water and There] (1897, rewritten 1923) where we read of Dottor Calajò that 'gli pare [...] che pianga come un commediante sulla scena' [*NA*, II, 356] [he seemed [...] to be crying like an actor on the stage].[23] A more radical verbal variant is found in *Il fu Mattia Pascal*, where Terenzio Papiano, who likes the sound of his own voice, speaks with 'inflessioni da provetto filodrammatico' [*TR*, I, 465] [the inflexions of an experienced amateur actor].

The image of the actor is sufficiently frequent in Pirandello's prose to be regarded as a distinctive if dicreet feature of his narrative language. More frequent, though (occurring about forty times in all), and thus more distinctive, is his use of figurative language involving the actor's role (*parte*) or a whole performance, characteristically accompanied by the verb *rappresentare*. This is not surprising when one considers how basic to Pirandello's view of human behaviour the notion of role-playing is (as expressed in the title *Il giuoco delle parti* [The Game of Role-Playing; often translated as The Rules of the Game]). The two young men in *Pari* [Equals] (1907), for example, who both live and work together, know almost instinctively which of them should speak or act in any given situation: 'Subito, a ogni minima evenienza, si assegnavano le parti' [*NA*, I 440] [Immediately, at the slightest occurrence, they cast themselves in their roles]. The moribund Costanzo Ramberti, in *L'illustre estinto* [The Illustrious Dead] (1909), is determined to die with dignity, and the constant presence of his private secretary helps him achieve this: 'La presenza di quell'uomo squallido, allampanato, miope, lo teneva per un filo, esilissimo ormai, su la scena, investito della sua parte, fino all'ultimo' [*NA*, III, 144] [The presence of that dreary, lanky, myopic man kept him in his role on the stage, held by a thread which was now very slender, right to the end]. Serafino Gubbio reflects that if Varia Nestoroff knew of his friendship with the late Giorgio Mirelli her behaviour towards him would change: 'Si vestirebbe per me d'una parte che me ne nasconderebbe tante altre' [*TR*, II, 582] [She would take on a role for me which would hide very many others from me]. In *Zia Michelina* [Aunt Michelina] (1914), Marruchino marries his widowed stepmother in extremely odd circumstances which appear not to include love, and the narrator refers to 'la parte che s'era assunta d'innamorato' [*NA*, I, 681] [the role he had assumed of the man in love].

The same metaphor becomes more conspicuous when *parte* is the direct object of the verb *rappresentare*. Biagio Speranza, in *La signora Speranza* (1903; one of the sources of *Ma non è una cosa seria* [But It's Not Serious]) finds himself obliged to fulfil his role as husband in protecting his wife from the aggressive Bertolli even though he does not live with her (another extremely odd and loveless marital situation!), but tells his friends, 'Appena avrò finito di rappresentare la mia parte di fronte al Cocco Bertolli, partirò, cari miei, e non mi rivedrete mai piú!' [*NA*, III, 1093] [As soon as I've finished playing my part to Cocco Bertolli I shall go away, dear friends, and you won't ever see me again!]. [24] Roberto San Romé, a character in *Di guardia* [On Guard] (1905), is temporarily responsible for his sister-in-law, whom he finds difficult even though he has tried very hard to make life enjoyable for her; and he suddenly feels 'quanto fosse ridicola la parte che rappresentava da circa tre mesi' [*NA*, I, 720] [how ridiculous the role was that he had been playing for about three months]. When the retired Martino Lori in *Tutto per bene* [All for the Best] (1906) realizes after over twenty years that his late wife betrayed him and that his married daughter is not his daughter, he reflects, referring to his daughter, her husband and her natural father: 'Non glielo avevano lasciato intendere con garbo forse, che oramai non aveva piú nessuna parte da rappresentare? Aveva rappresentato la parte del marito, poi quella del padre ... e ora basta' [*NA*, I, 380] [Hadn't they perhaps politely shown him that now he no longer had a role to play? He had played the role of the husband, then that of the father ... and now it was over]. Serafino Gubbio in his sixth notebook (reflecting Pirandello's constant interest in furniture) writes with distaste about houses with 'mobili piú o meno ricchi, disposti con arte, come in attesa d'una rappresentazione' [quite expensive furniture, carefully arranged, as though waiting for a performance]. Then, after setting forth his own views on furniture, he describes such houses as:

> case fatte per gli altri, in vista della parte che vogliamo rappresentare
> in società; case d'apparenza, dove i mobili attorno possono anche farci
> vergognare, se per caso in un momento ci sorprendiamo in costume o

in atteggiamento non confacenti a quest'apparenza e fuori della parte
che dobbiamo rappresentare. [*TR*, II, 687]
[houses arranged for other people, in consideration of the part we
want to play in society; houses where appearances count, where the
furniture around us can even make us ashamed, if for a moment we
catch ourselves dressed or behaving in a way not in line with those
appearances and outside the role which we have to play.]

Rappresentare is a keyword in Pirandello's expression of the theatrical
quality of everyday life; its direct object is not always an individual *parte* but
can be a whole scene or spectacle. In *Formalità* [Formalities] (1904; rewritten
1922) Flavia Orsani reproaches her husband with the way she has been
sacrificed, 'condannata qua a rappresentare per te la rinunzia alla vita che tu
sognavi' [*NA*, I, 153-154] [condemned here to represent for you the
renunciation of the life you dreamed of]. When Marta Ajala, a teacher and the
protagonist of *L'esclusa* [The Excluded Woman] (1901), is on her way to
school, where she thinks she will have to handle a difficult situation with three
male colleagues, one of whom is in love with her, she anticipates the encounter
thus:

> Già vi entrava col pensiero; vedeva il Nusco e il Mormoni come
> spettatori della scena ch'ella andava a rappresentare là dentro; e il
> Falcone che l'attendeva, piú cupo del solito. [*TR*, I, 137]
> [In her mind she was already going in; she saw Nusco and Mormoni
> as the spectators of the scene that she was going to act inside there;
> and Falcone waiting for her, gloomier than usual.]

In *Leviamoci questo pensiero* [Let's Have Done With It] (1910; rewritten late
in the author's life) a gathering of relatives around the bed of a woman who has
just died is described as 'quello spettacolo di morte, ch'essi stavano lí a
rappresentare' [*NA*, III, 394] [that spectacle of death, which they were
performing there]. Signora Léuca, in *Pena di vivere cosí* [The Anguish of
Living Like This] (1920, but partly rewritten just before Pirandello's death),
gives herself an illusory reason for not looking in the mirror to comb her hair,
'rappresentando la commedia davanti a se stessa' [*NA*, II, 260-261] [acting the
comedy to herself]. Marta Ajala, regarding herself as a lost woman, wishes her

mother and sister would accept this view of her and says, 'Volete farmi impazzire con codesta tragedia che mi rappresentate attorno?' [*TR*, I, 43-44] [Do you want to drive me mad with this tragedy you are performing around me?]. The verb becomes an abstract noun in *I pensionati della memoria* [The Pensioners of Memory] (1914; one of the sources of *La vita che ti diedi* [The Life I Gave You]) when a funeral procession is called 'l'ultima rappresentazione' [*NA*, II, 737] [the final performance].

There are one or two passages where the idea of life's theatrical quality is presented in extended form and several keywords such as those identified above occur together. A good example is found in *Suo marito* [Her Husband] (1911) when Giustino Boggiolo first shows his wife Silvia, who has been away for several months, the house he has bought and furnished in what he considers impeccably fashionable style. Silvia, however, sees it differently:

> [...] quella casa, che non le pareva sua, ma estranea, fatta non piú per viverci come finora ella aveva vissuto, ma per rappresentarvi d'ora in poi, sempre e per forza, una commedia; anche davanti a sé stessa, obbligata a trattar coi dovuti riguardi tutti quegli oggetti di squisita eleganza, che la avrebbero tenuta in continua suggezione; obbligata a ricordarsi sempre della parte che doveva recitar tra loro. E pensava che ormai, come non aveva piú il bambino, cosí neanche la casa - ecco - aveva piú, qual essa la aveva finora intesa e amata. Ma doveva esser cosí, purtroppo. E dunque presto, via, da brava attrice, si sarebbe impadronita di quelle stanze, di quei mobili là, da palcoscenico, donde ogni intimità familiare doveva essere bandita. [*TR*, I, 746-47] [25]
> [...] that house, which didn't seem hers to her, but alien, no longer made to be lived in as she had lived up to then, but from then onwards to act there, always and necessarily, a comedy; even to herself; forced to treat all those exquisitely elegant objects, which would keep her continuously in awe, with due respect; forced always to remember the part she had to play among them. And she thought that now, just as she no longer had her child, so - that was it - she no longer had even the house, as up to then she had understood and loved it. But so, unfortunately, it had to be. And so very soon, certainly, as a good actress she would take charge of those rooms, of that furniture there, as though they were a stage from which all familiar intimacy must be banished].

A different aspect of Pirandello's interest in theatre is displayed in *Il sonno del vecchio* [The Old Man's Sleep] (1906), in that here the protagonist, Vittorio Lamanna, is a playwright [*NA*, I, 1029-1038]. The setting is the fashionable 'salotto *intellettuale*' [*NA*, I, 1030] [salon for *intellectuals*; Pirandello's italics] of Signora Alba Venanzi, where Lamanna reads *Conflitto* [Conflict], a one-act play that he has just written, though he is ashamed of himself for going there 'a cercare la lode, la protezione, l'ajuto di quella gente' [*NA*, I, 1031] [to seek the praise, the patronage and the help of those people]. An outline of the plot is included:

> S'era proposto di rappresentare un conflitto d'anime, diceva lui. Un vecchio benefattore, ancor valido, aveva sposato la sua beneficata; questa, presa poco dopo d'amore per un giovane, si dibatteva tra il sentimento del dovere e della gratitudine e il ribrezzo che provava nell'adempimento de' suoi doveri di sposa, mentre il suo cuore era pieno di quell'altro. Tradire, no; ma mentire, mentire neppure! [*NA*, I, 1036]
> [His idea had been to represent a conflict of feelings, he said. An old man, a benefactor, still in good health, had married the woman he had helped; shortly afterwards she fell in love with a young man, and was torn between her feelings of duty and gratitude and the disgust she felt at having to fulfil her marital duties when her heart was full of the other man. She would not be unfaithful, but she would never never lie, either!]

In the small talk accompanying the event, and the journalistic prose recording it, Lamanna is described in clichés such as 'futura gloria del teatro nazionale' [*NA*, I, 1030] [future glory of the national theatre] and 'giovane commediografo di belle speranze' [*NA*, I, 1038] [a very promising young playwright]. But his play-reading goes disastrously, as he is distracted by the fact that the most distinguished of the guests - an eighty-six-year-old physicist - falls asleep almost as soon as he has begun. Although the play-reading is prominent, the story is ultimately a satire on salon society and a meditation on the respect still paid to the famous scientist in his dotage.

Suo marito satirizes much the same social world of literati and glitterati as *Il sonno del vecchio* (this is underlined by the reappearance in the novel of one of the short story's minor characters, the journalist Casimiro Luna), but its scope is vastly greater and to a large extent it is actually set in the theatre. One of the protagonists, Silvia Roncella, is a young and successful playwright. Whether or not Pirandello approved of *Conflitto* by his fictional character Lamanna in *Il sonno del vecchio* was not made clear; but there is little doubt that he identifies with the artistry of Silvia Roncella, since he attributes to her two of his own plays (one of them not yet written). Her first play, in four acts, is *La nuova colonia* [The New Colony], the plot of which is summarized at length in the novel but which Pirandello himself did not write as a play until 1926-1928 [*TR*, I, 677-679, 699]. [26] Her second play is drawn from one of her own short stories, *Se non così* [If Not Like This], the plot of which is also summarized; in addition, we are told some of Silvia's thoughts about how the short story might be made into a play [*TR*, I, 773-779], [27] and a more established playwright subsequently suggests *Nibbio* [Kite] as a possible alternative title [*TR*, I, 809]. The evolution of the corresponding texts by Pirandello is more complicated. In November 1895 he had published quite a long short story, *Il nido* [The Nest], which he had immediately transformed into a four-act play; in due course he had thought he might call this play *Il nibbio*; later still - apparently (*guarda caso!*) in 1911 - he rewrote the play in three acts as *Se non così...*, which was first performed in 1915 and published in 1916. Marco Praga then persuaded him to rewrite the play again, and this version, still entitled *Se non così*, was published in 1917; in its next edition (1921) the play was given its definitive title, *La ragione degli altri* [Other People's Reason]. [28] Silvia's short story, as described in the novel, is very different from *Il nido* and much closer to the play that Pirandello made of it, which begins - as Silvia decides hers will [*TR*, I, 775] - with the arrival of the female protagonist's father (who has no role at the corresponding point in *Il nido*). Her *La nuova colonia*, on the other hand, develops rather differently from Pirandello's, particularly in its dénouement. Both Silvia's plays focus on the bond between mother and child threatened by a new liaison on the part of the father.

It could be noted that chronologically *Suo marito* coincides with Pirandello's first practical encounter with theatre as a dramatist. [29] It is thus fitting that Silvia, to a certain extent Pirandello's *alter ego* in the novel, should wonder how her first play (which she wrote purely as an act of creative self-expression) will transfer to the stage. Indeed, in describing the stage and the 'quinte di carta' [paper wings] as 'una realtà fittizia e posticcia' [a fictitious and artificial reality] [*TR*, I, 679] she reflects the negative view of theatre which Pirandello had committed to print only three years earlier, in his essay *Illustratori, attori e traduttori* [Illustrators, Actors and Translators] [*SPSV*, 207-224]. It is also perhaps hardly surprising that considerable space is devoted in the novel to the rehearsals of Silvia's two plays, in passages which seem to show that by the time of writing Pirandello was no stranger to such events. In the novel *La nuova colonia* is first produced at the Teatro Valle in Rome by the Carmi-Revelli company. Silvia's husband, who attends the rehearsals on her behalf (because she is pregnant), is thoroughly disheartened by what he sees there [*TR*, I, 680]. 'Le brighe d'una prima rappresentazione' [*TR*, I, 669] [The problems of a first performance] and the tensions and typical foibles of the acting profession are highlighted. A certain amount of technical terminology and jargon is used, such as 'figurini' [sketches for costumes] or 'ne avrebbe fatto una "creazione" ' [she would have "created" the part] [*TR*, I, 680-683]. Directors' cuts in the script are mentioned, together with the need for actors to take slight liberties with their lines [*TR*, I, 839-843]. Then there is a long passage devoted to the première of *La nuova colonia* [*TR*, I, 686-697], during which, in the wings, rubbing shoulders with 'pompieri di guardia', 'macchinisti' and 'servi di scena' [firemen on duty, scene-shifters and stage hands], Silvia's husband, who has organized everything within his power on her behalf and knows all the lines of the play by heart, 'involontariamente per poco non le ripeteva ad alta voce' [*TR*, I, 691] [involuntarily almost repeated them out loud] (this would appear to be autobiographical). [30] And he experiences a 'fenomeno mostruoso' [monstrous occurrence] when the play seems to rise up like a hot-air balloon, detaching itself from all those involved with it (a remarkable passage but too long to reproduce here; see *TR*, I, 691-692). This 'trionfo della vita dell'opera d'arte' [triumph of the life of the work of art] is also 'il miracolo d'arte' [the miracle of art] [*TR*, I, 698, 694].

Interesting, too, in *Suo marito* are certain remarks made by theatre professionals about plays and about the theatre. Laura Carmi, the leading actress in the Carmi-Revelli company, displays 'un profondo disprezzo per tutte le miserie del palcoscenico' [*TR*, I, 676] [a profound contempt for all the shortcomings of the stage] and declares that her son will never set foot on the stage [*TR*, I, 683]. Revelli, the director of the company, 'detestava cordialmente, come tutti i suoi colleghi direttori e cavalieri capicomici, i lavori drammatici italiani' [like all his fellow directors and actor-managers cordially loathed Italian dramatic works], finding 'una sconcia farsaccia parigina' [a bawdy bad farce from Paris] much more profitable [*TR*, I, 675-676] (the *capocomico* in *Sei personaggi in cerca d'autore* would be another case in point; see *MN*, II, 676). Laura Carmi, on the other hand, 'ostentava una fervorosa predilezione per gli scrittori di teatro italiani' [*TR*, I, 676] [displayed an ardent preference for Italian playwrights]. She particularly likes Silvia's *La nuova colonia*, partly because it does not contain what she disparagingly and paradoxically calls *teatro*; 'Né personaggi, né stile, né azione, *qui sentent le "théâtre"* ' [*TR*, I, 683] [No characters, style or action *qui sentent le "théâtre"*]. She hears, however, that *Se non così* is less impressive: 'Qualche scena, qua e là, pare che sia buona ... il finale dell'ultimo atto, specialmente, sí, quello ... quello ha salvato il lavoro ... ' [*TR*, I, 845] [It seems that the odd scene, here and there, is good ... the ending of the last Act, especially, yes, that ... that saved the work]. This is confirmed when a performance of the play is described [TR, I, 848-854], and may be read as a tongue-in-cheek judgement by Pirandello on his own play *La ragione degli altri*. [31]

All in all, then, *Suo marito* is quite a comprehensive theatre novel.

Some of the theatre elements of *Suo marito* are carried over into *Il pipistrello* [The Bat] (1920), the only one of Pirandello's short stories to be set in the theatre. Again a playwright is one of the protagonists; again his play is

at least partially summarized; again the characters include actors and their
capocomico; again, during a première, the playwright is concealed 'dietro le
quinte tra i pompieri di guardia e i servi di scena' [*NA*, I, 229] [in the wings
among the firemen on duty and the stage hands]. If one were looking for
further evidence of intimacy on Pirandello's part with the workings of theatre,
one would notice his references to 'la luce della ribalta, delle bilance e delle
quinte, le luci della scena' [*NA*, I, 224] [the footlights, batten and wing lights,
the stage lights] and to a 'lampadario che pendeva dal tetto con otto globi di
luce' [*NA*, I, 230] [chandelier which hung from the roof with eight light
globes]. The bat of the title makes its appearance every evening during the
performance and, attracted by the lights, flies around the stage, to the acute
consternation ('pazzo terrore'; *NA*, I, 224) of the leading lady, Signorina
Gàstina, and the consequent concern of the playwright, Faustino Perres, whose
new play is due to be premièred some evenings after the bat begins its
intrusions. Attempts are made to eliminate the bat, but to no avail. During the
first performance of Perres's play, which is admitted to have artistic
weaknesses, the bat duly appears, Signorina Gàstina screams, faints and is
carried off stage, and the audience, thinking this is part of the play, applauds
wildly, making the play a success even though its performance cannot be
completed. The story's point, however, lies in the superimposition of one
reality (that of the bat) on another (that of the artist's creation) - analogous to
the juxtaposition of characters and actors in *Sei personaggi in cerca d'autore*,
which Pirandello wrote at about the same time. Signorina Gàstina, adopting a
Pirandellian line of reasoning, seeks to persuade Perres to accommodate the
problem of the bat within his play. She implies that the character whose part
she is playing - like Dottor Fileno in *La tragedia di un personaggio* [The
Tragedy of a Character] (1911) - has taken on a life of her own outside her
author's imagination, [32] and cannot reasonably be expected to focus exclusively
on her pre-ordained role in the presence of the bat (one is struck at this point
by the interchangeability of the actress and the character whose part she

plays). [33] Perres finds the dilemma insoluble and decides that his play shall not be performed again. *Il pipistrello* thus tackles a far-reaching aspect of Pirandello's conception of art - a full discussion of which lies well beyond the scope of this chapter.

Evidence of Pirandello's interest in cinema is confined to one of his narrative texts, *Quaderni di Serafino Gubbio operatore*, though this novel's singularity is compensated for by the abundance of such evidence it contains. In only one other narrative text by Pirandello is cinema even mentioned: this is *Maestro Amore* [The Teacher Love] (1912), where a character, in Rome, expresses an inclination to go 'al cinematografo' [to the cinema] and subsequently escapes to 'un cinematografo sotto i portici dell'esedra di Termini' [*NA*, III, 1126, 1130] [a cinema under the arches of the portico of the Termini]. The reason for the cinema's general absence from Pirandello's fiction is, of course, partly chronological: the first film show in Italy did not take place until 13 March 1896 (Pirandello appears to have attended it); the first cinematic production company in Italy was not established until 1905; the development of the Italian film industry was slow until 1911, when technological advances allowed the first full-length films to be made - and by that time more than half of Pirandello's fiction had been written. [34] From about 1918 onwards, Pirandello's considerable contact with cinema is amply documented, but relevant biographical clues regarding the years preceding the first publication of *Quaderni di Serafino Gubbio operatore* are scarce. He was a close friend of the cineast Giustino Ferri, and Massimo Cardillo has shown that at least one passage in the novel is based on a passage in an article Ferri wrote about the Cines production company in 1906; Pirandello had other friends in cinema, such as Lucio d'Ambra and Ugo Falena; it would appear that he was present at part of a filming of Manzoni's *I promessi sposi* in 1911, which gave him the idea of deriving a scenario from Nievo's *Confessioni di un italiano* (though the idea was never acted on); he lived virtually next door to another production company, Film d'Arte Italiana, and entered its premises on more than one occasion; in 1913-1914 (though partly, at least, because he was acutely short of money) he was very keen to submit scenarios derived from his own short stories to production companies, which did not, however, reciprocate his enthusiasm. Sergio Raffaelli suggests that Pirandello's disappointment in this regard is expressed in the novel in the grotesque characterization of Fabrizio Cavalena, an unsuccessful writer of scenarios. [35]

Quaderni di Serafino Gubbio operatore amply reflects an experience of cinema on Pirandello's part that was probably rather fuller than the available evidence suggests. It is largely set in the premises of a major Rome production company, La Kosmograph, the organization of which is explained in detail (the company is in fact a thinly disguised reproduction of Cines); [36] and, as far as its cinematic content is concerned, it focuses almost exclusively on the production end of the continuum. As the title indicates, the first-person narrator is a cameraman at La Kosmograph, and Pirandello is able to provide him with an impressive array of genuine technical terminology, including expressions such as *pezzo* (segment of film recording one take), *legatura* (montage, that is, the selection, cutting and piecing together of *pezzi* to form a continuous whole), *teatro di posa* (indoor area equipped for film-making), *segnare il campo* (to mark out the area within which the actors must confine their movements), *tenere in fuoco* (to keep the camera in focus by having the actors remain the appropriate distance from it) and *sala di prova* (the room where a test copy of a completed film is screened). [37] Most of the other characters are also employees or associates of La Kosmograph - especially actors and directors - and they are often seen at work, both in their studios and on location. But the overall view of cinema evinced by the novel is a negative one. There are various references to the stupidity of the films produced; the popularity of cinema is seen as a threat to theatre; the actors choose to work in cinema only because it pays better than theatre, while they find it intellectually less demanding; they are also restricted to mime (in the age of the silent film) and miss 'la comunione diretta col pubblico' [the direct communion with the audience] which theatre would afford them; they are exiled, alienated [*TR*, II, 585]. The camera on its tripod is repeatedly referred to in the metaphor of the predatory spider ('grosso ragno nero in agguato'; *TR*, II, 598). More broadly, cinema is presented as symptomatic of a new machine age [*TR*, II, 519-521 and 573-574] which is hostile to art [*TR*, II, 690]; indeed Franca Angelini has seen the novel as a curt answer to the Italian Futurists. [38]

It is often suggested that Pirandello is a repetitive writer - that his many creative works constantly return to a limited range of themes, attitudes and preoccupations. From one point of view, our survey of theatre and cinema in his fictional writings has tended to confirm this view. Pirandello is never more himself than when he is writing about human behaviour in terms of theatre, and the habit of mind this represents regularly colours his prose from his earliest short stories onwards, if only to the extent of a single word used figuratively - conveying most typically the image of the mask behind which life is lived or the role one assigns oneself on the stage where every man must play a part. There is thus little development in the interest in theatre displayed by Pirandello's fiction, though - predictably - his exploration of the practical aspects of theatre deepens after about 1908, and his use of theatre language becomes more sophisticated. From another point of view, however, the restricted field surveyed in this chapter would seem to show that Pirandello is anything but repetitive. He wrote just one cinema novel and one theatre novel, one short story set in the theatre (*Il pipistrello*), one other where the spotlight is on a playwright and his play (*Il sonno del vecchio*), one in which the *personae* of Sicilian puppet theatre are prominent (*La paura del sonno*), one which is strongly coloured by opera (*'Leonora, addio!'*), and so on. This collection of unique items suggests that Pirandello was forever probing his themes in different ways, continually experimenting with new artistic forms in which to cast his vision of human life. It would be instructive to test the hypothesis that every one of his many short stories is in some sense similarly unique.

JOHN C. BARNES

[1] All references to Pirandello's short stories are to the critical edition of the *Novelle per un anno* edited by Mario Costanzo with an introduction by Giovanni Macchia and published by Mondadori, Milan, in the series 'I Meridiani'. The dates of publication are: volume I, 1985; volume II, 1987; volume III, 1990. Page references to this edition of the *Novelle per un anno*, using the abbreviation *NA* and volume number, are given in the text of this essay. Since *Le tre carissime* was heavily rewritten before its definitive publication in 1926, the variants on pages 1342-1350 of *NA*, II, also need to be consulted.

[2] Both the Teatro Valle and the Teatro Costanzi were active theatres in Rome at the time.

[3] *NA*, II, 839. These lines appear to have been written by Pirandello rather than taken from an existing play - in which case they parody what Pirandello would have called 'teatro vecchio' [old theatre].

[4] G. Giudice, *Luigi Pirandello*, Turin, UTET, 1963, facing page 96.

[5] See Luigi Pirandello, *Maschere Nude*, I, edited by Alessandro d'Amico, introduction by Giovanni Macchia, Milan, Mondadori, series 'I Meridiani', 1986, lii-lv.

[6] G. Giudice, *Luigi Pirandello*, cit., pp. 99-100.

[7] G. Giudice, *Luigi Pirandello*, cit., pp. 100-101; O. Ragusa, *Luigi Pirandello: An Approach to His Theatre*, Edinburgh, Edinburgh University Press, 1980, pp. 64-65.

[8] G. Giudice, *Luigi Pirandello*, cit., p. 40.

[9] In *Personaggi* [Characters] (1906) the first-person narrator characterizes himself only as a writer of short stories ('personaggi delle mie future novelle' [*NA*, III, 1474] [characters in my future short stories]); but this is perhaps explained by the fact that the context of these words is itself a short story. In his daily life Pirandello really did affect complete indifference to theatre; see G. Giudice, *Luigi Pirandello*, cit., pp. 305-306.

[10] Apart from *Le tre carissime* these are: *Lontano* [Far Away] (1902), *Pianto segreto* [Secret Tears] (1903; incorporated in the novel *I vecchi e i giovani* [The Old and the Young] (1909); see Luigi Pirandello, *Tutti i romanzi*, 2 vols, edited by Giovanni Macchia and Mario Costanzo, Milan, Mondadori, series 'I Meridiani', vol. II, pp. 270-300), *Tutto per bene* [All for the Best] (1906; the source of the play of the same title),

' *"Leonora, addio!"* ' [Leonora, Farewell!] (1910; re-used in *Questa sera si recita a soggetto* [Tonight We Improvise]), *Leviamoci questo pensiero* [Let's Have Done With It] (1910), *Notte* [Night] (1912), *La veste lunga* [The Long Dress] (1913), *La morte addosso* [Marked by Death] (1918), *Pena di vivere cosí* [The Anguish of Living Like This] (1920) and *Niente* [Nothing] (1922).

[11] Apart from *Le tre carissime* the others are *Lumie di Sicilia* [Sicilian Limes] (1900), *Scialle nero* [Black Shawl] (1904), *Felicità* [Happiness] (1911), *I nostri ricordi* [Our Memories] (1912) and *Il pipistrello* [The Bat] (1920).

[12] All references to Pirandello's novels are to the edition of *Tutti i romanzi* (abbreviated in the text to *TR*) described in note 10.

[13] These are characters, respectively, in Meyerbeer's *Les Huguenots*, Verdi's *Ernani* and Verdi's *La forza del destino*. I thank Deirdre O'Grady for helping me unravel some of the allusions to operas. In this one story Pirandello refers to opera about as extensively as he does to teatro di prosa in the whole of his fiction. As will be seen shortly, Sophocles' *Electra* and Shakespeare's *Hamlet* are mentioned in *Il fu Mattia Pascal*; Saverio Càrzara, in *La paura del sonno* [Fear of Sleep] (1900), reads the plays of Goldoni as well as the *Romanzi dei Reali di Francia* in the service of his art as a puppet-maker [*NA*, III, 54]; an unidentified (and perhaps imaginary) French dramatist is paraphrased in *Il sonno del vecchio* [The Old Man's Sleep] (1906) to the effect that sleeping through a play represents a comment on it [*NA*, I, 1034]; *Suo marito* [Her Husband] (1911) contains a reference to Shakespeare's *Julius Caesar*, *Coriolanus* and Antony and Cleopatra [*TR*, I, 622]; and in the same novel one of Silvia Roncella's plays is dismissed by a critic as 'la *Medea* tradotta in tarentino' [*TR*, I, 685] [*Medea* transposed to Taranto]. But these are the only references to real plays and playwrights in Pirandello's fiction.

[14] G. Giudice, *Luigi Pirandello*, cit., pp. 164-165.

[15] See F. M. Guercio, *Sicily, the Garden of the Mediterranean: The Country and Its People*, London, Faber, 1938, Chapter 11, 'The Sicilian Marionettes' (pp. 247-62); F. De Felice, *Storia del teatro siciliano*, Catania, Giannotta, 1956, pp. 43-68; C. Alberti, *Il teatro dei pupi e lo spettacolo popolare siciliano*, Milan, Mursia, 1977.

[16] The original edition (*Ariel*, 1, xvii [10 April 1898], p. 1) has 'Adolfo' rather than 'Astolfo'; the critical edition makes the alteration without comment, but 'Astolfo' would appear to be correct.

[17] The defeat at Roncevaux was one of the high points of the traditional cycle. See C. Alberti, *Il teatro dei pupi*, cit., pp. 55 and 99.

[18] The illustrated edition of Elio Vittorini's *Conversazione in Sicilia*, Milan, Bompiani, 1953, with photography supervised by the author and executed by Luigi Crocenzi, includes three photographs of a puppet *Macbeth* (pp. 11, 192, 196), as well as photographs of a puppet Marfisa (p. 87) and puppet paladins (p. 199). Compare C. Alberti, *Il teatro dei pupi*, cit., pp. 96-97.

[19] For a consideration of Paleari's authority, see J. C. Barnes, 'La portata della metapsichica ne *Il fu Mattia Pascal*', in AA. VV., *Pirandello e l'oltre*, Milan, Mursia, 1991, pp. 277-287 (280-282).

[20] L. Richards, ' "Il buco nel cielo di carta": Pirandello's *Enrico IV* and Sophocles' *Philoctetes*', *The Yearbook of the Society for Pirandello Studies*, 12, 1992, pp. 55-63 p. 59). See also L. Pirandello, *Il fu Mattia Pascal*, edited by R. Bertacchini, third edition, Milan, Edizioni Scolastiche Mondadori, 1970, pp. 207-208; A. Leone de Castris, *Storia di Pirandello*, revised edition, Bari, Laterza, 1971, pp. 71-73; C. Vicentini, *L'estetica di Pirandello*, second edition, Milan, Mursia, 1985, pp. 121-122; G. Mazzacurati, '*Il fu Mattia Pascal*: l'eclissi del tempo e l'interdizione del romanzo', in *Il romanzo di Pirandello*, edited by E. Lauretta, Palermo, Palumbo, 1976, pp. 49-76 (71-73); G. Corsinovi, *Pirandello e l'espressionismo: analogie culturali e anticipazioni espressive nella prima narrativa*, Genoa, Tilgher, 1979, pp. 157-164; R. Luperini, *Introduzione a Pirandello*, Rome-Bari, Laterza, 1992, p. 57.

[21] See Pirandello's essay *L'umorismo*, in *SPSV*, pp. 15-160, and especially pp. 146-157.

[22] The definitive title was first used in the revised edition of 1925.

[23] Virtually the same wording occurs in *Berecche e la guerra* (1934 version): *NA*, III, 608.

[24] The collocation *rappresentare + parte* occurs three times in this story; see also pp. 1070 and 1097.

[25] Until recently *Suo marito* was generally known as *Giustino Roncella nato Boggiòlo*. This is because at the time of his death Pirandello was about half-way through revising it with the latter title, and for decades thereafter published editions incorporated the revised text as far as it went, with the new title. Pirandello, however, never authorized the publication of the half-revised text; and since the critical editor's task is to print the last version of a text that the writer authorized, Mario Costanzo, in the critical edition, rightly reprints the 1911 edition (*Suo marito*) with the revisions and the new title in his critical apparatus (see *TR*, I, 1048-1049).

[26] In the partially rewritten version of the novel (*Giustino Roncella nato Boggiòlo*) the title of this play is changed to *L'isola nuova* [The New Island], presumably because by the time of the rewriting Pirandello's own *La nuova colonia* had been written, performed and published.

[27] Clues regarding the text of the play she creates from the short story are given at *TR*, I, 850-854.

[28] See *NA*, III, 935-992, 1461; *MN*, I, liv-lv, 739-740; F. Càllari, *Pirandello e il cinema*, Venice, Marsilio, 1991, pp. 25-26.

[29] Pirandello was presumably involved in the production of his first two plays to be publicly performed (*La morsa* and *Lumie di Sicilia*, premièred together on 9 December 1910) - though *Suo marito* may well have been written by then. On the other hand, it is plausible to imagine that he had previously been involved in productions of plays by other playwrights, since a number of his best friends - such as Edoardo Boutet, Lucio d'Ambra and Nino Martoglio - were directors. See G. Giudice, *Luigi Pirandello*, cit., pp. 145-151; *TR*, I, 1048, where Costanzo dates the writing of *Suo marito* 'circa 1909'.

[30] Compare F. V. Nardelli, *L'uomo segreto: vita e croci di Luigi Pirandello*, 1932, second edition, s.l., Mondadori, 1944, p. 256: 'Durante le prime rappresentazioni, si metteva in un palchetto, solo solo, e seguiva i gesti degli attori, gesticolando anche lui; diceva le battute, movendo le labbra senza suono; quasi per aiutar quei manichini lassú, a muoversi, a parlare, a soffrire. La faccia dell'autore infatti, a volta a volta, era irata, accorata, intenerita, secondo la parte; no, secondo le parti. Ché tutte le riverberava. Poi, al calar del sipario, esciva in corridoio per correre in palcoscenico a far le sue osservazioni,' [During the first rehearsals he would go into a box, all by himself, and follow the actors' gestures, gesticulating himself as well; he said the lines, moving his lips almost soundlessly; almost as though to help those dummies up there to move, to speak and to suffer. Indeed, by turns the author's face was angry, sorrowful, tender, according to the role, no, according to the roles. Because he reflected all of them. Then, when the curtain fell, he would go out into the aisle and run up onto the stage to give his comments].

[31] In which case this judgement of 1911 is remarkably prophetic: such problems surrounded the first production in 1915 ('It failed utterly,' writes Olga Ragusa), that Pirandello was prompted to preface the published text with a 'Lettera alla protagonista signora Livia Arciani', presumably intended in part to minimize such problems in the future. See G. Giudice, *Luigi Pirandello*, cit., pp. 307-308; O. Ragusa, *Luigi Pirandello*, cit., p. 65; *MN*, I, 742-743.

[32] See *NA*, I, 816-824, and compare *L'umorismo*, *SPSV*, p. 101: Certo, quando un poeta riesce veramente a dar vita a una sua creatura, questa vive

indipendentemente dal suo autore, tanto che noi possiamo immaginarla in altre situazioni in cui l'autore non pensò di collocarla e vederla agire secondo le intime leggi della sua propria vita, leggi che neanche l'autore avrebbe potuto violare' [Certainly when a poet really succeeds in giving life to one of his creatures, this creature lives independently of his author, to the extent that we can imagine it in circumstances other than those in which the author thought of placing it, and see it acting according to the inner laws of its life, laws which even the author could not have violated].

[33] This is a consequence of the actor's autonomous appropriation of his role. See Pirandello's 1918 article *Teatro e letteratura*, in *SPSV*, 1018-1024: 'L'attore [...] bisogna che riconcepisca, come sa, il personaggio, lo concepisca cioè a sua volta per conto suo [...]. Quel dato personaggio sulla scena [...] non sarà mai quello del poeta, perché l'attore l'ha ricreato in sé [...]' [*SPSV*, 1022-1023] [The actor [...] must reconceive the character as best he knows, must conceive it, that is, in his turn and in his way [...]. That particular character on the stage [...] will never be the author's character, because the actor has recreated it in himself [...]].

[34] F. Càllari, *Pirandello e il cinema*, cit., p. 17 and note; S. Raffaelli, *Il cinema nella lingua di Pirandello*, Rome, Bulzoni, 1993, pp. 29, 36.

[35] G. Giudice, *Luigi Pirandello*, cit., pp. 510-513; M. Cardillo, *Tra le quinte del cinematografo: cinema, cultura e società in Italia, 1900-1937*, Bari, Dedalo, 1987, p. 17; F. Càllari, *Pirandello e il cinema*, cit., pp. 25-28; S. Raffaelli, *Il cinema nella lingua di Pirandello*, cit., pp. 34-35, 40-50.

[36] Cosmograph was the name of a major French company which briefly projected its films in Rome late in 1905 and returned to Italy on a larger scale in 1914. See S. Raffaelli, *Il cinema nella lingua di Pirandello*, cit., p. 38.

[37] Pirandello's use of such terms in the novel has been exhaustively studied by Sergio Raffaelli. See his *Il cinema nella lingua di Pirandello*, cit., pp. 65-109 and 123-127.

[38] F. Angelini Frajese, 'Serafino Gubbio, la tigre e la vocazione teatrale di L. Pirandello', in *Letteratura e critica: studi in onore di Natalino Sapegno*, 5 vols, Rome, Bulzoni, 1974-1979, vol. II, pp. 855-882 (p. 870); reprinted in her *Serafino e la tigre: Pirandello tra scrittura teatro e cinema*, Venice, Marsilio, 1990, pp. 9-36 (p. 24).

PIRANDELLO'S ONE-ACT PLAYS

Short plays, whether satyr plays, intermezzi, interludes, sketches or *levers de rideau*, have in their various guises been part of the theatrical repertoire from the earliest times. But it is only in the late nineteenth century that the one-act play acquires its own autonomy and becomes what Terry Hodgson calls a 'respected form'.[1] The work of the actor-manager André Antoine, who in 1887 founded the Théâtre Libre in Paris with a group of amateur actors, is generally regarded as vital in the move away from the theatrical conventions, and restrictions, of farce and melodrama. From eclectic beginnings, Antoine's work at the Théâtre Libre became particularly associated with naturalism in the theatre, as part of that battle for renewal which, he later wrote, had already been fought and won for the novel, painting and music.[2]

The one-act play was one of the major vehicles for reform used by Antoine with his avant-garde group. Differently from what was happening in other theatres of the time, he wanted to be able to offer his public, in a single evening, a variety of authors and plays dealing with contemporary issues. The programme of the opening night at the Théâtre Libre consisted of four one-act plays, including a dramatization of Zola's short story *Jacques Damour*. It was through evenings such as this, in which the *quart d'heure* no longer functioned as a preparation for the main, full-length play but as a work with the same status as the others in the programme, that Antoine and his company reacted against the notion associated with Eugène Scribe of the 'well-made play', breaking up the unity of the evening's theatrical experience into short, independent episodes.

From its foundation until 1894, when bankruptcy forced Antoine to close, the Théâtre Libre was an experimental theatre for an elite, instrumental in introducing new plays and authors, including the work of Ibsen and Strindberg, to the Paris stage. Its influence also went well beyond France, so that the German director, Otto Brahm, followed Antoine's example when he founded his Freie Bühne in 1889, and in 1891 in London J.T. Grein opened the Independent Theatre, which alongside performances of the great naturalist playwrights brought the new symbolist theatre to London. As Franca Angelini says, there are clear links between the various Free or Independent theatres of the end of the nineteenth century. In particular, the role of the star actor was diminished, and the emphasis was placed on the entire theatrical company working together instead of having to accommodate itself to one or two great names. As a result the whole of stage space came to be used, as the hierarchical distinction between star and supporting cast, and so between front and rear of stage, disappeared. [3]

The one-act play was an essential part of this process. At once a reaction against the theatrical conventions of the nineteenth century and an anti-bourgeois, elitist, form that encouraged new authors and independent, including amateur, companies it also lent itself to much of the vital experimentation in the theatre of the times. Peter Szondi writes of the one-act as one of the 'rescue attempts' in the crisis facing drama at the end of the century, [4] and he points out that, because of its brevity, and in order to maintain tension, the modern one-act must:

> ' ... elect a borderline situation, a situation verging on catastrophe - catastrophe that is imminent when the curtain goes up and that later becomes ineluctable'. [5]

Szondi's analysis at this point is related in particular to the one-acts of Maeterlinck and Strindberg, and to their 'drama of the unfree'.[6] Later,

Pirandello made conspicuous use of the borderline situation in his one-acts, as
we shall see particularly in relation to *L'uomo dal fiore in bocca* [The Man
with the Flower in his Mouth]. As Szondi says, dramatists as diverse as Zola,
Schnitzler, Hofmannsthal, Wedekind, Hauptmann and Chekhov also used this
form. This list, to which could be added many others including Verga, Bracco,
Giacosa, D'Annunzio, Svevo and Pirandello in Italy, bears witness to the status
the one-act had acquired and to its dominant presence in the innovations of
naturalist and symbolist theatre at the time. From its origins in the naturalist
theatre the modern one-act became in turn, in the hands of these very different
playwrights, symbolist, surrealist, allegorical or parabolic,[7] or indeed, as in the
case of Pirandello, a form reflecting many of the literary trends of the period.
In the rest of this essay I shall examine Pirandello's two earliest published one-
act plays, then discuss the relationship between his short story *Lumie di Sicilia*
and the one-act play which he derived from it, to show some of the changes,
and so choices, Pirandello made as a playwright when transforming his stories.
Next, I shall discuss Pirandello's theories on the links between short stories and
drama texts, to conclude with an analysis of *L'uomo dal fiore in bocca*.

Pirandello's earliest one-acts

Pirandello published fourteen complete one-act plays, that is, if we count the
five one-acts of which he wrote two versions, in Italian and in Sicilian dialect
(not necessarily in that order), as five, rather than ten, plays[8] , and if we
exclude his dialect play *'U Ciclopu*, based on a translation of Euripides' satyr
play. Of the one-acts Pirandello published, only four, *Perchè?* [Why?], *Cecé*
[Chee-Chee] *All'uscita* [At the Exit] and *Sogno (ma forse no)* [A Dream (but
maybe not)] are not transformations of his short stories, and even then there are
some narrative sources, although no single one, for *All'uscita*. According to
evidence drawn in particular from his letters, in the early stages of his activity
as a dramatist he also planned other one-acts, but never wrote them, or wrote
only fragments, or destroyed them, or they have been subsequently lost. The
first one-act he published was *Perchè?* (1892), and, so far as we know, it was

never performed or included in any edition of his works.[9] Essentially it is a dialogue between wife (Giulia) and husband (Enrico) about his jealousy of her friendships and affairs before they met and whether or not they should have married. Its structure is that of the psychological and verbal games they play and which are the real basis of their relationship. At one moment, for example, as Enrico looks through his wife's old love-letters and photographs, he uses the situation to reassert his dominance over her as, unlike her cousins, he gave her the legitimacy and status of marriage:

> ENRICO. Come? perchè? io sono allegro, ora. Ti giuro, che mi diverto. Fa il piacere, Giugiù! Via ... mostrami il piccolo Attilio! ...No? allora cerco io? permesso? (*piglia, fra le altre, una lettera*) "Giulia mia cara!" questi non vezzeggia. Oooh! guarda: *collegio* scritto con due *g*! Chi è che ... e *affliggere* con una sola! ... (*volta il foglio e legge la firma*) Filippo; bravo Filippo! Quest'altro tuo cugino, si vede, non era molto forte in ortografia. Curioso! tu avevi la specialità dei cugini. Dì la verità: credo che dessi retta, così per giuoco, a tutti del lato paterno e materno! Che imbecilli! non ti sposò nessuno ... [10] [ENRICO. What? Why? I've cheered up now. I'm really enjoying myself. Please, Giugiù! Come on ... show me little Attilio! ... You won't? Shall I look? May I? (*he picks up one of the letters*) "My dear Giulia!" This one doesn't use baby talk. Ooo! Look: he's written *college* with two g's. Who's done that ... and *afflict* with one *f*! ... (*he turns the sheet over and reads the signature*) Filippo; well done Filippo! It's obvious this other cousin of yours wasn't very good at spelling. How strange! You specialized in cousins. Admit it: I think you played at encouraging all of them, on both sides of the family! What idiots! None of them married you ..]

First of all, he symbolically appropriates and mocks the nickname (Giugiù) one old flame gave her, then he uses the 'male' images and letters she has kept in order to deride her own childhood and adolescence. Finally, his reference to his willingness to marry her highlights his own importance in saving her from rejection and spinsterhood.

Pirandello, here, may well be close to staging a 'psychic murder' of a Strindbergian kind, although at the end of the play the tables are turned, as the wife succeeds in leaving her husband in a state of suspense and uncertainty.

Also, so far as his theatre is concerned, he begins that series of 'doubles' which appear in so many of his plays, as in his narrative works. Giulia/Giugiù has a name which, like that of many other female characters in Pirandello's work, indicates her tendency to be, or become, two people, or to live suspended between two identities.[11]

The theme in *La morsa* (The Vise),[12] Pirandello's second published one-act, is female infidelity within marriage, not that imagined and constructed retrospectively by a jealous husband. As the play opens Giulia sees her lover, Antonio Serra, who is also the family lawyer, returning alone and unexpectedly early from a business trip with her husband, Andrea. Antonio has come to tell her that he fears Andrea has discovered their affair. He and Giulia then reveal the basis for his fears: Andrea may have seen them kissing on the stairs when the two men were leaving, and at the hotel where they were staying Andrea insisted on sharing a room and made what Antonio thought was a series of allusions to the affair. Antonio leaves, after trying to blame Giulia for what has happened, and in a brief, linking scene Giulia shows her anxiety and hesitation first alone and then with the maid, Anna, telling Anna to fetch the children and then changing her mind. Andrea himself returns, and he proceeds to extract his revenge, not in what he sees as the old, violent way of wronged husbands but by a much more subtle and cruel method. He uses, presumably invents, the method he attributes to a young man he met on his train journey home which involves adopting a much more psychological approach in order to expose a wife's guilt. In effect, Andrea 'spells out' the method, after spelling out the word 'psi-co-lo-gia',[13] forcing Giulia to react and watching her reactions until she herself becomes, as the young man in Andrea's story wanted for errant wives, the living proof of her own guilt. When he orders her to leave the house and refuses to let her see their children again she goes into another room, and shoots herself. Antonio returns at this moment and, in an apparently perplexing ending, Andrea accuses *him* of killing Giulia. Differently from *Perchè?*, the psychological drama in this play leads to suicide and an accusation of murder.

The theme of marital infidelity was, of course, not new at the end of the nineteenth century. [14] Pirandello's treatment of this, and other, themes in his one-acts does, however, lead him to far-reaching innovations in the form itself. Very important for the whole of Pirandello's theatre is his use, in these two early plays, of a highly ambiguous and allusive language which we, as readers or audience, have to decode in order to understand the character's mood or motivation. I have touched on this point with regard to Enrico's speech from *Perchè?*.

In *La morsa*, in reply to Giulia's anxious questions as to why Antonio thinks that her husband may be suspicious of them, Antonio replies:

> Che vuoi che ti dica? In questo stato, le parole più aliene ti pajono allusioni: ogni sguardo, un accenno; ogni tono di voce un ... [*MN*, II, 164]
> [What do you expect me to say? In this state, the most insignificant words seem like allusions; every look is a sign; every tone of voice a ...]

I have chosen here to translate 'parole aliene' by 'insignificant words', as this interpretation is confirmed both by reference to Sicilian dialect [15] and by Pirandello's choice of words when he later wrote a dialect version of this play. Here, his character says: 'Nni stu statu, ogni cosa di nenti ti pari 'nu montagna' [16] [In this state every little thing seems a mountain]. Andrea is a character who uses everyday, banal words to show his own state of mind, to play on Antonio's feelings of guilt and to indicate, without saying so openly, that he understands exactly what is going on. He is, therefore, like Enrico in *Perchè?*, an early version of those later characters for whom, to use Altieri Biagi's phrase, the most ordinary word contains unsuspected abysses, and among whom she numbers the Man with the Flower in his Mouth and Enrico IV. [17] We can also see here how, in these early plays, Pirandello seeks for what in 1899 he called the 'parola che sia l'azione stessa parlata', the words which will give his characters their unique identity and be at one with their actions. [*SPSV*, 1015].

Short stories and one-acts

Ten of Pirandello's one-acts were based on his own short stories. The chronological relationship between *La morsa* and the short story *La paura* [Fear] is problematic. While until recently it seemed an established fact that the story was written before the play, the latest evidence we have to date is inconclusive on this point.[18] I shall, therefore, take the example of the second 'pair' of texts in chronological terms, that is, the short story *Lumie di Sicilia* [Sicilian Limes], [19] published in 1900 and the play of the same name, probably written in 1910, where there are no doubts as to which came first.

The transformation of part or whole of a narrative work into a play was a recurring practice in the nineteenth century. Taking just the later part of the century, among naturalist writers such transformations are part of Zola's attempt to impose naturalism in the theatre,[20] while Chekhov, too, used his own short stories as the basis for many of his one-acts,[21] and in Italy Verga adapted *Cavalleria rusticana* [Rustic Chivalry] and *La Lupa* [The She-Wolf] for the stage. It was a practice Pirandello noted, and of which in 1899 at least he disapproved, as is shown by the opening of his essay *L'azione parlata* [*SPSV*, p.1015].

Lumie di Sicilia, as a story and as a play, remains within the general area of naturalism.[22] In the story a young peasant, Micuccio, arrives from Sicily at a luxurious house in a large town in northern Italy looking for Teresina. She is still at the theatre, and overawed by the servants, Micuccio is too embarrassed to say that he is Teresina's fiancé, so he watches in silence as preparations are made for a splendid dinner.

The central section of the story consists of a long narrated monologue by Micuccio, in which he realises that Teresina has made her fortune, and remembers the poverty in which she and her mother, zia Marta, lived five years previously. He saved them from starvation, and then encouraged, and paid for, Teresina to train as a singer. To allow her to train in Naples, Micuccio sold a small farm, and quarrelled with his family when he did so. He and Teresina agreed not to meet for five or six years, to let her make her own way in her career, and from writing to Micuccio herself, Teresina later merely wrote a few words at the end of the letters zia Marta wrote to him. When he was recently ill the two women sent Micuccio money, and it is ostensibly to return this money that he has made his journey. At the end of his reflections, Teresina returns home, but it is zia Marta who comes to talk to, and eat with, Micuccio.

For a brief moment, Teresina leaves her guests and comes to see him. When she goes back to her dinner, he realises that the gulf between them, caused by time, distance, wealth and the fact that (in his terms) Teresina is no longer morally worthy of him cannot be bridged, and giving zia Marta the money and the limes he has brought from Sicily, he goes to weep on the steps leading to Teresina's house. Teresina herself comes back to find that Micuccio has left, and she takes the limes in to her guests. The plot of the 1910 version of the play follows that of the short story very closely.

The short story itself is unitary, set mostly in Sina's house, taking place on the same evening and with the events between the arrival and departure of Micuccio as its plot. [23] Pirandello needed to do little to these aspects of his story in order to adapt them to the exigencies of a one-act. When he wrote the Sicilian script of the play, however, he changed the ending and he then retained this new ending in the definitive version of his Italian script. I shall return to this point later. He also used a type of transformation which greatly facilitates the passage from narrative to theatre, and that is to include some of the descriptive passages in the story as stage- and acting-directions. [24] In the short story, for example, when Teresina and zia Marta return from the theatre the servants take baskets of flowers into the reception. Micuccio is so astonished and agitated at this point that his eyes fill with tears, and he closes them, withdrawing into himself to contain his anguish. At the end of this sequence, Micuccio hears Teresina laughing. In the play, most of this description is transferred into the stage-directions, punctuated by a brief exchange between Micuccio and Dorina, the female servant, and Pirandello uses Teresina's shrill peal of laughter as a kind of 'ready-made' acoustic effect in the theatre. Another moment which lends itself to direct transference from narrative to theatre comes a little later. Micuccio and zia Marta are served food separately in a small, scantily-furnished room, and in the short story Micuccio *thinks* (my emphasis) that his hands are dirty after his long journey. He is too embarrassed to help himself from the dish the waiter offers him, and zia Marta has to help him instead. In the stage directions, Pirandello enhances the visual, and therefore the psychological, impact by making Micuccio first raise his hands and then look at them to see that they are dirty. [25]

The setting, and space, of the action are already established in the short story, where Micuccio looks beyond the small room, across another room in semi-darkness and into a huge, brightly-lit reception room. He remains in the same small room in the play, but the middle room is in darkness, and the reception room is glimpsed through a glass door. This inner door opens and closes when the servants move between the kitchen and the reception, and when Teresina comes out to see Micuccio. This organization of theatre space is naturalistic, and allows movement and lighting effects, but is also symbolic of the two worlds of the play and of the dark space between them.

In *La morsa* the characters evoke the two very important scenes and spaces of the kiss on the stairs and the hotel room, so taking the audience beyond the physical set to a creation of these scenes in the imagination. There is a similar use of evocation in *Lumie di Sicilia*, this time of rural Sicily, in the dialogue between Micuccio and zia Marta, as they talk nostalgically of the objects and faces of the past. Pirandello here uses, and develops, part of Micuccio's narrated monologue in the short story. I shall return to this point when discussing how Pirandello conveys information about the past to this audience.

Two of the major differences, though, concern the characters of Dorina and Micuccio. At the beginning of the short story, the male servant shows Micuccio in, while Dorina is sleeping, and snoring, behind a curtain. Micuccio only sees her briefly when Teresina comes home and she helps to carry flowers into the reception. Her appearance helps to increase his sense of foreboding, but that is as far as her function goes. In the play she is much more active. She appears earlier, coming out from behind the curtain to help make Micuccio feel ill-at-ease from the outset, and to question him slyly and mockingly about his relationship with Teresina. Her malevolent character, briefly indicated by description in the short story, becomes apparent in the drama text particularly through what she says.

Micuccio in the sort story is shy and reserved, easily cowed by the luxury of Teresina's rooms and the condescending mockery of her servants. After similar initial embarrassment, in the play he is much more assertive, saying it is not his fault if the train arrived when it did, asking if he can stay and declaring his certainty that all will be well when Teresina arrives. For zia Marta, in both the short story and the play, he has remained the same, firmly rooted in his Sicilian identity. In the play Micuccio's homogeneity is further underlined when we discover that his baptismal name is Domenico, but:

> MICUCCIO: Domenico o Micuccio, è la stessa cosa. Noi diciamo
> Micuccio. [*MN*, II, 340]
> [Domenico or Micuccio, it's the same thing. We say Micuccio].

Pirandello also conveys the same information by the introduction into his play of an object, a device, obviously, particularly appropriate to theatre. Micuccio, in the short story, is a flute-player. In the play, his instrument becomes a piccolo (*ottavino*, in Italian; which recalls his surname, *Bonavino*), and he carries it with him all the way from Sicily as:

> Facciamo una cosa sola, io e lui! [*MN*, II, 340]
> [We're one and the same, me and it].

This more confident Micuccio does not suffer from the same split identity, or live suspended between identities, as do so many of Pirandello's female characters, including Teresina/Sina. [26]

104

The changes in the character and function of Dorina and Micuccio, together with the redistribution mentioned earlier of part of Micuccio's reflections to zia Marta, enable Pirandello to find for his play a way of communicating the events and emotions which precede Micuccio's arrival, a knowledge of which is vital to an understanding of the plot. I shall use the term 'antefact', chosen by Laura Lepschy, to describe this necessary information. [27] As I have said, in the short story the antefact is conveyed in the middle section through the a mixture of reported dicourse and free indirect discourse in Micuccio's narrated monologue. In the play the much less reserved, and much more ingenuous, Micuccio tells his story in answer to the increasingly malicious, even malevolent, questions of Dorina and Ferdinando. The question-and-answer session shows what has shaped Micuccio, and what he still is. The information, though, is here made known to two characters who come from the very different world Teresina now inhabits. By choosing dialogue rather than the other potential solution of soliloquy Pirandello is able to juxtapose, and contrast, the two worlds of the play, and to show how unimportant the past is to the absent Teresina.

This sequence closes with a final, brief scene which is present in the play alone. The servants ask Micuccio to play his piccolo so that they can mock and disparage him and all he represents. The stage-directions read at this point:

> Micuccio siede e si mette a sonare con grande serietà. Ferdinando e
> Dorina fanno sforzi per non ridere. Sopravvengono ad ascoltare
> l'altro cameriere in marsina, il cuoco, il guattero, a cui i due primi
> fan cenni di star serii e zitti, a sentire. La sonata di Micuccio è
> interrotta a un tratto da un forte squillo del campanello. [MN, II, 345]
> [Micuccio sits down and starts to play with great seriousness.
> Ferdinando and Dorina try not to laugh. The other waiter in tails, the
> cook and the scullery-boy come on to listen, and the first two make
> signs to them to listen seriously and quietly. Micuccio's playing is
> interrupted all of a sudden by a loud ring of the bell].

This moment, epiphanic for reader and audience, is conceived entirely in terms of sound, gesture and movement, that is, in terms specifically intended for exploitation in the theatre. Micuccio's playing is halted by the bell ringing to announce the arrival of Teresina's guests, a sound which triumphs over the music of the simple song which Teresina used to sing in Sicily. A corresponding analysis could be made of the epiphany of Teresina, when she briefly leaves her reception to see Micuccio for the first time. The narrative and drama texts are, nevertheless, very similar, and Pirandello uses the costume and lighting of what is already a 'theatrical' moment in his short story.

The changes Pirandello makes surrounding Teresina's second appearance, however, lead him to alter fundamentally the balance of the play's ending. In the short story, as I have said, Micuccio leaves the limes and the money with zia Marta, and goes out to sit weeping at the top of the steps leading to Teresina's house. Teresina then appears, gives a cry of joy on seeing the fruit and, in spite of zia Marta's protests, takes the limes to the guests at her reception.

The picture of the disconsolate and weeping Micuccio is omitted in the 1910 version of the play, which ends with Teresina's cry. In 1915, when Pirandello adapted his play for Angelo Musco's dialect company, writing the parts of Micuccio and zia Marta in Sicilian, he also changed the play's climax. Now Micuccio gives the limes to zia Marta, but remains on stage when Teresina makes her second entrance. This time, he is the one who forbids her to touch the fruit, and before leaving, in a gesture with which he labels Teresina as a prostitute, he stuffs the money into the front of her dress. In a reversal of roles by comparison with the short story, it is Teresina who is left to weep. Pirandello then used this ending for the 1920 version of his play, which became the definitive text in Italian.

This final version brings the play to a dramatic close, but it also shifts the accent from a joyous, and heedless, Teresina absorbed in her success to a confrontation, and clash, between Micuccio and Teresina. Perhaps because Pirandello first wrote this ending for the dialect theatre, it is the Sicilian male code which triumphs, but the ending is also the result of the changes made in Micuccio's character. The threads which indicate that Teresina is a 'fallen' woman, as well as a singer, are drawn together and Micuccio, and the society he represents, achieve moral superiority. In the light of Pirandello's theatre in general we should also note that he discards an, at least partially,'happy ending' for his female character in favour of male superiority at this early stage. The questions which might occur to us, including why Micuccio waited for so long before seeking Teresina out, and why he wanted to preserve his illusion for so long, are not raised. [28]

Pirandello's theatrical vocation

From what has been said so far, we can see how the short story *Lumie di Sicilia* can provide Pirandello with material which he successfully transforms for the theatre. This play, and probably *La morsa*, provided him with a flexible set of devices which he used, and added to, when transforming other short stories into one-acts. It is also clear that, well before he wrote his best-known plays, he was keenly aware of what makes a good drama text. This being the case we should, in relation to his one-acts, briefly consider some of the more contradictory aspects of what has been called Pirandello's 'theatrical vocation'. As Franca Angelini says, evidence both old and new explodes the myth that Pirandello became interested in the theatre relatively late in his career, and that at an earlier stage he was reluctant, or half-hearted, about it. [29] Between 1875 and 1879 he wrote two plays, one destroyed and the other incomplete. [30] In letters written in 1886 and 1887 he also wrote to his family about his earliest attempts at writing plays, and the fascination theatre held for him. [31]

However, Pirandello also entertained many doubts about theatre. He expressed misgivings about transforming narrative works into plays, and later about short stories which contained so much dialogue as to be indistinguishable from theatre. In *L'azione parlata* he writes that in general it is difficult to condense and adapt a narrative work for the stage [*SPSV*, 1015]. In 1908 he concluded another essay with criticism of what he called the 'novella dialogata' (short story in dialogue form). [32] Among his targets are what he saw as the detrimental effects in Italy of copying French writers and theorists, and in particular of importing the 'novella dialogata' into Italy. This form, he wrote, can only be successful if the dialogue or conversation in it give 'l'illusione di una rappresentazione' [the illusion of a performance] [*SPSV*, 187], that is, if it can be sufficiently 'theatrical'. Later in the same essay he asserted that it was impossible to distinguish any longer between a short story of this kind and a a genuine short play [*SPSV*, 205].

And yet it is precisely the presence of so much dialogue in Pirandello's short stories that helped to facilitate their transformation into one-acts. Perhaps, in his essay, we can see Pirandello approaching the matter negatively, but at the same time implicitly weighing up the idea of drawing on his own work, and of capitalising on the 'theatrical' qualities of his short stories.

His ambivalent attitude towards the relationship between short stories and plays became further apparent when he defined his one-act *La patente* [The Licence] a 'novella sceneggiata' (dramatized short-story). [33] It is a formulation which clearly relates to his theorising in this area, and also to the complex origins of the play itself. The short story *La patente* was written in 1911. Pirandello then transformed it into a one-act in Sicilian in 1917. At the beginning of 1918, he was asked to send a short story for publication to the periodical *Rivista d'Italia*, at which point he translated his play into Italian and submitted it, adding his own definition to it. His one-act *All'uscita* [At the Exit] went through the reverse process. Conceived as a play, or at least as a dramatic work, it was apparently not originally intended for the stage, since after first publishing it in 1916 in the periodical *Nuova Antologia* Pirandello included it at the end of *E domani, lunedì...* [And Tomorrow, Monday ...], a volume of short stories. From these two examples we can perhaps see Pirandello, in a more positive key this time, working out through his own short stories and plays some of his ideas on the 'novella dialogata' and the 'novella sceneggiata', and the links between a particular form of narrative and a drama text.

L'uomo dal fiore in bocca [34]

In 1918 Pirandello published *Caffè notturno* [All-Night Café], a short story
written entirely in dialogue form, containing no narrative passages at all.
Then, after one intermediate change of title, he used this story with almost no
changes for the dialogue in his one-act *L'uomo dal fiore in bocca* (The Man
with the Flower in his Mouth), which was published in 1923. He called this
play a dialogue, possibly ironically, as for the most part it has the form of a
monologue.

The plot of the short story and that of the one-act are, therefore, identical.
Two men meet in an all-night café. These two, who in the short story have no
names or designations, are called in the play the Man with the Flower in his
Mouth and the Peaceful (or Pacific) Customer. I shall refer to them,
respectively, as the Man and the Customer. A third, non-speaking character,
the Man's wife, appears later on.

The Man begins the conversation, but at first it is the customer who
speaks most, recounting the series of trivial events which have led him to miss
his train: he and his family are on holiday in the countryside; his wife and
daughters nagged him until he came back to the town, where they live, to do
some shopping for them; because he had so much to do, and carry, he just
missed his train; he hadn't brought the keys to his house, so he had dinner in a
restaurant, went to the theatre and now, at midnight, has come to the café to
wait for his next train, which leaves at 4 a.m.

We only learn gradually in the play what has brought the Man to the café,
but as he is able to assure the Customer that it does not close he seems to have
been there before. What we see when he takes over the conversation is that he
has a great desire to talk, to others and, increasingly, to himself, and as the
play proceeds we wonder how many times he has told his story before. [35]
Through a series of images and analogies, whose meaning, as he says himself,
is not immediately apparent, his voice comes to dominate. The Customer talks
of banal happenings in a logical sequence which enables us to see the links

between cause and effect. The Man, instead, evokes familiar scenes (shop windows, a doctor's waiting room) in a way which defamiliarises them, and in so doing he gradually reduces the initially garrulous Customer to a terrified silence.

The Man's first flight of fancy comes after a misunderstanding (one of many) about the safety or otherwise of the Customer's parcels, now in the left-luggage office. The Man goes off at an apparent tangent, to describe a scene, familiar enough in itself, where shop assistants are skilfully wrapping parcels for their customers. He lingers over the minute details of their actions, and then says that he watches the assistants at work because he needs to cling to life through his imagination, like a climbing plant, but to the lives of others, not his own. From early on in the dialogue, then, we have a sense of a character who needs to fill his time, but as an observer, an outsider and a voyeur; and also of one who when speaking is capable of a switch of viewpoint which leads to an almost Brechtian estrangement.

Further incomprehension follows when the Customer, already becoming tentative in his views, suggests that the Man must get great pleasure from his imagination. To this, the Man reacts with irritation. As Altieri Biagi says, these two cannot possibly understand each other when even the word 'pleasure' (and later the word 'doctor') has a vastly different significance for each of them. [36]

The next scene the Man evokes is again familiar, but the way in which he describes it makes it strange. His imagination turns to a doctor's waiting room, and having carefully established that the Customer has been at least once to such a place he focuses to begin with not on the patients but on the chairs in the room, endowing them with almost a personality of their own. A hint as to why he fixes his attention on the chairs comes when he asks if the Customer noticed the chair he sat on when he took his daughter to the doctor's, and when the Customer replies that he did not, the Man says: 'Eh già; perché non era malato ...' [MN, I, 528] [Ah yes; because you weren't ill]. Illness, or as in Pirandello's story Berecche e la guerra [Berecche and the War] the anguish felt by Berecche as he gradually realises that he and his ideals have been overtaken by the younger generation and their new masters in the first world war, are amongst the physical and mental states which make Pirandello's characters see objects and events in a new way. [37]

The estrangement, and surprise, at what the Man says are all the greater because of the conventional viewpoint of the Customer at the beginning of the dialogue, and are further increased when the Man himself admits that he doesn't understand what brought the chairs and the patients to his mind. He seems to acknowledge that his own very personal images and analogies cannot be communicated, at least to a listener like the Customer. However, with a play on the verb 'occupare' the noun 'occupazione', he then suggests what the particular analogy might be:

> Vengono tanti clienti, ed esse sono là, povere seggiole, per essere occupate. Ebbene, è anche un'occupazione simile, la mia. Ora mi occupa questo, ora quello. In questo momento mi sta occupando lei. [MN, I, 529].

A literal translation, which at least has the merit of indicating the play on words, is:

> So many customers come, and they are there, poor chairs, to be occupied. Well, my occupation is similar. Now this occupies me, now that. At this moment, it's you who are occupying me.

This explanation of the analogy leads him on to consider the paradoxical nature of our experience of life, and to reveal the contradictions inherent in his own position. He sees the futility of life, but also has a great desire for life; and yet he does not know what life is. Life cannot be savoured in the present, but only through memories, yet our memories are, precisely, of all the trivial things which make life up. His particular use of the dialectic shows him caught in a trap.

In contrast with the language of the philosopher, trying to rid himself implacably, as he says, of all attachment to life is the language of appetite and desire. He uses words like 'gusto' (taste), 'soddisfare' (to satisfy) 'ingorda' (greedy) 'assaporare' (to savour) 'sapore' (taste), which show his realisation that life is all the more desirable when you are about to lose it. It is a speech in which one of Pirandello's characters does, indeed, seem like the sum of his contradictions, and fully conscious of his own relativism. [38]

This is a position which is only achieved, and maintained, by rejecting, indeed despising, any claims that wife and home have on him. A woman's head appears round the corner, and the Man explains that this is his wife, spying on him. He would like to kick her, like a dog, but realises that would have no effect. She wants to take care of him, but because he refuses to behave conventionally and let her be a loving and caring wife she is unable to eat, sleep or look after herself, and her hair is turning prematurely grey

The contrast between the two men is again underlined in their reactions to the Woman. The Customer pities her, but the Man sees his silent, spotlessly clean house, where time is marked out by the ticking of the clock, as a prison. His justification of his misogyny, and cruelty, is made first through an analogy with the houses and people in the earthquakes in Avezzano and Messina, who would not have stayed where they were if they had known that they were about to be destroyed, and then with the revelation that he has a fatal tumour, the 'insect' which cannot be brushed off, the 'flower in his mouth' of the play's estranging title. The 'silenzio di specchio' (mirror-like silence) would show him the void in which he exists, leading him to madness and destruction, whereas wandering the streets, observing the minutiae of life, conversations with strangers are a shield against madness: a necessary, if fragile, mask.

This is Pirandello at his most bleak. Enough is said in the dialogue for us to see all points of view, the suffering of the Wife as well as that of the Man, so that the 'sentimento del contrario' operates for both. As Felicity Firth says, when we watch this play on stage we are ourselves held prisoner, and we participate personally and physically in the experience the man describes. [39] The final images, the sensuality with which he describes eating an apricot, the youth and purity of the girls in the meadow and the tuft of grass, all show the Man's ineradicable attachment to life. [40]

Pirandello changed the title of his short story twice, from *Caffè notturno*, where location and time are stressed to *La morte addosso*, which confronts us with the image of death from the outset. His choice of *L'uomo dal fiore in bocca* for his one act shifts the emphasis to the surprising image, and prefigures the images and analogies which the Man uses. It also creates more suspense than the other titles, as we have to wait for some explanation of the metaphor until towards the end of the play. Other changes are minimal, but nonetheless vital. The characters in the one-act are given generic names, and ones which show how very different they are. The Man with the Flower is the character who sees, the 'Gran Me' [Big Me], whereas the Peaceful Customer, completely and unthinkingly immersed in life, is a 'piccolo me' [little me], to use Pirandello's own terms. [41] In the name of the Customer there is perhaps an indication that a meeting of such vastly different types is frequent, almost inescapable. In Italian, he is the 'avventore pacifico', and 'avventore' usually means a good customer, one who frequently uses the same shop or café. Although this particular 'avventore' has come to the café for the first time, his name points to a recurring situation.

Titles and names are important, and so, also, are the (few) stage directions which Pirandello adds to his one-act. The scene is carefully set in a dingy café, which becomes a marginal zone between life and death, and to his brief description of objects and lighting Pirandello adds the distant sound of a mandolin, with which the play opens and closes. [42] There are also indications of the mood of the Man, particularly irritation and anger, which are implied but not stated in the short-story. The greatest difference lies, however, in Pirandello's use of silence. At the beginning of the play, the stage directions say that the Man will observe the Customer at length, in silence, before he begins to speak. The pauses which Pirandello introduces into his play create, as Altieri Biagi says, an 'echo chamber', which can be filled with the reactions of the characters and require intense involvement and interpretation on the part of the reader, and the audience. [43] Finally, this play in performance gives great scope for mime, particularly when the Man is describing the shop window, so that although 'static' it can also be very physical. [44]

Some of Pirandello's short stories provide him with material which, to a greater or lesser extent, he transforms for the theatre. In this essay I have focused on a naturalist one-act and a very experimental, philosophical play. A comparison of narrative and drama text allows us to see both how 'theatrical' some of his short stories are, and also how aware Pirandello was from early on of the different requirements of the stage. Only a lengthier study of his one-acts, including those not derived from short stories, would permit a full appreciation of their experimental, and dramatic, qualities. I hope to have said enough in this essay to invite such a study.

JULIE DASHWOOD

[1] T. Hodgson, *The Batsford Dictionary of Drama*, London, Batsford, 1988, p. 252. See also my article 'I "piccoli saggi" di Pirandello', in AA. VV., *Pirandello e il teatro*, Milan, Mursia, 1993, pp. 183-192..

[2] A. Antoine, *"Mes Souvenirs" sur le Théâtre Libre*, Paris, Fayard, 1932, p. 9.

[3] F. Angelini, *Teatro e spettacolo nel primo Novecento*, Bari, Laterza, 1988, p. 144.

[4] P. Szondi, *Theory of the Modern Drama* (trans. by M. Hays of *Theorie des modernen Dramas*, 1965), Cambridge, Polity Press, 1987, pp. 54-57.

[5] P. Szondi, *Theory of the Modern Drama*, cit., p. 56.

[6] P. Szondi, *Theory of the Modern Drama*, cit., p. 56.

[7] F. Angelini, *Teatro e spettacolo*, cit., p. 21.

[8] For a complete list of Pirandello's plays, including those which, for various reasons, have not come down to us, see the invaluable critical edition of Pirandello's plays, still in course of publication, by Alessandro d'Amico, *Maschere Nude*, I, Milan, Mondadori, ser. I meridiani, lii - lxix. I shall refer to this edition as *Maschere Nude*, I, (D'Amico ed.). The five one-act plays

which exist in Italian and Sicilian are: *La morsa, Lumie di Sicilia, Liolà, La giara*, and *La patente*. The Sicilian texts of these plays can be found in: L. Pirandello, *Tutto il teatro in dialetto* (2 vols), ed. S. Zappulla Muscarà, Milan, Bompiani, 1993. The Italian and Sicilian versions are not always identical.

[9] *Perchè?* was published in the weekly journal *L'O di Giotto*, Rome, III, No. 25, 12 June 1892. The text of the play is reprinted in E. Villa, *Dinamica narrativa di Luigi Pirandello*, Padua, Liviana, 1976, pp. 173-180.

[10] L. Pirandello, *Perchè?* in E. Villa, *Dinamica narrativa*, cit., p. 178.

[11] See Maria Luisa Altieri Biagi's excellent and stimulating article 'La lingua in scena: dalle novelle agli atti unici' in *Gli atti unici di Pirandello (tra narrativa e teatro)*, ed. S. Milioto, Agrigento, Edizioni del Centro nazionale di studi pirandelliani, 1978, esp. pp. 272-273, where she analyses Pirandello's use of proper names. She cites in evidence Teresina/Sina (*Lumie di Sicilia*) and Evelina/Eva/Iviù/Lina (*La signora Morli una e due*) as women with names which indicate their innate predisposition to be or become 'two' and Lina/Giulia (*Cosí è (se vi pare)*), Lucia/Cia/Elma (*Come tu mi vuoi*) and Flora/Fulvia (*Come prima, meglio di prima*) as examples of female characters who have different names and live suspended between two identities.

[12] I give the usual translation of the title of this play, but the vise/vice referred to is a tool for gripping, not a fault or sign of immorality. Using the American spelling removes ambiguity, but may be unfamiliar. It is difficult to suggest an alternative: 'The Trap' fails to indicate the way in which the husband grips and works on his wife to force her to confess her adultery; 'The Grip' would probably not bring the idea of a vice to mind, either. The original (1892) title was *L'epilogo* [The Epilogue]

[13] For the function in Pirandello's work of scientific, and particularly medical, words, and the ability of characters like the Man with the Flower in his Mouth to use this terminology to distance themselves from the word which condemns them, and from life itself, see M. L. Altieri Biagi, 'La lingua in scena', cit., p. 271. Andrea, in choosing this method, becomes devoid of humanity, ultimately telling his wife to kill herself and then accusing Antonio of her murder.

[14] As J. A. Henderson says: 'The most depressing feature of the vaudeville in general, and, indeed, of practically all theatrical production of the time, is the uniformity of its subject-matter That the question of marital infidelity, whether treated as *comédie* or *drame*, should be so universally important is no doubt due in the first place to its being a highly relevant problem for at least certain social classes in Paris during the Second Empire and the First Republic. But in spite of endless variations [...] the theme was wearing thin.' *The First*

Avant-Garde. 1887-1894. Sources of the Modern French Theatre, London, Harrap, 1971, p. 23.

[15] See M. L. Altieri Biagi, 'La lingua in scena', cit., pp. 264-265.

[16] *'A morsa*, in L. Pirandello, *Tutto il teatro in dialetto*, I, cit., p. 250. *'A morsa* was first performed in Rome on 6 September 1918.

[17] See M. L. Altieri Biagi, 'La lingua in scena', cit., p. 271. In the original Italian: 'la parola più comune ha in sé baratri insospettati'.

[18] See *Maschere Nude*, I, (D'Amico ed.) p. 7-8. Because *La morsa* draws on the short story and develops it, D'Amico favours the view that the story possibly came first. However, the precise relationship between the two texts remains unclear. For readings based on the view that the short story was written first, see G. Pullini, 'Il primo Pirandello' in *Gli atti unici di Pirandello*, cit., esp. pp. 26-32; M. L. Altieri Biagi, 'La lingua in scena', cit., esp. pp. 298-303.

[19] Translating the title of this play also presents problems. According to D'Amico, 'lumìa' is a word derived from Arabic, meaning both a fruit and a tree very like a lemon, but smaller and rounder, less juicy and sweeter. In Agrigento, however, 'lumìa' often means lemon, and the 'lumìa' itself is called 'limoncella'; *Maschere Nude*, I, (D'Amico ed.) 42, note 2.

[20] 'Leaving aside the more curious examples of Zola's plays, works of a mystical and symbolist tendency which were not performed, practically all his dramatic writing consists of inferior versions of his novels', J. A. Henderson, *The First Avant-Garde*, cit., p. 29.

[21] 'It is essential [...] to recognise the relationship and indebtedness of Chekhov's one-act plays to his short stories, not only as the source of material, but as a source of technique. [...] In dramatising some of his own short stories, it is evident that Chekhov himself relied in his vaudevilles not only on his experience as a prose writer but also on his narrative work.', Vera Gottlieb, *Chekhov and the Vaudeville*, Cambridge, Cambridge University Press, 1982, pp. 43-44. Gottlieb says that Chekhov set himself the task of bringing realism to the vaudeville, humanising the stock characters and criticising the prevailing conditions on the stage.

[22] There is a brief analysis of *Lumie di Sicilia* in Andrea Camilleri, 'Le cosiddette quattro storie girgentane: *Lumie di Sicilia, L'altro figlio, La giara* e la *Sagra del Signore della nave*', in *Gli atti unici di Pirandello*, cit., esp. pp. 82-4.

[23] I use 'plot' here to indicate the events of the story as they are represented, in the order they are communicated, as in the analysis of the terms 'story' and 'plot' given by M. Pfister, *The Theory and Analysis of Drama* (trans. by J. Halliday of *Das Drama*, 1977), Cambridge, Cambridge University Press, 1988. I have used the 1991 (paperback) edition, p. 197.

[24] For purposes of brevity, I shall use 'stage directions' as the global term for what is verbalized only in the drama text (what Ingarden called the 'secondary text'). For a discussion of the terms 'stage- and acting-directions' see E. Törnqvist, *Transposing Drama*, Basingstoke and London, MacMillan, 1991, pp. 9-10.

[25] Hands have a particular place in Pirandello's work. M. L. Altieri Biagi refers to the man with the flower in his mouth looking at the hands of the shop assistants, and the hand of Tommaso Corsi (*Il dovere del medico*), seen against his green bedspread and emblematic of his return to life to show how they are 'one of the objects of empathic identification most recurrent in Pirandello' (in the original: 'uno degli "oggetti" di identificazione empatica più ricorrenti in Pirandello'), 'La lingua in scena', cit., p. 243.

[26] She is called 'Teresina' or 'Sina' according to the point of view of the other characters, who see her in turn as the 'Sicilian' Teresina and the worldly 'Sina'.

[27] For a discussion many of the uses of antefact in Pirandello's one-acts see A. L. Lepschy, 'The treatment of antefact in Pirandello's theatre' in *The Yearbook of the British Pirandello Society*, 8 & 9, 1988-1989, pp. 68-90 and 'The Treatment of the Antefact in Pirandello's Theatre in the Theatre Trilogy', in *Writers and Performers in Italian Drama from the Time of Dante to Pirandello*, eds. J. R. Dashwood and J. E. Everson, Lewiston, Queenston, Lampeter, The Edwin Mellen Press, pp. 129-141.

[28] On this see G. Isotti Rosowsky, 'Atti unici o epiloghi?' in *Gli atti unici di Pirandello*, cit., pp. 357-358.

[29] F. Angelini, 'Pirandello, D'Annunzio e il teatro: storia di un rapporto', in AA. VV., *Pirandello e D'Annunzio*, Palermo, Palumbo, 1989, pp. 131-2.

[30] See Alessandro D'Amico, 'Cronologia' in L. Pirandello, *Maschere Nude*, I, (D'Amico ed.), xxviii.

[31] These letters are published in: L. Pirandello, 'Epistolario familiare', ed. E. Providenti, *Nuova Antologia*, July-September 1985, pp. 229-254.

[32] In *Soggettivismo e oggettivismo nell'arte narrativa* [Subjectivism and Objectivism in Narrative Art] [*SPSV*, pp. 183-206, esp. pp. 203-206].

[33] See L. Pirandello, *Maschere Nude*, I, (D'Amico ed.) p. 516.

[34] Two very interesting analyses of this play can be found in M. L. Altieri Biagi, 'La lingua in scena', cit., esp. pp. 286-297 and F. Firth, 'La fortuna degli atti unici di Pirandello in Gran Bretagna (con uno studio su *L'uomo dal fiore in bocca*), also in *Gli atti unici di Pirandello*, cit., esp. pp. 375-381.

[35] The Man with the Flower is in some ways very akin to Dostoyevsky's Underground Man, especially when the latter says: 'Do you know one thing, though? I am certain that underground people like me must be kept in check. Though we may be capable of sitting underground for forty years without saying a word, if we do come out into the world and burst out, we will talk and talk and talk'. F. Dostoyevsky, *Notes from Underground*, (1864) trans. J. Coulson, Harmondsworth, Penguin, 1972, p. 43. This suggestion arises from my reading of W. Krysinski's book *Il paradigma inquieto. Pirandello e lo spazio comparativo della modernità*, ed. and trans. C. Donati, Rome, Edizioni Scientifiche Italiane, 1988, esp. pp. 133-136.

[36] M. L. Altieri Biagi, 'La lingua in scena', cit., p. 293.

[37] Interestingly enough, in *Berecche e la guerra* chairs again are the objects which produce the alienation effect. Berecche looks at '...un tavolino e tre sedie da cui si levavano gli avventori. Li ha fissati a lungo, avvertendo di punto in punto sempre piú, per quelle tre sedie vuote e quel tavolino abbandonato, una strana, malinconica invidia.' [... a small table and three chairs which the customers were just getting up from. He looked at them for a long time, feeling increasingly from one detail to the next a strange, melancholic envy for those three empty chairs and that deserted table.] L. Pirandello, *Novelle per un anno*, ed. M. Costanzo, Milan, Mondadori, 1991, vol. III, part 1, p. 577.

[38] As W. Krysinski says in *Il paradigma inquieto*, cit., p. 138.

[39] F. Firth, 'La fortuna degli atti unici di Pirandello', cit., p. 379.

[40] As A. Alessio says: 'È nel filo d'erba in particolare che il personaggio pirandelliano si identifica, il filo d'erba che l'uomo insensibile, cieco, avido e vano non esita a distruggere' [The pirandellian character particularly identifies with the blade of grass, which the man who is insensitive, blind, avid and vain does not hesitate to destroy], 'Forma e vita: la foglia e il filo d'erba' in *Pirandello e D'Annunzio*, cit., p. 178. The difference here is that the Man *asks* the Customer to pick the tuft of grass.

[41] See the 'Dialoghi tra il Gran Me e il piccolo me' [Dialogues between Big Me and little me], written in 1895, 1897 and 1906, in L. Pirandello, *Novelle per un anno*, ed. M. Costanzo, cit., vol III, part 2, pp. 963-985.

[42] For F. Firth, the mandolin is 'una estensione fisica della nota del malinconico lirismo già nel testo' [a physical extension of the note of melancholic lyricism already present in the text], 'La fortuna degli atti unici di Pirandello in Gran Bretagna', cit., p. 376.

[43] In the original Italian, 'una camera di risonanza'; M. L. Altieri Biagi, 'La lingua in scena', cit., p. 289.

[44] I have had the privilege of seeing Philip Stone's performances of this play, and of seeing how he uses mime and gesture in his interpretation of the part of the Man. See also J. Lorch, 'Philip Stone; Pirandellian Actor' in *The Yearbook of the British Pirandello Society*, I, 1981, pp. 19-25.

HENRY'S LAMP

Pirandello's starting-point for *Enrico IV* [Henry IV] is often held to be his reaction to the failure of the first production of *Sei personaggi in cerca d'autore* (1921) [Six Characters in Search of an Author]. After giving a synopsis of the play I shall briefly consider this view, alongside our knowledge that Pirandello also wanted to write a new role for the actor Ruggero Ruggeri. For his reply to his critics Pirandello chose the figure of the German emperor Henry IV, and I have given some space to considering why. I then move on to the more general question of historical drama and its relevance to *Enrico IV*, before looking at the play in the light of more recent history, specifically the first World War. Finally I shall turn to what for me is the central analogue of the play. When in Act II Enrico tells his servants that he is no longer mad, they offer to turn on the electric light in the villa. Enrico replies: 'No: m'accecherebbe. - Voglio la mia lampa.' [*MN*, I, 375] [No: it would blind me. - I want my lamp]. This analogue tells us what kind of play Pirandello was writing, and that is why I have chosen it for my title.

1. Synopsis of the play

Enrico IV is set in a lonely villa in the Umbrian countryside, in time present (circa 1921). As the play opens, the audience sees a splendid, if anachronistic, set which is a reconstruction of the throne-room of the German emperor Henry IV. Explanation of the set comes in the first part of Act I when three young men known as Landolfo, Arialdo and Ordulfo, who are employed in the villa, explain to a new employee, Bertoldo, what the situation is. Their master is a madman who believes that he is the eleventh-century German emperor Henry IV and requires that everything around him should be in keeping with the character he thinks he is. Bertoldo has prepared for the wrong Henry IV, and in a lively, mocking opening scene the others delight in initiating Bertoldo into their secrets. They are even more delighted when the arrival of visitors is announced, as they look forward to further opportunities for play-acting and mockery.

The new arrivals are a group of family and friends of the man whose baptismal name we never know, and who is only ever called Enrico in the play. They include his nephew, Carlo di Nolli, Carlo's fiancée, Frida, Frida's mother, Donna Matilde, with whom Enrico was once in love, and Matilde's lover, Belcredi. Enrico's sister, who loved and supported him, paying for the villa and all that is in it, has recently died. Before her death she thought she saw signs of improvement in her brother's condition, and made her son promise to try to help him. So the visitors have come in the hope that a cure can be found for Enrico, and the group is completed by a doctor, Dionisio Genoni. Belcredi and Matilde, who were part of the group of young aristocrats at the beginning of the century which Enrico belonged to, tell the others how it was that Enrico went mad. He took part, with them, in an historical cavalcade, in which he chose to appear as the emperor Henry IV. He fell from his horse, hit his head, lost consciousness and when he came to was fixed in his part. These events took place some twenty years before the play opens. Matilde, Belcredi and the doctor then have to assume appropriate roles and dress in eleventh-century costume before they can meet Enrico. These two scenes are a preparation for dramatic entrance of Enrico himself in the third part of the Act.

At the beginning of Act II, set in another room in the villa, it becomes clear that the visitors and the doctor have formulated a plan to try to effect a cure for Enrico. The plan is to restore to Enrico a sense that time has passed, and that he is no longer the young man who took part in the cavalcade or, indeed the emperor Henry IV. The irony which is revealed at the end of the

Act is that Enrico has recovered his sanity. A final twist is that the Act closes with Enrico as Henry IV serenely dictating an account of his reign to his faithful servant, Giovanni.

The attempted cure, at the beginning of Act III, almost has the opposite effect from the one desired, as Enrico receives such a shock, and experiences such terror, that he almost goes mad again. The Doctor, Matilde and Belcredi have in the meantime been told by the servants/secret counsellors that Enrico is not mad, and they rush onto the stage to denounce him. Enrico tells them that he was really mad for about twelve years, then for the last eight years he has been sane. He also says that his fall during the cavalcade was not an accident, as someone behind him stabbed his horse until it bled, and so it reared and threw him. Whether he is mad or sane, throughout this Act, becomes increasingly impossible to determine. At the end of the play he turns on Belcredi, the man who made his horse rear, and who has become Matilde's lover and lived the life which he denied Enrico, and kills him with a sword.

2. *The Madhouse*

Pirandello wrote *Enrico Quarto*[1] very quickly, between September and November 1921, and it was first performed at the Teatro Manzoni in Milan on 24 February 1922. With the sole exception, then, of the version in Sicilian dialect of *Tutto per bene* [All for the Best] it is the play which chronologically immediately follows *Sei personaggi in cerca d'autore* [Six Characters in Search of an Author], and as we know the first night of *Sei personaggi*, at the Teatro Valle in Rome on 10 May 1921, was marked by controversy and uproar. Gaspare Giudice writes that at this performance things began to go wrong from the start, that much of the play could hardly be heard and that when Pirandello left the theatre with his daughter he was greeted by the hisses, mockery and insults of the crowd. The play was called a 'manicomio' [madhouse], and Pirandello himself a buffoon and a madman.[2] The inital failure of *Sei personaggi*, and Pirandello's reaction to that failure, have been listed among the reasons which led him to write *Enrico IV* as his reply to those who had earlier made their incomprehension and hostility so apparent.

Only four months after the events of May 1921 Pirandello wrote to the actor Ruggero Ruggeri, whom he had first met in 1916 and for whom he had already written leading roles in three plays. In his letter Pirandello says that he had been thinking about another role for Ruggeri, and that he has had an idea for another play which he thinks is one of his most original works. He then goes on to sketch out the background and story of *Enrico IV*, and to ask for Ruggeri's views on the play before he settles down to work on it. [3] So Pirandello wrote this play with a particular actor in mind, and it is generally accepted that much of the play's success can be attributed to Ruggeri's interpretation of the role of Enrico. That he also had in mind the fiasco of the opening night of *Sei personaggi* has been demonstrated convincingly by Lucio Lugnani. [4]

Lugnani begins his argument by saying that *Enrico IV* is Pirandello's response to the accusation that *Sei personaggi* was a madhouse, so that the bare stage of the earlier play now becomes a 'manicomio in costume' [madhouse costume drama], disguised as a medieval throne-room. From this point of view it would seem that *Enrico IV* is Pirandello's ironic recantation of his earlier play, and is in a wider sense part of Pirandello's polemic with his theatre audiences. Lugnani then makes a detailed comparison of the first stage directions of the two plays. *Sei personaggi* opens in daylight; the curtain is raised and the stage is bare; the audience is not expected by the company preparing for a rehearsal, and in its turn the audience does not expect to find itself in a theatre where the stage is apparently not ready for the performance; the boundaries between stage and auditorium, the actors who work and the audience which comes to watch, listen and be entertained, and so between reality and fiction, are not established.

At the beginning of *Enrico IV*, however, the curtain is reassuringly down, and a play centred on one named character (not six unnamed ones) seems in prospect. When the curtain rises there is an elaborate set in place, which in most respects seems like the scene for an historical drama, a genre very popular at the time. However, the illusion is not allowed to last. We realise almost immediately that Pirandello is not aiming for a completely accurate reconstruction of the past; as he says in the first stage directions, the set is *'rigidamente parato in modo da figurare quella che poté essere la sala del trono di Enrico IV nella casa imperiale di Goslar.* [*MN*, I, 318] [*furnished and decorated with strict accuracy to represent what the throne room of Henry IV in the imperial palace of Goslar might have been like*]. Pirandello's use of 'rigidamente' and 'quella che poté essere' already suggest that he wants the set to appear as a construction. Then, in the same stage directions, we are alerted to the seeming anachronism of the two life-size modern portraits in oil, which stand out boldly against the back wall. At the same time as the audience takes in the set and its implications the two valets complete the anti-historicist, and anti-naturalist, image by springing to life, as though startled, jumping down from the ledge on which they were stretched out and going to stand, like statues, on either side of the throne. It is almost as though Pirandello were 'editing' theatrical conventions in order to parody them, here as in his direction that the whole of the first scene should be acted with 'estrosa vivacità' [*MN*, I, 519] [inspired vivacity]. Pirandello does, indeed, edit himself, and his own tendency to give his characters long philosophical speeches, when he writes in a note to the play that: *'Sarà chiuso dentro una parentesi quadra [ ] un breve passo del I atto, che nella rappresentazione della tragedia sarà bene omettere per la necessaria rapidità dell'azione'* [*MN*, I, 311] [*A short passage in Act I, which it is perhaps as well to omit in order to allow the action to flow as it should when the tragedy is performed, will be enclosed in square brackets [ ]].*

We are faced, therefore, with what Lugnani calls a theatre of disguise, and have moved from the absence of a set in *Sei personaggi* to a 'double' (possibly 'multiple') set, or a set within a set, in *Enrico IV*. To add to the argument, the Characters in the earlier play have a story, a content, but are searching for an author to give them form, and therefore eternity, through art. The secret counsellors in *Enrico IV* have a form, as young men from the minor aristocracy with whom the Emperor surrounded himself, but, as Landolfo says, they have no story of their own, and have to wait on the whim of Enrico to be told which events they have to adapt to each day. Enrico's 'whims', paradoxically, appear to provide some order in the play, in contrast to the situation in *Sei personaggi*. More could be said on this theme, but we perhaps have enough evidence already to substantiate Lugnani's thesis.

3. Pirandello's sources

We have seen that in writing *Enrico IV* Pirandello wanted to reply to his critics, and also to create a new role for Ruggeri. The play is also the only example in Pirandello's work of historical drama, however much it parodies that genre. A surprise, duly signalled in the play by Bertoldo, who has studied the wrong century and ruler, comes when Pirandello, apparently deliberately, confounds our expectations as to which Henry IV we might anticipate seeing on stage. Bertoldo has had a fortnight to prepare himself for his new post, and has wasted his time by reading up on Henri IV of France. An English-speaking audience might reasonably prepare itself for one of Shakespeare's historical plays. Perhaps only those who know medieval Germany well might think of the Holy Roman Emperor. So is Pirandello possibly teasing his audience? The Henry IV he chooses is the most obscure of the three, and in theatrical terms any reference to Henry IV recalls Shakespeare's King. The question which should now be put is why, in 1921, Pirandello decided to use salient events in the life of an eleventh-century German emperor, whose long and troubled reign lasted from 1056 until 1106, for a play which is set in time present.

As Horst Fuhrmann says: 'Canossa is [...] an ever-recurring symbol', and he quotes Bismarck's declaration of 1872 to the Reichstag: 'We shall not go to Canossa' as 'only one example among many of its use'. [5] At Canossa, on Wednesday 25 January 1077, Henry IV appeared barefoot and in sackcloth to do penance before the Pope, Gregory VII. His immediate aim was to be released from excommunication, and in this he succeeded, but only after the humiliation of waiting in the snow and at the cost of visibly subordinating himself to the sovereignty of the church. [6] As Fuhrmann indicates, those who know little or virtually nothing about Henry IV of Germany may have heard of Canossa and know its associations. Pirandello was apparently aware of this as well, since Canossa is the name which Landolfo uses in Act I of *Enrico IV* in order to try to provide a reference point for the bewildered and disorientated Bertoldo.

Pirandello's interest in the figure of Henry IV goes back to his student days in Bonn, where he studied between 1889 and 1891 before graduating in March 1891. This was also the period when he wrote the poems which make up his *Elegie renane* [Rhenish Elegies], in No. X of which a family gathers around the fire to listen to an old man narrating some of the stories and legends associated with the Rhineland, including the saga of 'Enrico quarto, tragico imperatore' [*SPSV*, 567] [Henry IV, the tragic emperor]. In his letter to Ruggeri, already referred to, and in his play, Pirandello adds the adjective 'grande' to this description, making the emperor into a tragic hero. The influence of Heine on Pirandello's Elegy has been noted, and in particular the relevance of the ninth of his *Zeitgedichte* [Historical Poems]. In this poem Heine describes Henry IV's humiliation by Gregory VII and Countess Mathilda at Canossa, but also attributes to him a secret vow for revenge over the two who watch him from an upper window as he stands barefoot in his penitent's robe. [7] Pirandello's Enrico also meditates revenge, after the *tableaux vivants* scene in Act III of the play.

A source of Pirandello's knowledge of the stories of the Rhineland when he was in Bonn was a book by Karl Geib, *Die Sagen und Geschichten des Rheinlandes* [The Sagas and Stories of the Rhineland]. In his article 'Petrarca a Colonia' [Petrarch in Cologne], published in 1889, Pirandello draws extensively on one chapter in Geib's book, as Willi Hirdt has shown. [8] Two further chapters in the *Sagen und Geschichten*, 'Kaiser Heinrich IV. in Bingen' and 'Kaiser Heinrich IV. auf Hammerstein', are devoted to Henry IV. Geib's writing is a mixture of the historical and the legendary. He refers to many of the main events in Henry's life, including the consequences of the fact that Henry was only six when he became Emperor: there was no-one to control the

German bishops, and Henry himself was abducted by Archbishop Hanno of Cologne; his mother, Agnes, was too weak to fight against the bishops, and retired to a convent. Henry took over the government of the Empire in 1065, when he was 15, but, according to Geib, was taught damaging principles by Archbishop Adalbert of Bremen, who told him to enjoy his youth and do as he pleased, so Henry sold secular and church offices and squandered the proceeds, setting the German princes against him because of his youthful excesses, his wish to divorce his wife, Bertha, and the unlimited trust he placed in Adalbert.

Adalbert was forced from power but, says Geib, Henry began his pleasure-loving life again, and only mended his ways after rebellions in Saxony and Thuringia. Eventually Henry defeated his enemies and named his son Konrad as his successor. At this point he was threatened from Italy by the Pope, Gregory VII, who excommunicated him. Henry was forced to go to Italy, crossing the Alps in a terrible winter, to have the excommunication rescinded. A description of the events of Canossa follows. But for Geib the worst thing that happened to Henry was the disobedience of his sons, which degenerated into hostility and treachery against their father. Geib calls the betrayal of Henry by his sons, in particular his imprisonment by his younger son, another Henry, the saddest and most detestable picture of a time filled with unnatural behaviour and dark prejudices. The image Geib impresses on us is of a deeply offended father bowed down with age and sorrow faced by his triumphant, renegade son.

This image is reinforced in the second chapter on Henry where, in Geib's version, after escaping from imprisonment Henry dies of anguish because of the behaviour of his son. The narration of events becomes secondary, and the figure of the wronged, grieving and ageing father is central. So the reign of Henry IV is shown to be one of great drama in the public sphere, while in private the story is one of wild youth followed by enmity, humiliation, betrayal, a bereft old age and death of a broken heart. Pirandello knew more about the reign of Henry IV than is found in Geib's account. It is, for example, almost irresistible to suggest that he knew the comment, not in Geib, of the eleventh-century Augsburg annalist, who wrote: 'What a lamentable spectacle is presented by the Empire! As the comic poet [Plautus] puts it: all are doubled; so are the popes doubled, the bishops doubled.' [9] But the essential traits of Pirandello's Enrico seem to be present in Geib's account.

4. Historical drama

As Landolfo, frustrated in his ambition to make full use of his skills as wardrobe man, says:

> ... il nostro vestiario si presterebbe a fare una bellissima comparsa in una rappresentazione storica, a uso di quelle che piacciono tanto oggi nei teatri. E stoffa, oh, stoffa da cavarne non una ma parecchie tragedie, la storia di Enrico IV la offrirebbe davvero. [*MN*, I, 322] [... our costumes would be ideal for putting on a lovely production of an historical play, for the kind of play that's so popular in the theatre nowadays. And the material, oh, the material contained in the story of Henry IV would be enough for lots of tragedies, not just one].

The characters in *Enrico IV* have a good story (or stories), an elaborate set, an extensive library for studying the life and times of Henry IV and a complete wardrobe where the costumes, as poor Landolfo says later in Act I, are all perfect copies of costumes of the period from the best theatrical costumiers. Pirandello, therefore, provides his characters with everything necessary for staging an historical drama. Since his intention, as is clear from the beginning of the play, was not to write such a drama, we should ask why he provides such a superabundance, or possibly superfluity, of historical props.

By 1921 an historical drama of the kind which, as Landolfo says, was popular at the time had become a stereotype. In Italy, until the 1930s, the production of poetic costume dramas seemed a good way to ensure box office success, in the wake of D'Annunzio's *Francesca da Rimini* (1901) and Sem Benelli's *Cena delle Beffe* (1908) [The Supper of Jests]. [10] These two plays, and those whose authors eagerly followed the trend, exploited a then-fashionable taste for costume drama and dark deeds.

D'Annunzio was tireless, as well as finicky, in his attention to the staging of his plays. When writing about the sets for *Francesca da Rimini* to his friend the painter and designer Adolfo De Carolis he dwelt, among many other details, on the minutiae of the decoration of the slave's tunic and the need to have the eagle of the Polenta family on Ostasio's red surplice. His desire for exactitude and perfection were so great that specialists were used for the woodcarving and the armour, and even the president of the Académie Française de Coiffure was sent for to supervise the hairstyles.[11] D'Annunzio was intent on ensuring absolute veracity in all his plays, not just the historical ones. His description of the set of *La città morta* (1898) [The dead city] is, literally, archaeological (the dead city in question is Mycenae). Then, as Franca Angelini says, Virgilio Talli's production of D'Annunzio's *La figlia di Iorio* (1904) [Iorio's Daughter] has become legendary, because Francesco Paolo Michetti and his pupil and helper Ferraguti ransacked the countryside of the Abruzzo region, which was D'Annunzio's own and where the play is set, in search of the authentic costumes, furnishings and props which D'Annunzio insisted on for his play.[12]

Pirandello's aversion for D'Annunzio is well-known.[13] To remain within the context of historical drama, in a note of 1905 on G. A. Cesareo's *Francesca da Rimini* Pirandello takes the opportunity to attack the 'ambizioso armamento storico' [ambitious historical apparel] and the 'soverchia decorazione scenica' [excessively decorated set] of D'Annunzio's play of the same name.[14] Pirandello's attitude appears to have softened by 1934, when he agreed to mount a production of *La figlia di Iorio*,[15] but he would certainly have had D'Annunzio and his imitators among his targets in 1921 when writing *Enrico IV*.

I would argue that he also had in mind the various more general trends towards historical accuracy and historicism in the nineteenth century. To take just a few examples which, however, show how widespread these trends were, in England, James Robinson Planché designed accurate historical costumes for Charles Kemble's revival of *King John* at Covent Garden in 1823. Eleven years later, in 1834, Planché's researches culminated in the publication of his book on the history of British costume. Also, Charles Kean's productions in the 1850s were based on the huge amount of research he insisted upon into the historical context of each play. In turn, Kean was an influence on staging in Europe, as Georg II, Duke of Saxe-Meiningen, visited London in 1846 and 1857, where saw Kean's productions at the Princess's Theatre.

Georg II's father, Bernhard II, had presented the town of Meiningen with a theatre in 1831, and a resident company was established there some thirty years later. Georg himself took over personal responsibility for running the theatre from the end of 1869, helped by his third wife, the actress Ellen Franz whom he married in 1873, and the actor and director Ludwig Chronegk. The Meiningen Court Theatre gained national and international importance in the 1870s and 1880s, touring in Germany and beyond with productions especially of plays by Schiller and Shakespeare, and the company's productions are marked throughout by a concern for historical accuracy in the design of set and costume. [16] There seems to be more than an echo of all this in the throne-room in *Enrico IV* which, as we have seen, is 'rigidamente parato'. Moreover Landolfo, who at times partly understands something of Enrico's character but at others fails to understand him completely, seems to be trying to make of Enrico a character concerned above all with similar principles of external historical accuracy. In Act I he tells the doctor, Genoni, not to be overly concerned at the fact that his is an easy disguise which has already been used many times before as Enrico 'guarda piú all'abito che alla persona' [*MN*, I, 340] [looks more at the costume than at the person]. In this Landolfo is, of course, mistaken, as Enrico instantly recognises his visitors for what they are beneath their disguises.

5. *Theatre and Painting*

There is another way, I would suggest, in which Pirandello takes, parodies and transforms a convention, this time of nineteenth-century painting as well as theatre, and this is shown by the presence and use of the two life-size portraits which in *Enrico IV* dominate the stage, and much of the dialogue, until they literally become living portraits at the beginning of Act III. John Osborne writes that the 'preference for the static' in nineteenth-century theatre 'manifests itself in its most extreme form in the widespread use of the *tableau vivant*', and adds that the convention was to present the final scene of a play as a living picture, often modelled on a specific painting well-known to the audience. [17] The German victory in the Franco-Prussian war and its aftermath gave a boost to the interest in *tableaux vivants*, as artists commemorated the war and their paintings were often used in the theatre as models for the climax of scenes. These artists also helped to organise the processions and pageants held in honour of the victorious troops. [18]

In Act I of *Enrico IV* Bertoldo says that the portraits of Enrico and Matilde are 'una bella stonatura [...] in mezzo a tutta questa rispettabile antichità' [*MN*, I, 323] [really out of place ... in the middle of all these worthy antiquities]. He is told that the niches which the portraits now cover were originally intended to hold statues in the style of the period, and that the portraits came later. In a brief exchange, therefore, Pirandello rejects the 'archaeological' style. Instead, throughout the play he problematises the portraits and their significance, until the last *tableau vivant* where Enrico and three of his secret counsellors form what in theatrical terms is the final freeze.

Landolfo is the first to attempt a verbal interpretation of the portraits. He says to Bertoldo that, for Enrico:

> Immagini sono. Immagini come ... ecco, come le potrebbe ridare uno specchio, mi spiego? Là, quella (*indica il ritratto di Enrico IV*) rappresenta lui, vivo, com'è, in questa sala del trono, che è anch'essa come dev'essere, secondo lo stile dell'epoca. Di che ti meravigli, scusa? Se ti mettono davanti uno specchio, non ti ci vedi forse vivo, d'oggi, vestito cosí di spoglie antiche? Ebbene, lí, è come se ci fossero due specchi, che ridanno immagini vive, qua in mezzo a un mondo che - non te ne curare - vedrai, vedrai, vivendo con noi, come si ravviverà tutto anch'esso! [*MN*, I, 324]
> [They're images. Images like ... that's it, like reflections in a mirror, is that clear? That one there (*he points to the portrait of Henry IV*) shows him, alive, as he is, in this throne room, which is also as it should be, in the style of the 11th century. So why are you so

surprised? If you're put in front of a mirror, don't you perhaps see yourself alive, today, dressed up as you are in period costume? Well, there, it's as though there were two mirrors, which reflect back living images, right here in the middle of a world which - don't worry - you'll see, you'll see, living with us, how it all comes to life as well].

At this point Bertoldo, understandably, says that he doesn't want to go mad.

Landolfo tries to make the portraits mimetic, and he does provide some insight into their significance. Enrico's portrait does not resemble him as he is now, twenty years on, a point that is visually underscored when he finally appears on stage after the long build-up in Act I. It can, however, be seen as an inner portrait, as subjectively Enrico has supposedly not moved on from the time of his youth. So to this extent, perhaps, we can make something of Landolfo's explanation. Landolfo does not yet know, of course, that Enrico has recovered his sanity, and that the portraits for him are reminders of the time (circa 1901-1902) when they were painted. They therefore represent for Enrico what happened just before Belcredi's cruel joke (if that is what it was) when he chose and studied for his role in the cavalcade. Further, they are monuments to the cavalcade itself, when he was betrayed and humiliated. In Act I Belcredi says that before he suddenly went mad Enrico was a good actor and a great organizer of *tableaux vivants*, dances and charity shows. During the cavalcade the former producer and actor becomes 'buried' in his role.

Later in the play, the portraits do 'come alive', when they are used as 'living statues'. But Landolfo's explanation hopelessly confuses the different time zones of the world in which he lives. He moves from Henry alive 'seeing' himself today as he was twenty years previously to the throne room as a mirror of the Middle Ages and then to Bertoldo alive in the present but in period costume. Finally, his interpretation breaks down, and he can only have recourse to telling Bertoldo to 'wait and see'. *Enrico IV* is a play where, repeatedly, interpretations lead nowhere, or alternatively have a meaning not understood by the character who utters them. In this instance we might indeed see the way in which Landolfo zooms from one time to another, confusing the different zones inextricably, as a paradigm for the play itself.

When the visitors, the group of family, friends and doctor, come to the villa the portraits are again the focus of discussion. Her portrait is the first thing which Donna Matilde notices after her entrance, and significantly enough she looks only at her portrait, not Enrico's. In this play, as throughout Pirandello's theatre, most of the characters see only what they want to see. For Donna Matilde, although not for Frida, the portrait is similar, to the point of being identical with, her own daughter. Faced with this uncanny resemblance she shivers; then, with what seems a gesture of maternal pride and affection, draws Frida to her, putting her arm round her daughter's waist. This gesture, though, acquires a different meaning when, in Act II, Frida tries on the costume that Matilde wore for the cavalcade. She finds it tight, and remarks what a small waist her mother must have had when young. So we might conjecture that Matilde's earlier gesture was indicative, not so much of affection (for Matilde is not an affectionate mother), but a desire to reassure herself that her daughter's waist was indeed bigger than that of the figure in the portrait.

It is a gesture which, if this interpretation is correct, reveals Matilde's thoughts, which are hidden from the other characters. The uncanny, the *unheimlich,* the 'name for everything which ought to have remained secret and hidden but has come to light' [19] lies at the heart of Pirandello's use of the portraits, the cavalcade and much else, in this play. The portraits do not commemorate a triumph; they are not part of a celebration to mark the return home of the victorious troops. Rather they are permanent reminders of humiliation, betrayal and loss, and of the tragic process of ageing. [20] The essential rhythm of the life of the German emperor can be found here.

At the end of Act II, Enrico composes his own tableau, a 'quadro notturno' [*MN*, I, 376] [night-time tableau] which contains himself and his four secret counsellors. I shall discuss this scene in greater detail in my final section. Following almost immediately, at the beginning of Act III, comes the *tableaux vivants* scene itself, and here again the uncanny is the keynote.

During the play, Doctor Genoni becomes increasingly fascinated with the portraits. From early on, though, and in spite of Belcredi's warnings, he shows his inability to comprehend the relationships between the visitors. Matilde's fear of ageing, shown by the very mixed feelings she has when she sees that the figure in her portrait is now that of her daughter, not of herself, leads her to ask Belcredi and then the doctor if they can see the likeness. Belcredi avoids the trap, but the doctor falls into it when he says: 'Mi pare che - dopo tutto - non ci sia tanto da stupirsi che una figlia somigli alla madre.' [MN, I, 329] [It seems to me - after all - that it isn't so surprising that a daughter resembles her mother]. Belcredi, with his onomatopoeic 'patatràc' (the noise of something falling apart, or breaking) shows what the doctor has done, and indeed what he continues to do for the whole play.

Genoni begins to elaborate a series of hypotheses in a high-flown language which marks him as the target of parody. He makes an effort to establish that Enrico was the originator of the idea for the cavalcade, but to no avail. Throughout, he is either wrong, or no-one knows the answers to this questions, so his dogmatic attempts to establish the truth are constantly disappointed. [21] His proposed cure for madness is that Enrico should be given 'la sensazione della distanza del tempo' [MN, I, 359] [the feeling of how far away that time was]. Frida, in Matilde's costume, is to take the place of her mother's portrait in the frame and Di Nolli, dressed as Henry IV, that of Enrico. They will step out of their frames, and Matilde will then appear, also dressed as Matilda of Tuscany. By this juxtaposition, Genoni hopes that Enrico will realise that time does not stand still, his mental clock will re-start and he will be jolted back into time present. When describing this shock treatment Genoni has recourse to a series of analogies, indicating that his kind of science and scientific language do not have the precision and solutions they claim, and that he cannot talk about the mind without metaphor.

The *tableaux vivants* scene is prepared, but ironically Genoni and the others do not yet know that Enrico has just revealed to his secret counsellors that he is no longer mad. At the beginning of Act III Enrico, sad and tired, makes his way across the darkened stage. Then, in a moment of sheer terror he hears Frida calling him, and is almost plunged back into madness. Frida jumps from her frame, also terrorised; the visitors return, and without paying any attention to Enrico rush to help Frida. For Enrico the moment is decisive. Threatened by a new onset of madness, the plaything of those around him, betrayed by his servants, overlooked and ignored, he meditates revenge for this fresh humiliation. He then decides, as the stage directions say, to pretend that the fiction the others have created is real, and so he returns to the role of Henry IV. After this experience, he can only return to and defend his own creation.

6. Enrico, Berecche and the first World War

Pirandello said in an interview with Benjamin Crémieux in 1925 that it was the first World War which made writing for the theatre essential for him. [22] Novels and short stories were no longer enough in a world where everything was 'in movement'; words themselves 'could no longer stay written on paper, they had to burst into the air, spoken or shouted aloud.' [23] Pirandello had written plays before the war, and been fascinated by the theatre from an early age. But it was the war itself, and all that happened to and around him, that made him a playwright.

In his book *Pirandello. Il disagio del teatro* Claudio Vicentini illuminates this stage of Pirandello's career, particularly in relation to the writing of *Sei personaggi in cerca d'autore*. [24] Vicentini argues that Pirandello's explosion of creativity during the war years springs from a profound artistic and psychological crisis. [25] The artistic crisis stems from Pirandello's own views on, and suspicions of, theatre. He found himself compelled to leave the safe confines of the narrative text and write plays. His dilemma, though, was that theatre requires the use of actors, stage, set, directors, technicians - the whole theatrical company. His texts, therefore, would of necessity be subject to interpretation, and the author's vision, and the superiority of art itself, would be jeopardised. So *Sei personaggi*, for Vicentini, becomes a practical demonstration of the arguments against theatre which Pirandello put forward in his essay *Illustratori, attori e traduttori* (1908)

[Illustrators, Actors and Translators], and which he continued to express even when writing his greatest plays. [26]

As we have seen, Pirandello wrote *Enrico IV* with a particular actor, Ruggeri, in mind, and so he may have felt that he had some control over the 'translation' of his play for the stage. But there were later some problems even with Ruggeri. Vicentini says that Ruggeri was horrified at at the proposal that he should give up his usual black costume, in which he had had all his greatest triumphs, for the 1925 production of *Enrico IV* at the Teatro d'Arte. [27] Picking up another thread of the argument, there are many ways in which this play, too, reflects the dilemmas of the war years.

Pirandello's psychological crisis during the war years has been amply documented. [28] It seems particularly relevant to the present essay to recall that his elder son, Stefano, was called up in 1915, taken prisoner in November that year and remained a prisoner until 1918. His younger son, Fausto, was also called up in 1915 when convalescing from a serious illness and subsequently contracted tuberculosis. His wife, Antonietta, had been subject to persecution mania since 1903. Her condition deteriorated badly, especially during the war years. Antonietta was committed to a nursing home in 1919, and she remained there for the rest of her life. War and madness touched Pirandello directly and personally.

Pirandello himself was too old to fight in the war. He suffered because of what happened to his sons, and because, like his first-person narrator in the short story *Colloquii coi personaggi* (1915) [Interviews with Characters] he belonged to the 'unfortunate generation' of those who saw their fathers fight for Italian unification, and now had to wait on one side as their sons left to fight in the first World War for the completion of Italian unification. [*NA*, III, 1143]. [29] The drama of the non-combatant, the non-participant can be found in other stories of this period, for example *Berecche e la guerra* [Berecche and the War] (written between 1914 and 1917), and the *Frammento di cronaca di Marco Leccio e della sua guerra sulla carta nel tempo della grande guerra europea* [Fragment of the Chronicle of Marco Leccio and of his Map War at

the Time of the Great European War] (written between 1915 and 1917).
These two *novelle* are particularly significant because in them Pirandello uses
the metaphor 'il teatro della guerra' [the theatre of war], which brings together
his artistic and psychological preoccupations at the time. In the map scene in
Berecche e la guerra the protagonist remembers himself as a nine year old boy
watching his father and some friends following the course of the Franco-
Prussian war. As their fingers trace the passage of the war on a map, it seems
to the young Berecche as though 'ognuno di quei diti [...] assumeva subito una
strana personalità' [*NA*, III, 583] [each of those fingers [...] immediately took
on a strange personality]. Here it is indeed as though the words in Pirandello's
narrative acquire a persona, a physical presence, and try to spring from the
page. Many aspects of *Berecche e la guerra*, in particular, are found later,
with some shifts of emphasis, in *Enrico IV*.

The protagonist of *Berecche e la guerra* [30] is an Italian who has tried to
construct his life, and his identity, on a 'German' model. Above all, he tries to
live according to what he regards as the virtues of German method, and so he
obstinately and methodically forces his unwilling family to live on the
outskirts of Rome in what is almost the countryside. The story is full of
replicas, and the villa Berecche chooses for his family is like a synthesis of an
ideal nordic image of Italy. Enrico's villa, transformed into the throne-room
of Goslar, recalls Berecche's villa as it, too, is a German insert into an Italian
setting. Then, like Berecche, Marco Leccio and the others of their generation,
Enrico is also a non-participant, in life itself, but specifically in the twenty
years which included the first World War. The cavalcade took place about
twenty years before the play opens; Enrico was mad for twelve years and then
recovered his sanity in about 1913-1914, just before the outbreak of the war.
His decision to stand aloof from life coincides with what Berecche calls the
'colossale bestialità' [*NA*, III, 1, 585] [colossal bestiality] which Germany
showed in precipitating the war.

Berecche is a retired professor of History, who feels anguish and
experiences the laceration of his ideals and identity because of the war. [31] So

he tries to find some bitter comfort in imagining how the war will be viewed in a thousand years, when all the sufferings of the insignificant people caught up in it will be forgotten. In his account, historians in this far-distant future will reduce history to a few lines. His leap into the future has as its counterpart the refuge which Enrico seeks in the past. [32]

Enrico tells his secret counsellors that they should live with conviction in the eleventh century, and from that perspective think of the men of the twentieth century who:

> ... si abbaruffano intanto, s'arrabattano in un'ansia senza requie di sapere come si determineranno i loro casi, di vedere come si stabiliranno i fatti che li tengono in tanta ambascia e in tanta agitazione. [MN, I, 377]
> [... in the meantime quarrel and struggle in an ceaseless anxiety to know how their lives will work out, to see what form the events which keep them in such anguish and tumult will take.]

The 'piacere della storia' [MN, I, 377], the 'pleasure of history', lies in the fact that even if a certain historical period is one of sorrow and disaster it is part of the past. So it can be studied safely, examined in terms of relationships of cause and effect, free from the uncertainties and emotions of the present. Yet the desire to place events in a logical sequence is something which Enrico only achieves when he is safely dictating an historical chronicle of his reign to Giovanni. Otherwise, as his secret counsellors indicate in Act I, history is played out as a random series of events, as from one day to the next they can be in Goslar, the castle of the Harzburg, Worms and so on, and the throne-room, says Landolfo, 'balza con noi, ora qua, ora là' [MN, I, 319] [jumps around with us, now here, now there]. Perhaps the real pleasure of history lies in being able to mimic the way things happen in the present from the safe refuge of of the past. This pleasure, though, is threatened in *Enrico IV* by the arrival of the visitors, who bring with them own inner drama in the present. They also bring back to Enrico the tragic recognition he had after twelve years of madness: life as it is lived everyday is full of uncertainty, travail and tumult, but it is also, paradoxically, a banquet which he has missed. [*MN*, I, 388]

Berecche is an authoritarian father-figure whose authority and prestige are based on the heroic, masculine 'German' identity he created for himself. When his love and admiration for Germany are suddenly challenged by the horror and chaos of the war the authoritarian, phallic finger he points at his family no longer has any power over them. The young men he calls 'figliuoli' [children/boys], who are his son, Fausto, and his daughter's fiancé, Gino, become adults, heroes who go off to fight. So they assume, or arrogate, the legitimacy, virility and authority of their father. For Berecche everything collapses, without and within.

In the villa in Umbria Enrico, too, has absolute power and authority, which are also based on, legitimised by, the maintenance of a 'German' identity. When he recovered from his madness Enrico realised that not only had his hair turned grey but 'doveva essere diventato grigio tutto cosí, e tutto crollato, tutto finito' [*MN*, I, 388] [everything else must have become grey as well, and everything have collapsed, be over], and so he decided to continue to play his role. His structure and identity are threatened, however, when the younger generation in the play, Frida and Di Nolli, symbolically take the place of their elders in the *tableaux vivants* scene. When Enrico claims Frida as his right at the end of the play part of his motivation, I would suggest, is the desire to make one last attempt to re-establish the authority, power and prestige which his nephew is trying to take from him.

The historians of the distant future, Berecche says, will remember, among the very few, the two emperors, Wilhelm II and Franz Joseph, who used the pretext of the assassination of Franz Ferdinand to start a stupid war. In the emperor's game of *Enrico IV* there is an oblique reference to Wilhelm II. In Act I of the play Belcredi says that the idea for the historical cavalcade was his, and that it came to him while he was leafing through an illustrated German magazine, looking only at the pictures as he doesn't know German. In it he came across a picture of the emperor (not named) dressed in one of the strange, traditional costumes of ancient student societies in Germany. This emperor (Wilhelm II) was accompanied by fellow aristocratic students and they were all in a procession on horseback. So Belcredi had the idea that he and his friends would organise a similar cavalcade in costume for the next Carnival. The stimulus for the cavalcade, which is itself the starting-point for the whole action, was therefore another image, another picture which comes to life in lateral fashion in the figure of Enrico.

The allusion to Wilhelm II establishes a tangential link between Kaiser Wilhelm, Henry IV and Enrico, who himself chooses to appear as an emperor. Pirandello could be suggesting that his own mad emperor reflects in some ways the characters - authoritarian, determined to maintain their prestige, convinced of their absolute power and divine right to rule - of both Wilhelm II and Franz Joseph. In Act III, almost at the end of his speech about the Irish priest, Enrico says that his role, his mental construct, requires him to be zealous in his defence of the hereditary monarchy. Historians generally characterise Franz Joseph as a man who lived in the past, who mistrusted things modern. [33] Even, intriguingly enough, we are told that in his palace of the Hofburg, in Vienna, he refused to countenance up-to-date improvements that would make life easier and more comfortable, including electricity, and that illumination was provided by kerosene lamps. [34]

A final possible satirical allusion to Germany, Austria and their part in Pirandello's play could lie in the name given to the new secret counsellor, Bertoldo. This is a 'nome del tempo', as is said in Act I, but possibly a name of the times in two senses: it refers to Bertold I of Carinthia, Henry IV's contemporary, but also to the Austrian foreign minister, Count Leopold von Berchtold. Just as Bertoldo in the play tries several times to resign his post, so Berchtold resigned, in 1915, from the Austrian government because of its refusal to make concessions to Italy. We might also speculate that Enrico's madness, which as Belcredi says 'costa fior di quattrini' [MN, I, 342] [costs a fortune] is a microcosm for the greater madness of the war. As Genoni says at this point, many other forms of madness are very expensive.

Berecche and Enrico live in a world which is shaped by their own phantasies, their own games and imaginings. Freud writes in his essay 'Creative Writers and Day-Dreaming' (1907): 'The motive forces of phantasies are unsatisfied wishes, and every single phantasy is the fulfilment of a wish, a correction of unsatisfying reality.' [35] Berecche phantasizes about participating in the war, restored to his central position between his two 'boys' to conquer Italy's 'unredeemed' territory. Enrico's whole world is based on phantasy, on his wish to avoid unsatisfying reality, and from what we know appears to have been so even before the cavalcade.

In the same essay Freud puts forward his view that the psychological novel 'owes its special nature to the inclination of the modern writer to split up his ego, by self-observation, into many part-egos, and, in consequence, to personify the conflicting currents of his own mental life in several heroes'. [36] Berecche and Enrico, I suggest, are two of the protagonists who personify such conflicting currents.

7. *The lamp*

We should now discuss Enrico's wish to keep his lamp, and his fear that the electric lighting in the villa would blind him. The lamp is, of course, one of the props for his role as Henry IV. It is, therefore, linked to that reconstruction of the remote past in which Enrico has chosen to live. The fact that Enrico prefers the lamp to electricity also locates him in the nineteenth century, or at all events in the time prior to the first World War, before electricity, in the theatre and in general, gradually became widespread. These are two of the time-frames, leading on to the third, which is that of his 'absence', at first enforced and then voluntary, which have shaped his mind and imagination

At the same time, Enrico's lamp can be seen as a metaphor for the creative mind. M.H. Abrams told us in *The Mirror and the Lamp* that writers such a Coleridge and Wordsworth 'revert to metaphors of the mind which had largely fallen into disuse in the eighteenth century' and 'behind these philosphers was Plotinus' basic figure of creation as emanation'. [37] The change which took place was 'from imitation to expression, and from the mirror to the fountain, the lamp and related analogues'. [38] So the lamp analogue is one which pictures the mind as active in perception, not just as imitative.

I shall now consider some of the implications of Pirandello's use of the lamp as metaphor for the past, on the one hand, and for the creative, emanating mind, on the other.

Enrico is the '*grande Mascherato*' in Pirandello's play of mirrors, doubles (or alter egos) and masks. Following his recovery, he made a deliberate choice to 'remain' Henry IV, on the eve of the first World War, to escape from the torments and afflictions of the present, both private and public. He has at his disposal all the material and spiritual resources he needs for his pretence, both the wealth which sustains the fiction and his own fertile mind, shaped by its phantasies. These resources are necessary physically for the historical drama on all levels which Enrico plays out, but also psychologically, to mask the solitude he experienced after twelve years of madness. Enrico says, he wanted to 'rivestirmela subito, meglio, di tutti i colori e gli splendori di quel lontano giorno di carnevale' [*MN*, I, 389] [dress it [solitude] up again straight away, in all the colours and splendour of that far-off day of carnival]. So he wanted to cover the emptiness, the lack, caused by his enforced humiliation and absence. But if his illusion is 'colorito' [richly coloured] it is also 'sepolcrale' [sepulchre-like] [*MN*, I, 377], so that Enrico can only mask solitude by re-burying himself in his role, and in his tomb. While he did this, the world around him changed irrevocably.

Now, we know from Fuhrmann that the emperor Henry IV was forced to stay in a castle near Verona for seven years, between 1090 and 1096, otherwise he risked imprisonment, and during that time 'events of epoch-making importance happened around him as if there were no longer an emperor, a German king, or a Henry IV'. [39] This seems precisely what happened to Enrico, when he chose a further eight years of voluntary carnival, imprisonment, or entombment. He seems, moreover, to become himself an analogue for those other emperors relevant to the play, Wilhelm II and Franz Joseph, who also lived in the past, believing in past grandeurs, rejecting the modern. This drama of 'absence' is clearly existential, but it also marks the inability of the older generation, the generation of the fathers, to provide a political ideology which would prevent, or withstand, the trauma of the first World War. [40] The old emperors and their totalitarian power-struggles are mimed and satirized in *Enrico IV*, but they are also shown to have created an unbearable void in the contemporary psyche. This is one - negative - set of significances of the lamp, and one outcome of the 'theatre of war', for Pirandello

To turn now to the lamp as an analogue for the creative, actively perceiving mind, we have seen that Enrico constructs, or creates, his own identity. Part of that identity, as Di Nolli says, is as 'un magnifico attore e terribile' [*MN*, I, 335] [a magnificent actor and terrifying]. In the play Enrico is able (as he has been able for many years) to hold his audience of visitors and servants in the palm of his hand. His powers extend to production as well. He is his own producer, as when he appears on stage in his penitent's habit, with hair dyed blond at the front but turned grey at the back and made up to look like a doll, or a white clown. More generally he is in charge of the whole production at the villa.

As a producer he seems versed in different kinds of theatre. When we first learn that he is no longer mad, he describes the effects he has created in the scene with his visitors in terms of synaesthesia:

> Buffoni! Buffoni! Buffoni! - Un pianoforte di colori! Appena la toccavo: bianca, rossa, gialla, verde ...[...] Non vedi come li paro, come li concio, come me li faccio comparire davanti, buffoni spaventati! [*MN*, I, 370]
> [Buffoons! Buffoons! Buffoons! - A pianoforte of colours! As soon as I touched her: white, red, yellow, green ...[...] Don't you see how I dress them up, how I make them appear before me, terrified buffoons!].

Here we see Enrico's active, organizing mind openly at work for the first time, as he organizes not just himself but his visitors, showing for them a contempt which is reminiscent of Hamlet's treatment of Polonius. It is as though he has turned the symbolist *correspondance* of sound and colour, or a kind of Wagnerian symbiosis, against them, to show that for him they exist in buffoons' dress.

Then, with his secret counsellors, Enrico composes the 'magnifico quadro notturno' [*MN*, I, 376] [magnificent night-time tableau] I have already mentioned. It is a scene which in some ways might have satisfied the Producer in *Sei personaggi* in his search for an impossible 'quadro armonico' [*MN*, I, 119] [harmonious tableau] which will contain his unruly characters. The Producer, the advocate of traditional theatre, cannot find a mimetic solution to his problems. Enrico, though, seems to achieve harmony as he poses his counsellors in 'belli e sciolti atteggiamenti' [*MN*, I, 375] [nice, relaxed attitudes]. So, we might ask, has Enrico resolved the Producer's dilemma? Is Pirandello here really recanting, and providing his audience with a satisfactory moment of fully-realized mimetic art? The 'night-scene', the nocturne, has, of course many romantic overtones, and could seem a suddenly familiar element in an otherwise destabilizing play. So perhaps Pirandello is again trying to tease his audience, providing reassurance for those who seek, or need, it while at the same time satirizing them. But if, like Landolfo, we feel the enchantment of this scene, are we falling into the same trap as Croce, who was moved to pity by the Stepdaughter's cliché-ridden description of her little sister? [41]

Throughout the 'quadro notturno' scene Enrico's lamp is on the table, and he and his counsellors are grouped around it as he creates the scene. It is as though the lamp becomes an analogy - positive this time - for his, and possibly the, creative mind. This interpretation is further justified by what immediately follows. Enrico tells his counsellors that each one of them should have lived his part for himself: 'non per rappresentarlo davanti a me , davanti a chi viene qua in visita di tanto in tanto; ma cosí, per come siete naturalmente, tutti i giorni, davanti a nessuno ...' [*MN*, I, 377] [not to perform it in front of me, or in front of those who come to visit from time to time, but like this, as you are naturally, every day, with no-one watching ...]. So Enrico's creation points forward to a theatre which can rely on good ensemble work, where theatre itself is magic and where theatre and life become inseparable.

The fact that we can interpret the lamp metaphor in such radically diverse ways provides us with the key to the play itself. *Enrico IV* is a great play for a great actor, and that fact alone gives it some unity. But suddenly the actor reveals that he is acting, only to appear no longer to be so, and to lose control when he kills Belcredi. All semblance of a unifying viewpoint is lost, and this, ultimately, is the significance of Enrico's lamp. Through the multiple allusions he has created around the metaphor of the lamp Pirandello puts his own conflicting and irreconcilable psychological and artistic preoccupations on stage, as he stages those afflicting the mind of his protagonist.

JULIE DASHWOOD

[1] To avoid some of the obvious confusions which Pirandello himself plays on in his text, I shall use the Italian title of the play throughout rather than the English translation *Henry IV*. For similar reasons, I shall refer to the protagonist of the play as Enrico, while the name Henry IV will be used for the eleventh-century German Emperor.

[2] See Gaspare Giudice, *Luigi Pirandello*, Turin, UTET, 1963, pp. 332-337.

[3] This is a famous, much-quoted letter. It was published in 1955 in *Il dramma*, 31, pp. 67-68, and can also be found in Leonardo Bragaglia, *Carteggio Pirandello-Ruggeri*, Fano, Biblioteca Comunale Federiciana, 1987, pp. 42-43. There is an English translation in *Luigi Pirandello in the Theatre. A Documentary Record*, eds Susan Bassnett and Jennifer Lorch, Switzerland etc, Harwood, 1993, pp. 73-74.

[4] Lucio Lugnani, 'Intorno a *Enrico IV*', in AA. VV., *Teatro e messa in scena di Pirandello*, Rome, La Nuova Italia Scientifica, 1986, pp. 85-103. The section of this essay comparing *Sei personaggi* and *Enrico IV* owes much to Lugnani's analysis.

[5] Horst Fuhrmann, *Germany in the High Middle Ages*, translated by Timothy Reuter, Cambridge, Cambridge University Press, 1986, p. 58.

[6] Horst Fuhrmann, *Germany in the High Middle Ages*, cit., p. 66.

[7] The first version of Heine's poem was written in 1821, and the final version published in 1844. Elio Providenti refers to the influence of Heine on Pirandello's poem in Luigi Pirandello, *Lettere da Bonn. 1889-1891*, introduction and notes by Elio Providenti, Rome, Bulzoni, 1984, p. 15.

[8] According to Willi Hirdt, Geib's book was first published in 1836, with a third edition in 1880. Hirdt points out that it is a much-loved book, as is shown by the publication of a further edition in 1980; see Hirdt's 'Pirandello a Bonn, ovvero "due autori in cerca d'un personaggio" ', in *Pirandello poeta*, ed. Paola Daniela Giovanelli, Florence, Vallecchi, 1981, pp. 69-94. I have only had access to the 1850 edition of the *Sagen und Geschichten*.

[9] Quoted in Horst Fuhrmann, *Germany in the High Middle Ages*, cit., p. 68.

[10] See Luigi Pirandello, *Three Plays*, ed. and introd. Felicity Firth, Manchester, Manchester University Press, 1969, pp. 192-193, n. 26.

[11] See William Weaver, *Duse. A Biography*, London, Thames and Hudson, 1984, p. 235.

[12] Franca Angelini, *Teatro e spettacolo del primo Novecento*, Bari, Laterza, 1988, p. 163.

[13] One of the most interesting examinations, in my opinion, of the antithetical natures of Pirandello and D'Annunzio can be found in Giuseppe Petronio, 'Pirandello e D'Annunzio tra arte e successo', in AA.VV., *Pirandello e D'Annunzio*, Palermo, Palumbo, 1989, pp. 9-29.

[14] This note, first published in the *Nuova Antologia*, 1 February 1905, can now be found in *SPSV*, pp. 976-985.

[15] See Sarah Zappulla Muscarà, 'Il Convegno Volta e la regia pirandelliana de *La figlia di Iorio*' in AA. VV., *Pirandello e D'Annunzio*, cit., pp. 347-367.

[16] A detailed account of this company and the context within which it worked can be found in John Osborne, *The Meiningen Court Theatre. 1866-1890*, Cambridge, Cambridge University Press, 1988.

[17] John Osborne, *The Meiningen Court Theatre*, cit., p. 52. See also Shearer West, 'Painting and theatre in the 1890s' in *British Theatre in the 1890s. Essays on Drama and the Stage*, edited by Richard Foulkes, Cambridge, Cambridge University Press, 1992, pp. 132-148.

[18] See John Osborne, *The Meiningen Court Theatre*, cit., p. 52

146

[19] Quoted in Sigmund Freud's essay 'The Uncanny' (1919), in *The Penguin Freud Library. Volume 14. Art and Literature*, translated by James Strachey, London, Penguin, 1985 (1990 reprint).

[20] Very pertinent to any discussion of Pirandello's tragedies is Suzanne K. Langer's definition of tragedy as as 'deathward advance' of individuals through 'a series of stations which are not repeated; growth, maturity, decline'; see her *Feeling and Form*, London, Routledge & Keagan Paul, 1953, p. 351.

[21] For a study of Pirandello and doctors see Angela Belli, 'Medical Ethics in the Plays of Luigi Pirandello', in *A Companion to Pirandello Studies*, ed. John DiGaetani, New York etc., Greenwood Press, 1991, pp. 82-92.

[22] The interview was published in *Le Temps*, 20 July 1925. There is an English translation of it by Susan Bassnett, with the title 'Interview with Luigi Pirandello' in *The Yearbook of the British Pirandello Society*, No. 4, 1984, pp. 48-55.

[23] Susan Bassnett, 'Interview with Pirandello', cit., pp. 51-52.

[24] Claudio Vicentini, 'La guerra e il teatro' in *Pirandello. Il disagio del teatro*. Venice, Marsilio, 1993, pp. 53-72.

[25] Claudio Vicentini, 'La guerra e il teatro', cit., p. 54.

[26] Claudio Vicentini, 'La guerra e il teatro', cit., pp. 69-70.

[27] Claudio Vicentini, 'Eutanasia dell'avanguardia', in *Il disagio del teatro*, cit., p. 126.

[28] Gaspare Giudice, *Luigi Pirandello*, cit., esp. pp. 246-303.

[29] All references to the *Novelle per un anno* are to the critical edition now available, published by Mondadori in the series 'I Meridiani' and edited by Mario Costanzo.

[30] For an analysis of this story, see J. Dashwood, 'Padri e figli: Pirandello e la prima guerra mondiale' in AA.VV., *Pirandello e la politica*, Milan, Mursia, 1992, pp. 287-298.

[31] Italy had been a member of the Triple Alliance, with Germany and Austro-Hungary, since 1882. Italy's ambition to gain Trieste and the Trentino however, was in conflict with the interests of Austria-Hungary. When the war broke out, Italy announced its neutrality. Then, in May 1915, after an

interventionist campaign in Italy, the king of Italy declared war on Austria, entering the war on the side of the Triple Entente.

[32] There are similarities also in the 'filosofia del lontano' of Dr Paulo Post in *Da lontano* (1909) [From Afar] and of Dr Fileno in *La tragedia di un personaggio* (1911) [The Tragedy of a Character].

[33] See Jean-Paul Bled, *Franz Joseph*, translated by Teresa Bridgeman, Oxford, Blackman, 1992 (first published 1987), p. 199.

[34] See Arthur J. May, *The Habsburg Monarchy 1867-1914*, Cambridge, Mass., Harvard University Press, 1951, pp. 144-150.

[35] In Sigmund Freud, *Art and Literature*, cit., p. 134.

[36] Sigmund Freud, *Art and Literature*, cit, p. 138.

[37] M.H. Abrams, *The Mirror and the Lamp*, London, Oxford, New York, Oxford University Press, 1953 (1977 reprint), p. 58.

[38] M.H. Abrams, *The Mirror and the Lamp*, cit., p. 57.

[39] Horst Fuhrmann, *Germany in the High Middle Ages*, cit., p. 69. I have no evidence that Pirandello knew of Henry IV's imprisonment at Verona.

[40] Robert Dombroski makes this point about the 'absence' of Vitangelo Moscarda; see his 'Moscarda e l'esistenza: lettura politica di "Uno, nessuno e centomila" ' in AA.VV., *Pirandello e la politica*, cit., p. 225.

[41] This is the persuasive interpretation given by Emanuele Licastro, '*Six Characters in Search of an Author* and Its Critique of Traditional Theater: Mimesis and Metamimesis' in *A Companion to Pirandello Studies*, cit., pp. 215-216.

PIRANDELLO'S MYTH PLAYS

When the Centro Nazionale di Studi Pirandelliani organized a Conference at
Agrigento on 7 and 8 December 1974 entirely devoted to a study of
Pirandello's Myth Plays, it opened the way for further research, including
individual studies and more general works, on the three plays which their
author himself had designated by the very problematic and polysemic term of
myths. These, in chronological order of their respective first performances, are
La nuova colonia [The New Colony] (1928), *Lazzaro* [Lazarus] (1929) and *I
giganti della montagna* [The Mountain Giants] (1936). In this brief study we
shall consider what is (or might be) the meaning of the term myth as used by
Pirandello and what the differences and analogies are between these three
plays; in particular between the 'minicycle' of the first two and the third which
is incomplete and has as its pivot a never-accomplished performance of a play
in verse (which, however, is called a 'fable' not a 'myth'.)

To begin with we wish above all to stress the importance of the initiative
undertaken by Enzo Lauretta, Director of the Centro Nazionale di Studi
Pirandelliani, who was the first to give serious attention to the 'myths'. In so
doing he rescued from the limbo of embarrassing works plays which, either as
projects or in the writing occupied and accompanied their author, if not for the
whole of his life, then for a large part of it. The volume of the *Acts* in which
under the title *I Miti di Pirandello* [Pirandello's Myths][1] the Conference papers
and discussions are published is the first critical work entirely devoted to a part
of Pirandello's writing which up to that time, with a few rare exceptions, had

caused perplexity rather than enthusiasm and been reduced to the rank of marginal activities, of clumsy attempts to return to a 'thesis theatre' which, it was said, was alien to the subversive, reasoning method of the more authentic pirandellian style.

It is also true however that the speakers at the Agrigento Conference in 1974 make assertions and offer conclusions which in subsequent years, up to the very recent *Bianche statue contro il nero abisso. Il teatro dei miti in Pirandello e D'Annunzio* by Anna Meda, [2] have been very carefully examined, both in studies of one or other of the 'myths' and in general works on Pirandello's writing and its evolution over time, often with different, or even widely diverging, results. The work of situating the 'myths' within the chronology of Pirandello's production, whether theatrical or narrative, is now becoming increasingly exacting and problematic. This is because the discovery and study of new material is leading us to change the dates of the conception, planning and various attempts at drafting the three works which we propose to examine. The only certainties concern the dates of the first performances of *La nuova colonia* and of *Lazzaro*, and also of *La favola del figlio cambiato*, some scenes of which are performed by the actor-characters of *I giganti della montagna*, that is, of the play whose last Act Pirandello was incapable, in all senses, of writing before he died.

As we discover more and more about the chronology of the 'myths' the need to rethink their dating means, for example, that we can no longer, as was the case for many years, relegate them to the end of the author's life and work. If, for example, we accept that 1924 is the year in which Pirandello began to write *La nuova colonia*, this means that in the precise period in which he wrote the second, and definitive, version of *Sei personaggi in cerca d'autore*, the most subversive text in modern theatre, he nevertheless did not, deep down, abandon a dramatic form which was apparently more traditional. He must, therefore, have been in a position to alternate the insoluble problems of the reasoning individual with the prospect - which, however, a careful reading shows to be contradictory and polysemic - of messages having a universal value. These latter are entrusted to apparently veristic *fabulae* where the irrationality of miracle and magic takes the place of the excessive, and destructive, rationalizing which characterizes 'humoristic' reflection.

All of this is particularly true of the two works performed, respectively, in 1928 (*La nuova colonia*) and 1929 (*Lazzaro*), while the long and incomplete gestation of *I giganti della montagna* means that it requires separate consideration. The first of the two 'myths' develops themes and contains characters which Pirandello had been thinking of since 1909 (but the idea probably goes back to 1905) when he began to write his novel *Suo marito* [Her Husband]. In this a female writer, Silvia Roncella, [3] writes a play called *La nuova colonia* (and is destined to give birth on the very night of the first performance). Pirandello, that is, close to the beginning of the century had taken on the guise of a pregnant woman in order to invent himself as the author of a plot which he tells in detail in the novel. The plot, based on that of Euripides' *Medea*, is set on an island where some outcasts try to create a new society. Silvia Roncella is a housewife who is naturally gifted but uneducated. Because of this, almost as though fertilised by the Greek breezes of her native city, Taranto, she grafts the classical myth onto the notion of the utopia where the island is seen as a social experiment, which Carlo Dossi had revived when he wrote *La colonia felice* [The Happy Colony]. [4]

Pirandello devotes a good two pages of *Suo marito* to a narration of the plot: a colony of sailors from Otranto has taken possession of an island in the Ionian Sea, a former penal colony abandoned after an earthquake, where they live outside the law and almost outside time. Among them there is only one woman, La Spera, a redeemed prostitute, who on the island is respected as a queen and venerated as a saint. Currao, the man she lives with and by whom, on the island, she has had a son is the only man to 'possess' her, basing his authority as leader on this privilege. When a second group of sailors - a 'new colony' - lands on the island with wives, mothers, daughters and sisters La Spera, although transfigured by motherhood, becomes again a prostitute in the eyes of the others. Like Jason in the ancient myth Currao abandons the woman who helped and supported him in his first conquest of power, and wants to marry the daughter of the head of the 'new colony' in order to become his successor through a kind of reinvented dynastic law. As part of his plan he demands that La Spera should give him the child who, by the dictates of the 'law of the father', belongs to him. As in the old legend, La Spera-Medea kills her son, and the cry which accompanies her gesture causes a landslide so great that huge rocks crash down and a gulf opens which swallows up the community.

We have dwelt on this plot because a comparison with the play, which, as we have seen, Pirandello probably began in 1924 and finished only very shortly before the first performance, allows us to identify what for the author are the traits which differentiate the elaboration of an 'ancient fable' from the writing of a 'modern myth'. To begin with, the play opens with a *Prologue* in a tavern frequented by ex-prisoners, small-time smugglers and prostitutes in rags who, even when they accomplish some act of generosity, are despised and persecuted by 'respectable' people and by the authorities. Amongst them is Tobba, who speaks with nostalgia of the island where he was imprisoned no less than six times when it was a penitentiary, and which has now been abandoned because it is threatened by earthquakes. Tobba describes it, paradoxically, as a place of freedom where the poor could live in communion with nature, far away from the oppressive city. At this point La Spera, described in a stage direction as a kind of witch-like apparition, ageless, her face masked by layers of make-up, her hair dishevelled and with large, well-shaped breasts, incites the outcasts to leave for Tobba's island. She wants them to choose freedom, even at the risk of dying during the journey, and calls on God, in a kind of personal pact, as witness to the strength of her commitment. It is, therefore, La Spera (endowed with the arcane powers traditionally attributed to prostitutes) whose words persuade the other marginalised inhabitants of the City to undertake the journey across the sea and to accept the initiatory adventure of the search for salvation. The sign which seals acceptance of La Spera's existential bargain by the divinity invoked is the milk which flows from the woman's breasts. So she, who had previously had to send her child to a wet-nurse, now gains the ability to breast-feed him. Until she chose freedom she was only biologically his mother, but now she becomes actively a mother, able to suckle her child, in intimate symbiosis with the son she had with Currao.

In the *Prologue*, therefore, the protagonists of the ancient story are placed in a veristic setting where there are the poor, the rich, customs officers and prisoners (and La Spera, who in the three Acts of the play seems at times to echo the exalted redemption of Jorio's daughter [5] could, at the beginning be the Lia of Verga's novel *I Malavoglia*, [6] lost in the sailors' brothels). They are then thrust outside history, which is symbolised by the rousseauist topos of the corrupt city, and go to the island which has been abandoned by men and their institutions but which is threatened by that very nature in which they seek their salvation. Then, in Act I Pirandello picks up the thread of Silvia Roncella's play, but every word and every gesture is seen in the perspective of La Spera's choice and pact. No longer wearing make-up, and with her child in her arms, she comforts the afflicted, cares for the sick and preaches equality and self-denial when the group of men which has landed on the island is tempted by the demon of private property. Currao, their leader, would like to introduce a kind of 'social contract' based on common ownership of the colony's few resources, on work and on chastity. However, the only woman in the group is La Spera, and even if she refuses all sexual approaches she nevertheless 'belongs' to Currao. The desire she arouses in the others leads to discord and the flight of one of the colonists to the city, from where the rich and middle-class set out for the island with wine and women. They found a new colony, no longer based on equality but on hierarchy and the restoration of the institutions and rites of the mainland. As in Silvia Roncella's play, Currao wants to marry the daughter of the leader of the new colonists and to take La Spera's son away from her by force. La Spera is no longer the only woman on the island, the 'queen' and 'saint', but is despised by everyone, and in Act II she accepts that her stature is, so to speak, diminished; she becomes an ordinary woman, no longer the 'Mother with Son' but a much more modest 'mum with little Nico'. However, the threat that her son will be taken from her leads her to regain, not just the prophetic tones of the *Prologue*, but also the dark powers of the sorceress belonging to her ancient, sacred status as a prostitute. Her words become active, and destructive: she has no need to cry out like Silvia Roncella's La Spera for the sound-waves to produce the landslide naturalistically. All she does is to repeat 'Trema la terra!' [The earth is shaking] four times, and then in the stage-directions we are told:

> *E la terra veramente, come se il tremore del frenetico, disperato abbraccio della Madre si propagasse a lei, si mette a tremare. Il grido di terrore della folla con l'esclamazione "La terra! La terra!" è ingoiato spaventosamente dal mare in cui l'isola sprofonda. Solo il punto più alto della prominenza rocciosa, dove La Spera s'è rifugiata col bambino, emerge come uno scoglio.*
> [MN, II, 1157-1158]
> [*And as though the tremor of the Mother's frantic, desperate embrace spreads to it, the earth really begins to shake. The crowd's cry of terror, as they exclaim "The earth! The earth!", is terrifyingly swallowed up by the sea into which the island sinks. Only the highest point of the rocky prominence, where La Spera has taken refuge with her child, remains like a rock.*]

Then, in her last line the woman standing on the rock which emerges from the waters which have covered the world, in the void left by a humanity incapable of finding an equitable form of social contract, addresses God directly once more, as she did in the *Prologue*, with words which are a skilful blend of references to the Old and New Testaments: 'Ah Dio, io qua, sola, con te figlio, sulle acque!' [MN, II, 1158]. [Ah God, I am here alone with you, my son, on the waters]. The Mother, has escaped from the disastrous failure of the two successive colonies which were corrupt from the outset in symbiosis with her son. In this, she can be distinguished from the couple, man and woman, who are the sole survivors of a universal cataclysm and whom Pirandello had conceived of in 1926 as the protagonists of a novel, *Adamo ed Eva* [Adam and Eve], of which only a fragment exists. [7] In *La nuova colonia,* indeed, the only real protagonist is the woman-mother, the first of a whole series of female characters who, alone or as part of a couple with men, Pirandello places at the centre of his plots after 1925. This was the year when he met Marta Abba, and when he took the bold step of writing an unusual choral work, *Sagra del Signore della Nave* [Festival of Our Lord of the Ship], in which rites of of the Christian religion, founded on the kingdom of the Father, and customs going back to the cult of the Mother present in proto-historic societies are brought face to face. [8]

At the end of *La nuova colonia* the God of the Testament, who had been invoked at the end of the *Prologue*, is again called upon when the supreme manifestation of the *maleficent* power of the destructive mother is followed by the hope of palingenesis based on the vital symbiosis of the *good* mother with her son. The archetype of motherhood presented in *La nuova colonia* is shown in its dual aspect, positive and negative, a fact which stands out all the more if it the play is compared to the almost contemporaneous 'inner play' of *Sei personaggi in cerca d'autore*. Here the Mother, a passive being, an inert 'lump of flesh' pursues her obsessive aim to re-establish contact with the Son who rejects her, and in so doing brings only ruin and death to her other children. In *La nuova colonia* Pirandello on the one hand omits the infanticide which was in Euripides' play and also in Silvia Roncella's, and, on the other, accentuates the cosmic nature of the myth's final catastrophe. Therefore he rediscovers in the archaic tradition the, at times, dark and subterranean ambivalence of motherhood in opposition to the authoritarian clarity of the Fathers.

The first performance of *La nuova colonia* took place in 1928, and Pirandello finished writing the last scenes only very shortly before the première, in close collaboration with the scenographer and architect Riccardo Marchi. [9] It now appears from a letter to Marta Abba that in that same year *Lazzaro* , too, was almost finished, although it was performed in 1929, the year in which, on 11 February, the Concordat was signed between Mussolini's Italy and the Vatican. According to some, rather too precipitate, critics, Pirandello wrote his 'religious myth' with the precise intention of celebrating the return to order of the State within the Church of Rome, by placing on stage a priest who, after a brief period of rebellion, once more accepts the symbols of Catholicism. *Lazzaro* is, in fact, a very complex play (even if at certain crucial points it is too rushed and contrived) whose title might deceive those who had read, for example, G.A. Borgese's *Lazzaro* where chapter XI of the Gospel according to St John is dramatised. Just as Henry IV is not the penitent of Canossa, so there is no trace of Jesus's friend in the second of Pirandello's myths, which is set in modern Agrigento.

The evocative vagueness of the mediterranean setting of *La nuova colonia* gives way, although only on a superficial level, to an emphasis on the veristic traits of setting and characters. The flight from 'inner' to 'outer' - from the city of ill omen to a place offering salvation - seems to become singularly impoverished, reduced to a simple transfer from an urban dwelling to a rustic farm nearby. And yet the meaning of the move from a place of degradation to a haven of salvation is perhaps even more subtle and complex than in the 'myth' called 'political' on which the playwright meditated for so long. The title, transcending the individuality of a single character, symbolises the great theme of resurrection which, as well as Borgese, others of Pirandello's contemporaries chose to treat, [10] fascinated, their curiosity aroused by the experience of a man (and not a god) who after having died returns to life. He is a kind of *mort vivant*, who reveals the probable non-existence of a God as a being and can drive some to despair and others to a pantheist, immanentist view of life.

Moreover, writing *Lazzaro* also signified Pirandello's return, but no longer in a 'humoristic' way, to one of the themes of the inner play in *Sei personaggi in cerca d'autore*: that of the omnipotent Father who disposes of the existence of others, steeped in pseudo-nietzschean ideas of the superman, when he separates the Son from the Mother. As a result the Father arouses the Son's hatred towards her and towards the children born of the illegitimate union for which he himself was the matchmaker. In *Lazzaro* Pirandello experiments with a similar plot, but gives the mother the 'sublime' impulse towards rebellion, which leads her to cross a threshold which, on one level, is just the

156

gate of a farm but on another is a crossing to another world of salvation, reached after a long and painful initiation. The mother, Sara, is the wife of Diego Spina, a deeply fervent catholic, who sacrifices all earthly joys for himself, but also for others, in the hope of eternal salvation. For this reason he destined his son, Lucio, to become a priest from his earliest years, and he entrusted his daughter, Lia, to nuns in a convent, taking her away from her mother. Sara has, therefore, lost both her children and suffers on seeing her pale, emaciated son and her daughter, whose legs have become paralysed but is still cared for by the nuns. After having appealed in vain to a tribunal for the right to bring up at least her daughter, like Nora in Ibsen's *A Doll's House* (but in other respects the two plays are substantially different) she leaves her house and the town whose institutions sanctify the law of the father and makes a very brief journey, which is nevertheless the prelude to a radical, if gradual, metamorphosis out of the city walls and into the countryside.

It does not matter that Sara takes refuge within the boundaries of one of her husband's farms (even the island in *La nuova colonia* was under the jurisdiction of the mainland) as, on contact with the earth, she dies and is reborn. This she explains in a long speech in Act II, where she describes her initiatory journey of transfiguration. She speaks of the risk she ran of damnation through self-destruction:

> Buttai via tutto e mi feci contadina - contadina qua, sotto il sole, all'aperto! Un bisogno mi prese, un bisogno d'essere selvaggia; un bisogno di cadere a terra la sera come una bestia morta sotto la fatica - zappando, pestando le spighe sull'aia con le mule, a piedi nudi, sotto la canicola, girando a tondo con le gambe insanguinate e gridando come un'ubriaca ... [*MN*, II, 1199]
> [I threw everything away and became a peasant - a peasant, here, under the sun, in the open air! I was seized by a need, a need to be wild, a need to fall on the ground at night like a beast worked to death - hoeing, treading the grain on the threshing-ground with the mules, barefoot, at the height of summer, round and round with my legs stained with blood and shouting like a drunk ...]

She speaks also of the salvation which is offered to her by a kind of beneficent rustic divinity - the peasant Arcadipane, whose eyes are laughing and candid like those of a child, and who wears a shaggy, goatskin cap. Sara calls him: 'quest'uomo puro - puro [...] come una creatura uscita ora dalla mani di Dio ...' [*MN*, II, 1199] [This pure man - pure [...] like a child who's just come from the hand of God] and declares that he prevented her from destroying herself by teaching her: 'le cose della campagna, la vita, la vera vita che ha qui, fuori della città maledetta, la terra;' [*MN*, II, 1199] [the things of the countryside, life, the real life he has here, outside the accursed city, the earth.]. Arcadipane enables Sara to live according to nature by initiating her also into a simple and fertile sexuality (she recalls with horror Diego's viscid, limp, never-satisfied desire). Two healthy children, simple, like the earth, are born to this new couple in which the man represents a kind of ingenuous bulwark both against primitive chaos and against decadent disintegration, and the woman the fertility of nature itself where the divinity lives eternally, denying death. Sara erupts onto the stage: '*tutta rossa e col manto nero, sembra un'irreale apparizione di ineffabile bellezza: nuova, sana, potente*' [*MN*, II, 1179] [*dressed all in red and with a black cloak, she seems an unreal apparition of ineffable beauty: new, healthy, powerful*].

This scene takes place in Act I, which is set in Diego's house on the day he has decided to evict Arcadipane and Sara from the farm which they, through their work and the water they have miraculously found, have made fruitful and fertile (they give almost all the produce to the hospital). Diego intends to offer the farm to the city beggars and to go and live with them together with Lia. Sara has come, not to entreat God the Father to alter his decision to drive them out of the terrestrial paradise, but to announce to her husband that Lucio has abandoned the priesthood in order to be 'reborn' from her, his mother. He has become a convert - after his long, damaging experience in the seminary - to that dionysiac pantheism which Sara had found by going through the painful and exalting stages of her own liberation. Diego runs out of his house to find his son, is hit by a car and declared dead by a passing doctor. Lia asks a rather science-fiction scientist, who has already used adrenalin to resuscitate her pet rabbit, to inject the remedy into her father as well, while being fully conscious of her father's anger when she had shown him the reanimated creature. Diego (but perhaps he only apparently died) returns to life and when he discovers he has been dead he realises he has experienced the void of an afterlife in which he did not meet God and in which there is, therefore, no hope of a final recompense for suffering on earth. Previously he had accepted, in a spirit of sacrifice, that Arcadipane and Sara were cohabiting but now he shoots Arcadipane (without, however, killing him). Lucio saves his father from despair by declaring that he has rediscovered his faith in the life to come through a kind of sudden illumination, and by pretending to forget that shortly before he had said:

> per non finire noi, annulliamo in nome di Dio la vita, e facciamo regnare Dio anche di là (non si sa dove) in un presunto regno della morte, perché ci dia là, un premio o un castigo [...] questo dovrebbe essere [...] il vero risorgere dalla morte: negarla in Dio, e credere in questa sola immortalità, non nostra, non per noi, speranza di premio o timore di castigo: credere in questo eterno presente della vita, ch'è Dio, e basta. [*MN*, II, 1195]
> [so that we don't come to an end we annihilate life in God's name, and we make God rule also in a world to come (we don't know where it is), so that there he will give us our reward or our punishment [...] this should be [...] the true resurrection from the dead: to deny that there is death in God and believe in this single immortality, not ours, not for us, not hope of reward or fear of punishment: to believe in this eternal present of life, which is God and nothing else.]

Differently from the Son in *Sei personaggi*, Lucio has not rejected his mother's second family, and now he comforts his father by accepting the priesthood again and so acting as a link between the two ways of living a religious life symbolised by his parents. Of them, however, it is Diego who loses, as he had induced Lia to bear with her restricted life so that after death she would have 'alucce di angeletta' [*MN*, II 1209] [funny little angel's wings] and now has to accept that Lucio will induce the mother to call her daughter, restoring to her (by magic or by curing a psychosomatic illness?) the use of her legs so that she can walk on the earth.

At the end of the play Lucio is a traditional priest for Diego, for whom he is guarantor of the life to come. For Sara, though, he is an adept of the archaic cult of the earth mother and, just as Demeter brings Persephone out of Hades, so she is authorised to call Lia, curing her of the illness which was to have opened for her the gates of eternity. Uranus gives way to Gea, but between the two is the son, the double-faced herm, an angel for one of them, Dionysus for the other and perhaps 'per sé nessuno' [for himself, no-one], as in almost the last words of Pirandello's other great example of total dedication, Signora Ponza in *Cosí è (se vi pare)* [Right You Are (If You Think So)] (1917) [*MN*, I, 1099].

Until 1929 Pirandello uses myth to experiment with plots based on social and family relationships seen in an a-historical present and in settings which are initially banal, everyday and conventional. But they then become symbols of an 'elsewhere' through invoking metahistorical values imprinted on an (albeit hypothetical) archaic purity. If the inner coherence of the protagonists in the myths distinguishes them from the 'humoristic' characters, then also there is nothing rationalistic, and even less positivistic, about the evolution of La Spera or Lucio. They react to situations which require abrupt changes, obeying impulses which in the 'myths' are free to emerge from those dark depths of the self which some identify with 'the mothers'. Pirandello himself alluded to this shortly before his death in 1936:

Nietzsche diceva che i greci alzavano bianche statue contro il nero abisso, per nasconderlo. Sono finiti quei tempi. Io le scrollo invece per riverlarlo ... "In questo nulla spero di trovare il tutto" - dice Faust avventurandosi nella regione inferna delle Madri. Per poter scendere in fondo all'abisso ci vuole almeno la speranza di trovarvi Elena ... Bisogna abituarsi a vedere nel buio. [11]
[Nietzsche said that the Greeks raised white statues over the black abyss, to hide it. Those times are over. I shake the statues, instead, to reveal the abyss... "In this nothingness I hope to find everything", said Faust, venturing into the infernal region of the Mothers. To be able to

go down to the bottom of the abyss you need at least the hope of finding Helen there ... We must get used to seeing in the dark.]

The search for a inner truth leads Pirandello to create in his theatre figures, above all of women, who are the holders of inner, instinctive, absolute truths. This rules out any intention on his part to act as a supporter of the Fascist regime when it was consolidated between 1925 and 1929 and Mussolini praised the countryside and launched the demographic campaign. Pirandello as a writer of myth is not a 'strapaesano' [12] just as Massimo Bontempelli is not a vulgar 'stracittadino' [13] when, between 1926 and 1929, through his Franco-Italian review *'900. Cahiers d'Italie et d'Europe* he launches the idea that novelists of all nationalities should create the myths of the Third Age of humanity.[14] Certainly his is an ontological as well as a literary project: in opposition to idealist solipsisms the writer must construct solid realities in the newly-found space he has acquired by inaugurating the new course of history. It matters little that Bontempelli should ingratiate himself with the censors by writing that in Italy, in 1926, politics had preceded literature in the work of reconstructing the objective world. What counts above all is that, according to him, it is the task of the writer to provide the new reality with founding myths, focused on characters and events capable of 'modifying the earth's crust', just as magic allows a kind of knowledge of reality which is different from that provided by empirical science. There are certainly substantial differences between Pirandello and Bontempelli, the two Italian 'mythographers' of the 'twenties. However, that does not prevent Pirandello's last, very troubled, and incomplete myth from containing echoes not only of the 'magic realism' of Bontempelli as a theorist of literary creation but, as we shall see, of certain very original achievements of Bontempelli's theatre. [15]

We learn from Pirandello's letters that in 1928 (that is, the year of the first performance of *La nuova colonia* and the writing of *Lazzaro*) he was already working on *I giganti della montagna*,[16] the first Act of which he published in 1931, and that at the same time he was expanding the *Favola del figlio cambiato* to make it into an autonomous play. [17] It was originally intended only to function within the 'myth' as a support, in the same way as the 'inner plays' in each of the plays making up the so-called 'trilogy of the theatre-within-the theatre'. In fact, this should be called a 'tetralogy' because the final variant is *I giganti della montagna*, where the theme of myth is grafted on to that of the relationship between actor, text and audience.

In the traditional fable as a literary genre, order is restored at the end after having been overturned at the beginning. The opposite happens in the 'myth', based on the rejection of the initial situation, on a voyage of initiation beyond a threshold and on the impossibility of return, with the risk of the failure, reversal or ironic undermining of the outcome to which the protagonists aspire. In order to save her son, La Spera causes a huge catastrophe; to be able to exercise the magic virtues of her motherhood on her daughter, Sara defers to her son. *La favola del figlio cambiato*, on the surface, respects the conventions of the genre, adopting one of its most frequent topoi, that of the child snatched from its cradle. [18] In this play, in a country in the south, beside the sea, a Mother realises that during the night the 'Women', that is the witches, have replaced her beautiful, healthy baby with another ugly, frail child. A Sorceress reveals to her that her child will be raised in a far-off royal palace in the place of the true prince, for whom he has been exchanged. The true prince grows up deformed and stuttering, the laughing-stock of the village, and having been crowned as a joke he is called 'the king's son'. One day a boat arrives in the small mediterranean port carrying a handsome, blond and ailing prince, who has left his life of drudgery in his misty northern kingdom where smoke-stacks abound in order to regain his health. In the end he gives up the crown after being recognised by his mother at whose side he wants to be 'reborn' in the sun in communion with nature. The young idiot, crowned as a joke, will be the one to return to his native-land and to take the throne now vacant after the old king's death. Order, overturned at the beginning by the snatching of the blond baby who was exchanged for the little dark prince, is re-established, and since the 'joke' king was in fact the 'real' king, the people of the northern kingdom will have a legitimate sovereign, and it matters little that he is an idiot.

Indeed, in words which were considered subversive when *La favola* was performed, the young man who renounces power says:

> Credete a me,
> non importa che sia
> questa o quella persona:
> importa la corona!
> Cangiate questa di carta e vetraglia
> in una d'oro e di gemme di vaglia,
> il mantelletto in un manto
> e il re da burla diventa sul serio,
> a cui voi v'inchinate. [*MN*, II, 1301]

[Believe me,/ it doesn't matter if it is this person or that:/ what matters is the crown!/ Change this one of paper and glass/ for one of gold and precious jewels,/ his short cloak for a royal mantle/ and from being a joke he becomes the real king,/ to whom you bow.]

The handsome, healthy, intelligent young man stays in the south, refusing to succeed his supposed father of whom he speaks without affection:

> Vedo mio padre nella sua reggia
> in un fastoso deperimento.
> Addormentato nel capo ogni idea,
> nel petto ogni sentimento,
> nel fegato ogni ira,
> [...]
> La voce di mio padre, per me,
> è come vedere
> uno specchio nell'ombra. [*MN*, II, 1280]
>
> [I see my father in his palace/ in magnificent deterioration./ All ideas are asleep in his head,/ all feelings in his breast,/ all anger in his liver,/ [...] For me my father's voice/ is like seeing/ a mirror in the shade.]

The young man condemns the northern civilisation of technology and factories:

> Via la nebbia amara, e quel fumo,
> quel fumo forato da lampade,
> architetture di ferro,
> forni, carbone, città
> affacendate da cure
> cieche e meschine [*MN*, II, 1303]

[Away with the bitter fog, and that smoke/ that smoke pierced by
lamps,/ iron structures,/ furnaces, coal, cities/ busy with blind, mean
cares.]

and he chooses the woman who for him is 'the' mother, so that in *La favola*,
too, the 'mythical' archetype of instinctive, primeval motherhood is present.
Moreover, it is taken to the extreme of the rejection of biological fatherhood,
never repudiated in the first two 'myths' where fatherhood is, rather, at the
centre of the conflicts in the plays. La Spera rebels at the end of the play when
Currao claims possession of her son; Sara has two sets of children conditioned
by the personalities of their two respective fathers. In *La favola* the fatherhood
of the widowed king, nordic and absolute in its sterile affirmation of political
power, is opposed to the absolute, southern motherhood of the triumphant
Mother, as ardent in reclaiming her handsome son as she was cruel in
neglecting the 'other son'. [19]

This hyperbolic motherhood is assumed, lived and endured by Ilse, the
female protagonist of *I giganti della montagna*, both as an actress whose first
words are the opening lines of *La favola* and as the 'mother' of *La favola* itself:
La favola was written for her by a poet who committed suicide, who loved her
and to whom she never gave herself physically in order that he should be
driven to create a masterpiece. This is a complete reversal of the situation of
Silvia Roncella, who had given birth to a son and a myth; in *I giganti*, the poet
generates a myth so that Ilse can be doubly the mother of it, and on dying he
gains the ever-present immortality of phantasms. [20]

In Act I of *I giganti della montagna* Ilse's company (or, rather, the
company of the Countess, as the actress has married a Count who follows the
troupe and, to help her in her desperate enterprise, has spent all his money) is
exhausted and impoverished by its vain attempts to perform the dead poet's
play to spectators who reject it. The company arrives at a mountainous island
where it hopes to find some public acclaim. The so-called giants, tireless
builders of acqueducts, reservoirs and mechanized farms have, with their
servants, become slow-witted and bestial because their complete devotion to

technical, material and physical activities makes them blind and deaf to art.
With names like those of D'Annunzio's characters (Uma di Dornio and
Lopardo d'Arcifa) and activities like those advocated by the futurists they loom
menacingly over the action even if they never appear on stage in the three Acts
which Pirandello completed.

Down below there is a village with its church and its theatre, the latter
now closed and destined, perhaps, to become a cinema. Half way up the
mountain - and this is where the Countess's company is heading - is the Villa
della Scalogna with an open space in front of it. This is a particularly complex
use of the opposition between inner and outer. In *La nuova colonia* it took the
form of the contrast between the city tavern and the island representing nature,
and in *Lazzaro* it became a polysemic intersecting of city-house and garden in
Act I and of farm and countryside, seen as the earthly paradise, in Act II. In
the third myth the space outside the house is a place of false prodigies
orchestrated to frighten possible intruders, while the inner spaces are places of
creative fantasy, of manifestations of the unconscious and of necromancy.
Inside the villa there is, indeed, a wardrobe where all choose, spontaneously,
disguises which best suit there own fantasies and, in particular, there is an
Arsenal of the Apparitions where space can extend towards imaginary horizons
and give life to creatures who spring directly from the imagination.

At the beginning of the play the remaining actors in Ilse's company push a
hay-cart onto the open space in front of the villa on which the Countess,
reciting the first lines of *La favola*, lies stretched out. They find themselves
faced with characters who are deformed, are like caricatures or who
hallucinate (like the old woman La Sgricia, who believes she is already in the
next world.). Exiles from the world, they live by dreams, prodigies and
imaginings which take the shape of phantasms; these are themselves released
in what is theatre in its purest state. So Ilse and her company have arrived
among characters who are no longer concerned with authors or audiences, and
are greeted by the strange figure of a 'wizard' (or, as has also been said, a
'shaman'), Cotrone, who is still very similar, physically, to the 'humans'

outside. Although 'his shoes look damp', [21] the description of him as mediator between the real and the imaginary, with his *'occhioni ridenti splendenti sereni, la bocca fresca splendente anch'essa di denti sani tra il biondo caldo dei baffi e della barba non curati* [MN, II, 1313] [*big serene eyes sparkling with laughter: his young mouth shining too with healthy teeth through the warm gold of his unkempt beard and whiskers*; 7] recalls that of Arcadipane, the rural demiurge of *Lazzaro*.

The fact that he dresses in city clothes is certainly unique among the inhabitants of the villa, but his clothes are loose enough to be clown-like, and he wears a fez on his head as a symbol that he has abandoned Christianity, that is, the conventions and convictions of the society from which he has exiled himself. In that society, where traditional logic rules, there is a rigid dividing line between dream and reality and the theatre is a fiction performed for the public by actors who, with their bodies, give substance to phantasms. In the villa, though, 'theatre' is the spontaneous creation of images for personal consumption by a community of beings who can become their own doubles in sleep and witness their own suicide, or raise a procession of souls from Purgatory led by an angel. Cotrone, introducing the wonders of the villa, speaks of a knowledge of nature based on magic and not on positive science. Referring to himself and to the community of the scalognati, [22] he says to the guests who have come from the world outside:

> Siamo qua come agli orli della vita, Contessa. Gli orli, a un comando, si distaccano; entra l'invisibile: vaporano i fantasmi. È cosa naturale. Avviene, ciò che di solito nel sogno. Io lo faccio avvenire anche nella veglia. Ecco tutto. I sogni, la musica, la preghiera, l'amore ... tutto l'infinito ch'è negli uomini, lei lo troverà dentro e intorno a questa villa. [*MN*, II, 1337]
> [Here we are on the very fringes of life, Countess. At a word the fringes disintegrate; the invisible world creeps in: misty apparitions form. It is natural. It is what happens in dreams all the time. I make it happen when people are awake. That's all. Dreams, music, prayer, love ... Everything that is infinite in man you will find here, round and about and inside the villa; 52]

166

He later says:

Respiriamo aria favolosa. [...] Udiamo voci, risa; vediamo sorgere incanti figurati da ogni gomito d'ombra, creati dai colori che ci restano scomposti negli occhi abbacinati dal troppo sole della nostra isola. Sordità d'ombra non possiamo soffrirne. Le figure non sono inventate da noi; sono un desiderio dei nostri stessi occhi. [*MN*, II, 1340] [23]
[We breathe the very air of fable. [...] We hear voices, laughter; we see enchantment taking shape in every shadowy corner, created out of colours which linger fragmented in our eyes dazzled by the excessive sunlight of our island. We cannot bear the dullness of the dark. The apparitions are not invented by us; they are the desires of our own eyes; 59]

Cotrone has 'resigned from everything'[68] [24] , and turned to a kind of entrancing Pythagorism:

Liberata da tutti questi impacci, ecco che l'anima ci resta grande come l'aria [...] Guardiamo alla terra, che tristezza! C'è forse qualcuno laggiù che s'illude di star vivendo la nostra vita; ma non è vero. Nessuno di noi è nel corpo che l'altro ci vede; ma nell'anima che parla chi sa da dove; [...] Un corpo è la morte: tenebra e pietra. Guai a chi si vede nel suo corpo e nel suo nome. Facciamo i fantasmi. [...] la maraviglia ch'è in noi la rovesciamo sulle cose con cui giochiamo, e ce ne lasciamo incantare. Non è piú un gioco, ma una realtà maravigliosa in cui viviamo, alienati da tutto, fino agli eccessi della demenza. [*MN*, II, 1345]
[Set the soul free from all these encumbrances and it is like the sky, limitless [...] We look down at the earth - what sadness! perhaps there is somebody down there who thinks he is actually living this life of ours: but he's not. None of us is really in the body that other people see, but in the soul, and who knows where the soul's words come from? [...] A body is death: darkness and stone. Pity the man who thinks he is there in his body and his name. We make these apparitions [...] We pour out our wonderment into our playthings and lend ourselves to their enchantment. It is no longer a game we live in but a wonderful reality, cut off from everything, free to the point of madness; 68-69]

Cotrone concludes by inviting Ilse to stay in the villa where she could perform *La favola*: 'come un prodigio che s'appaghi di sé, senza piú chiedere niente a nessuno.' [*MN*, II, 1346] [bring it to life as a complete and self-contained miracle, just as it is; 69]. The company's actors are exhausted and are tempted to accept the invitation, but the Countess resists. She wants to make the work of the dead poet known to a real audience, that is, she wants to make it live in the age-old, multiform, mysterious space which is hidden in the tradition of western theatre as the creator of codified illusions, and not confine it to the bowels of the villa. Cotrone has revealed that bodies are no obstacle to the oneiric orgies of the Scalognati: and indeed, while he reads the *Favola* in his room he conjures up in the Arsenal some of the secondary characters needed in the *Favola* in the form of marionettes. So Pirandello introduces onto his stage those mechanical beings which, created by nineteenth-century science fiction and experimented with by the futurists, were present in Bontempelli's theatre both as characters (in *Nostra Dea* [Our Dea]) and as projections of the fear of universal reification (in *Minnie la candida* [Minnie the Candid]). In the form of the marionettes, which are the final stage of the dehumanisation of the inhabitants of the villa, Cotrone's 'white magic' takes shape in the Arsenal of the Apparitions, and he invites Ilse to recite, in this place which is predestined to become a theatre, those first lines of *La favola* which she spoke at the beginning of the play. And then it is not puppets but real characters (the 'Neighbours') who materialise at the side of the countess, now identified with her role as mother, and reply to her.

In *Sei personaggi*, in an ordinary theatre, Madama Pace's appearance sprang spontaneously from the scene-setting. In *I giganti della montagna* the miracle of the appearance of a character called up by the requirements of a theatrical plot and dialogue occurs in a magic place, and no longer on a traditional stage from where pure (too much so?) poetry is now banished because of the obtuse materialism of the spectators. In this 'myth', where the antithesis between art theatre and commercial theatre is couched in terms which make any possible solution reductive and unsatisfying, the polemic about the mental deafness of every potential audience is taken to extremes. Cotrone offers Ilse the opportunity to perform *La favola* with the Scalognati, so that she can fully enjoy its message, or rather the invitation to return to the reassuring maternal womb, among connoisseurs in the welcoming depths of the villa. In spite of this, Ilse asks the 'wizard' to intercede so that she can perform the play for the giants.

Once he had expressed the irreparable conflict between the 'fanatics' of life and the 'fanatics' of art in such extreme terms, Pirandello could not provide a definitive solution to the dilemma which tormented him until the end of his life. On the basis of notes, drafts [25] and statements by the playwright's son, some of the ever-increasing number of directors in Italy who produce *I giganti della montagna* have Ilse die torn to pieces by the giants' servants who were hoping to see a variety show. Others, keeping strictly to the text which Pirandello himself finished, stop at the end of Act III after Ilse, in performing, has called up real characters whereas Cotrone, while reading, has only succeeded in creating marionettes.

The din of the procession of the giants going down to the valley is heard and it makes the walls of the villa tremble. And the play, whose tragic conclusion, as R. Alonge says, is Pirandello's own death [26] ends with the last, terrible words he spoke: 'Io ho paura! ho paura!' [27]

FULVIA AIROLDI NAMER

---

[1] *I Miti di Pirandello*, ed. E. Lauretta, Palermo, Palumbo, 1975.

[2] A. Meda, *Bianche statue contro il nero abisso. Il teatro dei miti in D'Annunzio e Pirandello*, Ravenna, Longo, 1993. Among recent critical works in Italian partly or entirely devoted to Pirandello's'myths' are: R. Alonge, *Pirandello tra realismo e mistificazione*, Naples, Guida, 1972; P. Puppa, *Fantasmi contro giganti*, Bologna, Patròn, 1987; U. Artioli, *L'officina segreta di Pirandello*, Bari, Laterza, 1989. Of particular relevance are some volumes of the *Acts* of conferences organised by the Centro di studi pirandelliani: *Pirandello e la cultura del suo tempo*, Milan, Mursia, 1984; *Testo e messa in scena in Pirandello*, Rome, La Nuova Italia Scientifica, 1986; *Pirandello e D'Annunzio*, Palermo, Palumbo, 1989; *Pirandello e l'oltre*, Milan, Mursia, 1991; *Pirandello e la politica*, Milan, Mursia, 1992; *Il teatro di Pirandello*,

Milan, Mursia, 1993. See also the *Acts* of the Conference *L'ultimo Pirandello*, ed. L. Granatella, Brescia, Comune di Brescia, 1988.

[3] L. Pirandello, *Suo marito*, now in *Tutti i romanzi*, Milan, Mondadori, 1990, vol I, pp. 677-679. In an incomplete new draft of the novel, which was to be called *Giustino Roncella nato Boggiòlo* [Giustino Roncella born Boggiòlo], *La nuova colonia* became *L'isola nuova* [The New Island].

[4] C. Dossi, *Il regno dei cieli. La colonia felice.* Naples, Guida, 1985.

[5] In the play of the same name, *La figlia di Jorio*, by Gabriele D'Annunzio, written in 1903.

[6] Verga's novel *I Malavoglia* [The Malavoglia Family] published in 1881.

[7] L. Pirandello, *SPSV*, 1097-1098. Here, too, a flood drowns humanity: 'Bisogna perdonare alle acque se ... sobbalzate tutte sulla faccia della terra ... se ne risucchiarono poi ... tutta la storia degli uomini ... L'irreparabile perdita di una storia più volte millenaria ... a misurarla nella totale calamità da cui era potuta appena appena scampare la terra, appare del tutto trascurabile'. [The waters must be forgiven if ... flung as they all were over the face of the earth ... they then sucked back ... the whole history of mankind ... The irreparable loss of a history which had lasted for many thousands of years ... if measured against the total calamity which the earth was only just able to avoid, seems completely negligeable.]

[8] In 1925 Pirandello, who for the first time ventured into directing for the theatre, opened the first season of the 'Teatro degli undici' [Theatre of the Eleven] founded by his son Stefano and other writers among whom were Massimo Bontempelli, whose play *Nostra Dea* [Our Dea], in which Marta Abba made her debut, Pirandello directed. The first plays performed were *Sagra del Signore della Nave* and *The Gods of the Mountain*. In this work *en plein air* a procession which follows a bloody and terrifying byzantine-style crucifix reaches the churchyard where the ritual killing of the pig is taking place. This means that the christian sacrifice of the Son of the Father and the sacrifice of the animal, whose name (*maiale* in Italian) recalls that of Maia, the mother in archaic rites, are being celebrated at the same time.

[9] *La nuova colonia* risked being given an unexpected 'happy ending' when Pirandello was asked (still in 1928) to write a scenario of it for an adaptation for the cinema.

[10] Particularly important, as well as the already-quoted G. A. Borgese, *Lazzarro, tragedia biblica* [Lazarus, a Biblical Tragedy] (1926), were E.

O'Neill, *Lazarus Laughed* (1927) and M. Gallian, *La casa di Lazzaro* [Lazarus's House], (1928).

[11] This quotation, taken from G. Giudice, *Luigi Pirandello*, Turin, UTET, 1963 is used by A. Meda, *Bianche statue contro il nero abisso*, cit., p. 198.

[12] A follower of the cultural movement in post-first World War Italy which advocated a return to regional traditions as opposed to cosmopolitanism.

[13] A follower of the movement in post-first World War Italy which advocated belonging to European cultural movements; the opposite of 'strapaesano'.

[14] For what the review has to say on 'myth', see M. Bontempelli, *L'avventura novecentista*, Florence, Vallecchi, 1974.

[15] *I giganti della montagna* [The Mountain Giants] - together with *La favola del figlio cambiato* [Fable of the Changeling Son], conceived of for use in the myth and then given independent existence - constitutes a kind of 'summa', at times ironical, of the culture of half a century: the giants, out of homage to futurist worhip of the modern, build huge, technically perfect constructions; however their names recall those of D'Annunzio's characters. In *La favola del figlio cambiato* a prostitute evokes the initial hypnotic state of Rosso di San Secondo's *Bella Addormentata* [Sleeping Beauty] (and Rosso is also the theorist who uses the opposition between north and south as an existential metaphor). There are traces of a regional kind of verismo in an episode of *I giganti* set in Sicily, where the story of a tragic infanticide is told. The 'triangle' consisting of the count, the countess and the poet is described in 'grotesque' terms by the actors. Bontempelli himself had written in 1916 a play called *Guardia alla luna* [The Moon's Guardian], in which the protagonist believes that the Moon has stolen her daughter who disappeared from her cradle. In *Siepe a nord-ovest* [Hedge to the North-West] (1918) he places actors, marionettes and puppets on stage all at the same time. As we shall see, particularly interesting here are *Nostra Dea* and *Minnie la candida*. Traces of Expressionism and of surrealist use of dream are particularly evident in *La favola* and *I giganti* (as in *Sogno (ma forse no)* of 1929).

[16] We should note that the first play to be performed when the 'Teatro degli undici' opened in 1925 was Lord Dunsany's *The Gods of the Mountain*.

[17] *La favola* is imagined by Pirandello as a play which the audience rejects, the work of a poet who has committed suicide. It so happened that *La favola del figlio cambiato* as a text by Pirandello (1932) set to music by G. F. Malipiero was in reality booed by the audience and slated by the critics, for reasons which were more political than artistic, first in Germany and then in Italy (1934). It is, however, interesting that, as the author of *La favola*, Pirandello

hides behind the character of a 'young poet', just as in 1933, in *Quando si è qualcuno* [When One Is Someone], he imagines that an anonymous 'great writer', imprisoned by critics and by general opinion in a definitive 'form', chooses to write poetry under a false name, leading others to believe in the existence of a 'young poet' who becomes the idol of the new generation.

[18] Pirandello often bases his plays on his narrative texts, as has been seen in the case of *La nuova colonia*. The source of *La favola* is his short story of 1902, *Le donne* [The Women], republished later with the title *Il figlio cambiato* [The Changeling]. The antecedent for one episode of *I giganti* is the short story *Lo storno e l'angelo centuno* [The Starling and the Angel One-O-One]. *Sagra del Signore della Nave* is based on *Il Signore della Nave* [The Lord of the Ship], just as *Liolà* (the first of Pirandello's works *en plein air*) (1916) has a precedent in a passage of his novel *Il fu Mattia Pascal* [The Late Mattia Pascal] (1904).

[19] It is not coincidental that we refer here to the play *L'altro figlio* [The Other Son] (1923) in which a mother hates the son she had because she was raped.

[20] For the presence of ghosts on the stage, see especially the one-act *All'uscita* [At the Exit] (1916).

[21] We owe this translation and interpretation of Pirandello's phrase 'ha i piedi un po' molli' [*MN*, II, 1313] to Felicity Firth's translation of *I giganti della montagna*, published in *The Yearbook of the Pirandello Society*, 10, 1990. Her translation has been used throughout, with page references in the text of the essay.

[22] '*Scalognato* [...] means both 'accursed' and 'pursued by bad luck' [...] intended to convey a suggestion of broken fortunes or blighted lives...', F.Firth, *op. cit.*, p.1.

[23] After this statement, almost as an illustration of it, the 'dama rossa' [red lady] appears on the stage. She is an unconscious sinner and happy to be so in spite of her name, Maria Maddalena, which would seem to indicate repentance. Unlike the other women in Pirandello's theatre she not only gives but also takes pleasure. From her frequent loves are born 'creatures' which she, with complete indifference, 'leaves on the grass'.

[24] 'Dimesso da tutto' [*MN*, II, 1345].

[25] See L. Pirandello, *SPSV*, 1199-1201 and *MN*, II, 1372-1376.

[26] R. Alonge, *Missiroli. I giganti della montagna*, Turin, Multimmagini, 1980.

[27] 'I am afraid! I'm afraid!'.

FREEDOM AND FRAGMENTATION: THE EXCLUDED WOMAN

The starting-point for this essay is Pirandello's predilection for the theme of
adultery (particularly female adultery), and two equations which recur
throughout his work: marriage as prison and adultery as freedom. These
equations are plainly perceptible in a number of his plays, for example, *Il
piacere dell'onestà, Il giuoco delle parti, Come prima, meglio di prima,
Questa sera si recita a soggetto, Come tu mi vuoi,* and *Trovarsi.* [1], and in his
novels *L'esclusa* and *Il fu Mattia Pascal.* [2] *L'esclusa* is a novel based on
paradox: it is the adultery novel in which adultery has not taken place. The
conclusion I draw from this novel is that its main concern is not adultery but
freedom, as Pirandello's interest in his theme is not primarily psychological,
sociological or personal, but philosophical.

Tony Tanner, in *Adultery and the Novel,* expounds his belief that there is
a special relationship between adultery and the bourgeois realist novel as a
genre. His thesis is that the age of the bourgeois realist novel coincided
exactly with what might well be termed the age of adultery, that is, the age
when the greatest threat to bourgeois society was constituted by the threat
posed by any rupture of the marriage contract. What he says is this:

> Marriage, to put it at its simplest for a moment, is a means by which
> society attempts to bring into harmonious alignment patterns of
> passion and patterns of property; in bourgeois society it is not only a
> matter of putting your Gods where your treasure is (as Ruskin accused
> his age of doing) but also of putting your libido, loyalty, and all other
> possessions and products, including children, there as well. For

bourgeois society marriage is the all-subsuming, all-organizing, all-containing contract. It is the structure that maintains the Structure, or System (if we may use that word, for the moment, to cover all the models, conscious and unconscious, by which society structures all its operations and transactions). The bourgeois novelist has no choice but to engage the subject of marriage in one way or another, at no matter what extreme of celebration or contestation. He may concentrate on what makes for marriage and leads up to it, or on what threatens marriage and portends its disintegration, but his subject will still be marriage. What he discovers, I will suggest, is that the bourgeois novel is coeval and coterminous with the power concentrated in the central structure of marriage. As bourgeois marriage loses its absoluteness, its unquestioned finality, its "essentiality", so does the bourgeois novel. On another level we may say that as the contract between man and wife loses its sense of necessity and binding power, so does the contract between novelist and reader. [3]

Marriage, then, is system and structure; adultery stands for rebellion against structure and system at the deepest level. In Pirandellian (Tilgherian) terms marriage is form and adultery, and indeed independence of any kind, is life. And Tanner shows the other side of the same coin, and illustrates at length from nineteenth-century literature the idea that adultery can lead to more freedom than perhaps was bargained for, to a loss of the sense of identity, to disorientation and disintegration of personality. One hundred and thirty pages are devoted to showing how this works in *Madame Bovary*. By the act of transgression the transgressor is fragmented, dissolved, denied any abiding conviction of possessing a consistent identity. Suddenly the transgressor does not know who he or she is. And here, indeed, we would appear to be on Pirandellian ground. I hope to show how *L'esclusa* would have illustrated Tanner's thesis equally well.

Marta Ajala

The novel is also stylistically disorientating. Pirandello's contribution to the literature of adultery subverts the genre and provides us with a kind of anti-novel by Tanner's definition, an ironic or 'humoristic' epitaph to the conventions of nineteenth-century bourgeois realist fiction. Adultery in

L'esclusa is emblematic: it stands for several freedoms, of which freedom from the institution of marriage is only one. It stands, then, for the spiritual, existential freedom which is multiplicity or fragmentation of consciousness, freedom from the past, freedom from other people's consciousness and departure from every kind of structure, including an independence of the genre Pirandello has borrowed as a vehicle for his demonstration. In *L'esclusa* Pirandello has written a transitional novel, subversive and parodic in its intertextual echoes, and concerned not with artistic verisimilitude but with revealing new modes of perception and representation. It is extraordinary to think that, until recently, the book was considered to be veristic. It was based on Capuana's *Ribrezzo* [Disgust] (1885) and a comparison of the two works is an effective way of measuring how far Pirandello has departed from the veristic convention. The plots are basically the same. In both stories a woman is wrongfully accused of infidelity. In both she is repudiated by her husband and rejected by her father and by society at large (rejection by the father is given prominence in both versions). In both she is driven into the arms of her supposed lover and becomes the adulteress she is publicly considered to be. They have different endings. Capuana's heroine, Giustina, dies of meningitis, abandoned by both husband and lover. Capuana's narrative is presented in a conventional idiom. It is evenly paced and his characters are closely observed. Plot is rooted in causality and characterisation based on psychological analysis. What Pirandello does with characterisation, narrative and plot I hope in some measure to show.

A vital point must be quoted from the dedicatory letter Pirandello wrote to Capuana when *L'esclusa* first appeared in book form in 1908. He insists on what he calls: 'la parte più originale del lavoro: parte scrupolosamente nascosta sotto la rappresentazione affatto oggettiva dei casi e delle persone; [il] fondo insomma essenzialmente umoristico del lavoro.' [4] [the most original part of the work: a part which is scrupulously hidden beneath the completely objective depiction of events and people; in short [the] essentially humoristic basis of the work]. Sipala, in his book *Capuana e Pirandello*, sees this dedication to

Capuana as having 'tutto il senso d'un commiato' [5] [sounding just like a farewell]. Pirandello is, in effect, declaring the representative guise of the novel to be a false trail. The attribution of a 'fondo umoristico' to *L'esclusa* in this letter of 1908, the year of *L'umorismo* [Humorism] itself, identifies the climate of the novel with the alternative reality of the essay on humour, the 'realtà diversa da quella che normalmente percepiamo, una realtà vivente oltre la vista umana, fuori delle forme dell'umana ragione' [SPSV, 152] [reality different from the one we normally perceive, a reality existing beyond human sight, beyond the forms of human reason.] Passages in *L'esclusa* echoing verbatim passages in *L'umorismo* reinforce this conclusion. It is easy to recognise in the novel the fragmented, upside-down reality later to be elaborated in *L'umorismo* and in *Il fu Mattia Pascal*, the dismantled, post-Copernican universe which has 'l'inestimabile privilegio di poter fare a meno di quella stupidissima verosimiglianza a cui l'arte crede suo dovere obbedire' [*TR*, 474] [the inestimable privilege of being able to do without that very stupid verisimilitude which art believes it is its duty to obey]. The idea of the world as a 'granellino di sabbia' [*TR*, 268] [tiny grain of sand] without significance or causality permeates Pirandello's work at the time of writing *L'esclusa*, as is apparent from his essay *Arte e coscienza d'oggi* [Art and Consciousness of Today] (1893) and his short story *Pallottoline* [Tiny Pellets] (first published in 1902). In comparison with this 'povera nostra terra [...] atomo astrale incommensurabilmente piccolo' [*SPSV*, 896] [poor world of ours [...] an incommensurably small astral atom], where human histories can only seem to be 'storie di vermucci' [*TR*, 269] [stories of mere worms], Capuana's *Ribrezzo* reads like Pirandello's own parody of conventional narrative, beginning: 'Il signor conte si levò per tempo...' [*TR*, 268] [The count got up early ...], so wittily mocked in the second introduction/premise to *Il fu Mattia Pascal*.

In the absurd world of *L'esclusa*, character is multiple and motivation fortuitous. Like *Il turno*, written two years earlier, it is a parody of causality. The husband, Rocco Pentàgora, finds Marta reading a letter. She drops it. He dives to pick it up and bangs his head on a cupboard door. Blind with rage and pain, and *without reading the letter*, he drives his wife from the house. Later, staring out into the night, he moans: 'Che debbo fare? che debbo fare?' [*TR*, 16] [What should I do? What should I do?], and his young brother, a boy playing with bread pellets at the kitchen table, says: 'Io, nel tuo caso, farei un duello.' [*TR*, 17] [In your situation I'd have a duel]. Nothing could be more casual than the procedures by which the three protagonists are cast into their roles of repudiated wife, vindictive husband and putative lover. At no point does Marta love her lover. Capuana's Giustina turns to *her* supposed lover for the rational reason that he alone in the world knows her to be innocent. Pirandello's Marta Ajala experiences loss of self when she eventually goes to Alvignani's house. It is even suggested that she leaves her *self* somewhere along the road outside and picks it up again afterwards. When she gets there, 'Aveva perduto affatto la coscienza di sé, d'ogni cosa.' [*TR*, 131-132] [She had completely lost consciousness of herself, of everything]. The deciding factor in her surrender is the position of the staircase: '...la scala scoperta. Ecco: se la scala non fosse stata cosí scoperta, forse non sarebbe salita.' [*TR*, 135] [the stairs were visible. That was it: if the stairs hadn't been so visible, perhaps she wouldn't have gone up.] As the critic Debenedetti says of this book: 'La psicologia non scende mai nei personaggi, non coincide mai con loro: non arriva ad essere la loro motivazione perchè è la loro punizione.' [6]

In other ways, too, there is a large measure of dislocation in Pirandello's presentation of his characters in this book. Not only are they unmotivated, they are realised on different levels and to different degrees. Marta is portrayed as raw consciousness, largely through the device of free indirect speech; her mother, sister and friend are portrayed with various degrees of sketchiness as rather colourless, straight characters; while the rest of the cast consists of a gallery of grotesques. Here, deliberate caricature has taken the place of portraiture, and caricature not as gratuitous entertainment but as a series of variations on the theme of the subjectivity of experience. The grimaces and antics of each distorted persona are physical projections of a whole gamut of possible mental attitudes to the central motif: adultery as a type of human experience. So Antonio Pentàgora, Marta's father-in-law, claims to revel in his own role of seasoned cuckold: 'Io di corna negozio' [*TR*, 65] [Cuckoldry is my speciality]. He is the first in a long line of Pirandellian characters to make the best of an enforced role. Marta's own father, Francesco Ajala, is another prototype. He knows of his daughter's innocence, but still persists in his role as victim of opinion, and locks himself away in a darkened room, demonstrating the human capacity to cling to an inauthentic attitude even unto death: 'Non ne uscirò che morto!' [*TR*, 29] [I shall only come out when I'm dead!] Matteo Falcone, the deformed and monstrously ugly schoolmaster who loves Marta, is burdened beyond the point of endurance. He deserves a study to himself, as indeed does the whole subject of physical ugliness in Pirandello. It is Pirandello's favourite concrete illustration of the role played by chance in human affairs (as witness the Monte Carlo chapter in *Il fu Mattia Pascal*). Matteo Falcone loves Marta, and knows that he hardly even exists for her. His mind literally disintegrates in the face of this non-existence, and he goes mad. He shares with Vitangelo Moscarda (*Uno, nessuno e centomila*) (1926) a claim to be the ultimate illustration of Pirandello's insistence on the awareness of others for a sense of his or her own reality.

The principles of distortion and parody are likewise applied to other key aspects of the genre. Plot and pace are parodied; so is background detail. Pirandello observes a formal chronology in his narrative, but let us consider the sixth chapter, once much criticised for its failure to be realistic. This is the chapter in which, at the same hour and in five short pages, Marta gives birth to a stillborn child and her father dies of self-induced apoplexy, while outside the crowd celebrates the election of Alvignani, the 'lover', as deputy. Described as inclement by Russo, [7] who cannot forgive Pirandello for not being Verga, this chapter provides us with a totally non-realistic condensation of events presented with cruel and comic speed. It is a tragedy delivered at the pace of a knockabout farce, accompanied by a superabundance of noise and action, crude physical detail, Grand Guignol automatism, and with an ever-multiplying cast of puppet-like figures dashing about: midwife, doctors, neighbours, priest, sacristan, acolytes, choirboys, mourners and voices off.

Another feature of realism that is parodied here is the old convention of plentiful representative background detail. The central assumption of realism is, of course, the tacit agreement between author and reader of the existence of a 'common phenomenal world which may reliably be described by the methods of empirical history'. [8] We have seen that Pirandello's belief in a reality which is different from the one we normally perceive knocks the bottom out of the whole principle of fiction as representation. So representative detail becomes redundant, and is either excised, condensed or, where it does occur, deformed for metaphorical purposes. Let us take, for example, the chapter of the religious procession, in which the townspeople terrorise Marta by banging the giant iron saint's head against her upstairs balcony. The *fercolo* [litter] is depicted as a many-headed monster, a rabid incarnation of society's will to punish the deviant, intoxicated with its own rage: 'Cento teste sanguigne, scarmigliate, da energumeni si cacciarono tra le stanghe della macchina' [*TR*, 62] [One hundred bloody heads, dishevelled, as though possessed of the devil, were thrust between the shafts of the litter]. The three or four pages describing the incident are studded with epithets denoting fury, delirium, violence and madness. This is not local colour, a veristic picture of late nineteenth-century Agrigento. It is the bare face of human injustice with the mask of realistic detail stripped away.

The claim that this novel is transitional, that it constitutes an epitaph to the mode of verismo, is strongly reinforced by the arguments of its theoretical counterpart written in the same year, *Arte e coscienza d'oggi* (1893) [Art and Consciousness of Today]. This is Pirandello's personal statement of his view of the cultural and moral crisis of the end of the nineteenth century, in which he considers and finds wanting the various and conflicting artistic modes of his time: verismo, French naturalism, determinism, symbolism, mysticism, decadentism and so on. He looks to a prophet who shall rise up and pronounce

the saving word, il *verbo nuovo*. One could say that Pirandello has indeed
alighted on his *verbo nuovo*, in the word which is the recurring motif of both
these works: *coscienza*, a word he recognises in both its meanings, both as
conscience and as consciousness. It is the prophet's word, in that what the
twentieth century then produces is a literature mainly preoccupied with the
exploration of the nature of consciousness.

The link between *Arte e coscienza d'oggi* and *L'esclusa* is very close; so
close, in fact, that Alvignani in the novel is preparing a study with the title *Arte
e coscienza d'oggi*. The novel is informed with the sense of disorientation
described in the essay which Pirandello finds prevalent in every sphere:
religious, social, ethical and political as well as artistic. The crisis described in
L'esclusa, like that in *Il fu Mattia Pascal* and in *Uno nessuno e centomila* is a
crisis of consciousness. These novels are essentially philosophical
demonstrations, whose premise is the impossibility of certainty as expressed in
Arte e coscienza d'oggi where Pirandello writes:

> ...è naturale che il concetto della relatività d'ogni cosa si sia talmente
> allargato in noi, da farci quasi del tutto perdere l'estimativa. Il campo
> è libero ad ogni supposizione. L'intelletto ha acquistato una
> straordinaria mobilità. Nessuno più riesce a stabilirsi un punto di
> vista fermo e incrollabile. [*SPSV*, 900]
> [...it is natural that the concept of the relativity of everything has
> become so widespread among us that we have almost entirely lost our
> sense of judgment. The field is open to every supposition. Our
> intellect has acquired an extraordinary mobility. No-one any longer
> can manage to establish a firm and unshakeable point of view.]

and:

> Nessuna conoscenza, nessuna nozione precisa possiamo aver noi della
> vita; ma un *sentimento* soltanto e quindi mutabile e vario. [*SPSV*, 897]
> [We cannot have any knowledge, any precise notion of what life is,
> but only a *feeling*, which is therefore changeable and varied.]

This is the uncertainty which becomes the hallmark of modernist, non-realist
fiction, the partial, fragmented viewpoint which is all the writer has left when

deprived of an ascertainable phenomenal world describable by the methods of history. In 1919 Virginia Woolf describes this restricted vision in the often quoted passage in her essay *Modern Fiction*:

> Life is not a series of gig-lamps symmetrically arranged: life is a luminous halo, a semi-transparent envelope surrounding us from the beginning of consciousness to the end. [9]

Pirandello had said the same thing fifteen years earlier in his *lanternino* passage in *Il fu Mattia Pascal*, where consciousness is:

> ... un lanternino che proietta tutt'intorno a noi un cerchio più o meno ampio di luce, di là dal quale è l'ombra nera [...] che noi dobbiamo purtroppo creder vera, fintanto ch'esso si mantiene vivo in noi. [*TR*, 397]
>
> [... a small lantern which projects all around us a greater or lesser circle of light, beyond which is the dark shadow [...] which we, alas, must believe is real for as long as the lantern remains alight in us.]

Both *L'esclusa* and *Il fu Mattia Pascal* are, I would claim, existential metaphors, philosophical demonstrations about the nature of awareness, identity and freedom. I would go further and maintain that, at a fundamental level, they are the same story. In both the central character reaches an impasse in his/her life. Both are lacking in emotional motivation and are described as being moved by chance impulses. Both are said to be 'outside life' at frequent intervals throughout their stories. Both abandon an authentic identity based on the structure of marriage, and in doing so experience a brief, euphoric honeymoon with existential freedom. Both undergo a long period of reflection and introspection in a darkened room, and at this stage in both narratives there occurs the image of a lamp shedding a fragile but consoling light at the centre of a menacing, encircling darkness. Both characters don a new persona in a new city, and there find the life behind the mask impossible to sustain. For both the stumbling-block lies in their inability to relate to others in their new, inauthentic role. Both finally, and with a sense of defeat, return to their place of origin in an attempt to recover their previous identity - their 'very being', one would say, if in Pirandellian terms such a thing could be said to exist.

As it is, they are bound for disillusion, for one's 'very being' for Pirandello is precisely the mirage, the *ignis fatuus*, that we are all in search of, and for which we have to substitute the mask. In both novels questions of 'coscienza' dominate. Not only is Alvignani working on his *Arte e coscienza d'oggi*, he has as his family motto the words 'Nihil mihi conscio', rather pragmatically interpreted by Nino Borsellino as 'la coscienza non mi basta'. [10] Tito Lenzi, in *Il fu Mattia Pascal*, fiercely attacks, in a long and often quoted passage, the Ciceronian dictum 'Mea mihi conscientia pluris est quam hominum sermo'. In the first version of *L'esclusa*, of 1901, Alvignani is given the same passage almost verbatim.

The stories of both Marta Ajala and Mattia Pascal are refutations of Cicero's 'ho la mia coscienza e mi basta' (Pirandello's translation) [I have my conscience and that is enough for me]. The conversation of men is shown to mean precisely everything to the outcast. Robert Dombroski, in his book on Pirandello's novels *Le totalità dell'artificio*, has convincingly made the point that every character in *L'esclusa* is an outcast, Marta Ajala's case being simply the most extreme. [11] *L'esclusa*, like *Il fu Mattia Pascal*, is a demonstration based on a hypothesis: 'Take the case of a character who makes a bid for independence of the consciousness of others'. Both stories demonstrate that it cannot be done. Towards the end of the book, Alvignani drives the message home:

> Oh, mia cara, quando io dico: "La coscienza non me lo permette", io dico: "Gli altri non me lo permettono, il mondo non me lo permette". La mia coscienza! Che cosa credi che sia questa coscienza? È la gente in me, mia cara! Essa mi ripete ciò che gli altri le dicono. [*TR*, 136]
> [Oh, my dear, when I say: "My conscience won't let me", I'm saying: "Other people won't let me, the world won't let me." What do you think this conscience is? It's people in me, my dear! It repeats to me what other people tell it].

Marta's immediate moral/psychological crisis is a metaphor for her, and our, existential/ontological crisis. Society in this novel is a metaphor for humanity. Marta's attempt is to be independent not of society but of humanity, her own humanity included, and it is for this reason that it fails. Ultimately, the alternatives facing her are not acceptance and rejection, but being and non-being. Shut out by others, she is shut out also from herself. Spontaneous human response begins to fail early, before the death of her father. Father, mother and sister, knowing her to be innocent, behave as if she were guilty. The house is shrouded in silence and darkness, 'quasi che il mondo fosse crollato' [*TR*, 36] [almost as if the world had fallen apart]; 'Marta infatti non piangeva più' [*TR*, 35] [Marta indeed didn't cry any more]. Disintegration is all about her; she loses her bearings even in relation to the inanimate world:

> ... le pareva che soltanto adesso le si chiarisse [...] il significato dei singoli oggetti, e li esaminava, ne concepiva quasi l'esistenza astraendoli dalle relazioni tra essi e lei. [*TR*, 42-43]
> [... she seemed only now to understand [..]. the meaning of individual objects, and she examined them, she almost conceived of their existence by abstracting them from the relationship between them and her].

After her illness she goes through a long period of torpor of the conscience, of not caring, of insensibility. She is described by her mother as 'impassibile', set apart, calm, as though nothing was wrong. She regards her struggle to become a teacher as a struggle not towards respectability but towards being itself. When Rocco tries to thwart her efforts she sees it as an attempt to destroy her: 'Questo vuole! Io non debbo più respirare.' [*TR*, 83] [This is what he wants! I mustn't breathe any longer]. One cannot enumerate all such references, but when she arrives in Palermo in her new persona she is, like Adriano Meis, devoid of authentic identity, and human contact is alien to her and deeply disturbing. The illusion of liberty accords her at first a deceptive sense of elation:

Pareva che l'anima delle cose, serenata finalmente dalla lieta
promessa della stagione, si componesse, obliando, in una concordia,
arcana, deliziosa. E quanta serenità, quale freschezza nello spirito ...
[*TR*, 97]
[It seemed as though the soul of things, serenaded at last by the glad
promise of the season, was reconciled, forgetting all, into an arcane,
delightful harmony. And what serenity, what renewal of the spirit ...].

There is a strikingly equivalent passage in *Il fu Mattia Pascal*.

But her sense of being reintegrated into the world does not last. As in *Il
fu Mattia Pascal* it is not long before 'un po' di nebbia' [12] begins to mist her
vision. She sees that her mother and sister have found their way back to life:

...e maggiormente, per forza di contrasto, sentiva penetrarsi dal
convincimento che lei sola era l'esclusa, lei sola non avrebbe più
ritrovato il suo posto, checché facesse. [*TR*, 102]
[... and all the more, by force of contrast, she felt herself pervaded by
the conviction that she alone was the outcast, she alone would never
find her place again, whatever she did.]

Why should she feel like that? She is among new people, has a job she likes,
admiring colleagues and a loving mother and sister. The explanation of her
anguish is found in the dilemma that was later to be at the heart of
existentialist thinking: is it possible to escape the prison of one's past?
Pirandello's answer, in the end, though with reservations, is no.

It is the same conclusion that Don Eligio draws from the predicament of
Mattia Pascal: '...che fuori della legge e fuori di quelle particolarità, liete o
tristi che sieno, per cui noi siamo noi, caro Signor Pascal, non è possibile
vivere' [*TR*, 472] [...that outside the law and outside those particular
circumstances, happy or sad, which make us what we are, dear Signor Pascal,
it is not possible to live]. And this is why Marta has to return to Rocco
Pentàgora; her motive is not sentimental reconciliation, nor a response to
social pressure: it is simply in order to avoid having to say, as Mattia Pascal
has to say, '... che non sono affatto rientrato né nella legge, né nelle mie
particolarità [...] e io non saprei proprio dire ch'io mi sia.' [*TR*, 472] [... that I

have not at all returned either within the law or within my own particular circumstances [...] and I would really be unable to say who I am.]

Ersilia Drei

Vestire gli ignudi (1922) [To Clothe the Naked] is the adultery play where the adultery has already taken place before the play begins, but is not revealed to the audience until a good two thirds of the play are over. The effect of this is that, for most of Acts I and II, we concentrate on Ersilia's state of mind, her search for identity and on the various attempts of the male characters in the play either to write her story or to impose an identity on her which fits in with their own preconceptions and needs. What happens, very briefly, is that at the beginning of the play Ersilia arrives at the rented rooms of the writer Ludovico Nota. It is apparent that these two have only just met, and we learn from the first stage directions and from their conversation that Ersilia had just left hospital after a suicide attempt. Nota read a newspaper article based on an interview which Ersilia gave when she thought she was dying, wrote to her at the hospital, and has just collected her from there. After bickering with his landlady, Signora Onoria, who regards Ersilia's arrival with suspicion, Nota tells Ersilia that he had thought of basing a short story or a novel on her interview. Now, however, he has seen that she is young and beautiful (but also deathly pale and with dark circles around her eyes, details he does not dwell on or even seem particularly to notice) he wants to seduce her and to find renewal, and home comforts, through her. He maintains, indeed, that since he has already imagined her whole story, from start to finish, he does not need to use her as a literary model. Ersilia, though, seizes on Nota's idea of making her into a literary heroine, seeing in it a chance to become 'someone', in fiction if not in fact.

Details of what was said in the interview, what was written in the newspaper and ultimately, as far as we are ever allowed to learn, what really happened are gradually revealed throughout the play. In Act I, the bare bones of the story are given: Ersilia was a governess in charge of the little daughter

of the Italian consul at Smyrna; the child fell from the balcony of the consul's
villa; Ersilia was dismissed without even her fare home; she returned to Rome
and went to the Naval Ministry to find her 'fiancé', Franco Laspiga, the young
naval lieutenant who seduced her in Smyrna and then proposed marriage to
her. She was told, however, that he was about to marry another woman; as a
result, she said, she attempted suicide.

The newspaper article has been read by others as well as Nota, and its
consequences become increasingly far-reaching. Cantavalle, the journalist
who interviewed Ersilia, has found out where she is and comes to tell her that
he put more in his article than she wished. In particular, and with a casuistry
that amounts to sheer bad faith, he wrote that Ersilia had been dismissed by her
employer, the Italian consul at Smyrna. To Ersilia, who had not wanted her
former employer,or any of the other protagonists, mentioned he insists that he
respected her wishes as he did not actually *name* the consul. However Grotti,
the consul, has himself come to Rome because of what happened in Smyrna,
has read the interview and has gone to Cantavalle's editor to demand that the
newpaper should publish a complete refutation of what Cantavalle wrote. The
journalist has now come to ask Ersilia what he should do about Grotti's
complaint.

Ersilia faints and is taken away to rest, and Cantavalle tells Nota about
another twist of events. Ersilia's story had been that she had attempted suicide
because she learnt that Franco Laspiga was about to marry another woman. A
further effect of his 'piece', as Cantavalle calls it, has been that Laspiga's
fiancée has called off the marriage, that her father has been to see Grotti and
that Ersilia is now being blamed for the death of the child who was in her care.

As the story, from being a romantic tale of blighted love set in the Orient
begins to assume the proportions of a public scandal, Nota's enthusiasm for his
love nest-with Ersilia wanes. When, towards the end of Act I, Laspiga arrives
in the guise of the penitent wanting to make amends, Nota is almost too eager
to hand over responsibility for Ersilia to him. The obstacle to this solution, as
becomes clear in Act II, is Ersilia herself, as she no longer wants to marry

Laspiga. She tries to make him understand her rejection of him, in terms he is quite unable, or unwilling, to understand, including the relevation that she lied when she said that disappointed love was the reason for her suicide attempt. At this point, Grotti himself enters. When he and Ersilia are left alone, we learn that after Laspiga had left Smyrna Ersilia and Grotti had an affair. Even more, they were in bed together when the baby fell from the balcony, and caught *in flagrante* by the consul's wife. As in *L'esclusa*, the plot becomes almost unbearably complicated, to the point of parody of the genre of adultery.

At the beginning of Act III, Ersilia has gone with Nota to collect her suitcase, left behind at her hotel. Laspiga returns, and tells Onoria and Nota of Ersilia's affair with Grotti. All three of them now turn against Ersilia, giving vent to their self-righteous indignation at the lies she has told. Grotti returns, and he and Laspiga have a duel of words which is, in reality, a duel to maintain their own versions of the story. When Ersilia comes back, however, she has again taken poison. She refuses all help and tells the others that, now that her lie has been exposed, she must die naked, alone and in silence, unable even to provide herself with a decent garment, a romantic tragedy, to clothe her death.

In Act I of *Vestire gli ignudi* Pirandello introduces a reference to *L'esclusa*. Ersilia asks Nota to write his novel, but about her as she is, not as the woman he imagined, and she wants the novel to be 'bello come quell'altro tuo romanzo che ho letto [...] "L'Esclusa", ecco, "L'Esclusa" '. [*MN*, I, 880] [... as good as that other novel of your I read [...] "The Excluded Woman", that's it, "The Excluded Woman"]. Nota is quick to disabuse her, saying that he cannot stand Pirandello's work, and that *L'esclusa* is a bad novel. We never discover what grounds Ersilia had for thinking that Nota was the author of Pirandello's novel. Those who know *L'esclusa* might, however, see this self-reference as a *mise en abyme*. Ersilia thought she had found an author who knew very well the feelings, aspirations and difficulties of an excluded woman, and so one who would write about her with similar sympathy and understanding. Nota, though, is a seedy character whose murky intentions are symbolised from the beginning of the play by the dark, shabby, dirty, smelly room he uses as his study. Further, the setting also suggests that he is not very successful as a writer, while his appropriation of Ersilia's story (and desire to appropriate her body) indicate his predatory, vampiric nature.

Nota is completely self-absorbed, self-congratulatory and self-interested, concerned, indeed, only for himself, as are the other male characters in the play. He had imagined Ersilia's story, but he never actually writes it, firstly because his intentions towards her have changed and then because the story, from being three columns in a newspaper in the silly season, comes alive. Ersilia can never be as Nota, at one stage, wants her to be: 'senza più memoria di tutte le cose tristi che ti sono accadute' [*MN*, I, 873] [without any memory of all the sad things which have happened to you]. The process set in motion by the chance interview Ersilia gave, in extraordinary circumstances, becomes ineluctable as the cortège of male characters walks on stage to force confessions from Ersilia which she does not want to make. In so doing, they strip her of the 'vestina decente' [*MN*, I, 937] [respectable little dress] she had wanted to wear as her own funeral garment.

Vestire gli ignudi can be seen as an extreme demonstration of what Ibsen wrote in his outline for *A Doll's House*, that is:

> There are two kinds of moral laws, two kinds of conscience, one for men and one, quite different, for women. They don't understand each other; but in practical life, woman is judged by masculine law, as though she weren't a woman but a man. [13]

In an almost incredible exchange, Cantavalle turns to Ersilia to ask *her* to sort out the tangle he himself has created, to 'regularise' his position now that Grotti has intervened with his editor. Cantavalle says: 'Sono venuto qua per sapere come debbo regolarmi contro il reclamo e la minaccia di questo signore' [*MN*, I, 887] [I've come here to find out how I should act in the face of this man's complaint and threat]. The translation loses the link in Italian between 'regolarsi' and 'regola' [rule], but its is clear that Cantavalle wants to lay the blame for the row developing on Ersilia and to rescue his own position by returning within the rules. The weight of masculine law is brought to bear on Ersilia she loses her human identity, her body jerks, she whinnies like a horse and then faints.

There are many examples in the play of the ways in which institutions and masculine law are used against Ersilia. The Admiralty and the Foreign Office become involved, and much of the play takes the form of an interrogation and trial of Ersilia, who is constantly accused of being the guilty party. Moral and social codes and conventions are used against her. Laspiga admits that in Smyrna he did not take Ersilia seriously, and that after seducing her he proposed because that is one of those promises 'che si fanno, perché ...sí, perché allora si devono fare - '. [MN, I, 892] [which are made because ...yes, because at times like that they have to be made]. The use of the third person plural in Italian, which I have translated by the English passive, enables Laspiga to place the blame for his cynical behaviour elsewhere, and so to exculpate himself. Laspiga presents himself, at first, as the penitent who feels the obligation to make reparation for the harm he has done, but his position, like Nota's, undergoes a radical shift. To begin with he says that remorse at his own conduct has led him to seek Ersilia out. In Act II, though, he reveals his anger and hurt pride at being thrown out by his fiancée and her family. He plays his role with a deal of satisfaction and egotistic pleasure. Of Ersilia's stated motive for suicide he says 'ha voluto uccidersi per me' [MN, I, 893] [she wanted to kill herself for *me*], a theme he repeats a number of times, always seeing Ersilia in relation to himself. Even before they meet again he declares that she is now his fiancée, giving her an identity without her consent. So he, too, is turning to Ersilia for legitimation, and this is why he completely fails to understand her rejection of him in Act II.

The importance Laspiga attaches to his own honour, which is what really motivates him, is exposed in the farcical, but also bitterly ironic, logic-chopping he engages in after he has found out about the affair between Ersilia and Grotti. At the beginning of Act III he returns to Nota's room and furiously calls Ersilia a whore (no such term is used of Grotti). All he wants now is to ascertain whether the affair began before or *after* he seduced Ersilia, and subsequently proposed to her; if the former is true, he says, then he will have been shamefully deceived. He is so completely bound up in himself that the obvious question is not raised: Ersilia says that he was her first lover, and if so Laspiga must have known that she was a virgin that night in Smyrna. In *Vestire gli ignudi* Laspiga, in particular, epitomises the dictum: 'ho la mia coscienza e mi basta'. He says, indeed: 'Ma io ho la mia coscienza' which 'non cangia' [MN, I, 911] [I have my conscience [which] doesn't change]. Laspiga uses the vocabulary of a religious penitent, but he completely rejects awareness of others. So it is Laspiga who most overtly shows that, like the other male characters, he will be one of the goats on the left of Christ at the last judgment. [14] He has one moment of true feeling, when Ersilia is dying, but by then charity comes too late.

It is, however, Grotti, with whom the adultery actually took place, who most threatens Ersilia. At the beginning of the dialogue between them in Act II Ersilia shrinks away from him, trembles with fear and protects herself with her elbow. Later, she turns on him like a whipped animal. Grotti shouts, terrorises her, shows contempt and becomes her interrogator, accuser and torturer. In a long sequence, the two battle again through the violent, sado-masochistic stages of their affair. In this battle, ultimately, Grotti wins. With extreme cruelty and brutality he uses all his authority as consul, employer and male against Ersilia, to the point where she breaks down in tears. Then, remarkably, he is able to move her to tenderness when he reminds her of how well he treated her when she first arrived in Smyrna, and goes on to describe his empty life and difficult marriage. After further threats and declarations of hatred he finally declares his need for Ersilia and his desire that they should be 'due infelici' [*MN*, I, 919] [two unhappy people] together. Once again, it is left to Ersilia to provide what solution, or resolution, she can. Grotti has used his whole range of identities and emotions to drive her to suicide.

Adultery in this play does not equal freedom, for Ersilia. In another of those moments in which one of Pirandello's male characters reveals the full extent of his egocentricity Grotti calls their affair 'quella stupidaggine d'ozio, d'un po' di vizio' [*MN*, I, 915] [that stupid moment of idleness, of a bit of vice]. Ersilia, though, loses what little she had through adultery and the death of the child. What claim she has to identity is, in any case, very precarious. She has no autonomy, no family and no friends. [15] She loses her job, and so her livelihood, and this in any case was one of a dependant. She cannot have the identity of a wife, the only one she says offers her happiness. She does not become the tragic/romantic heroine of either her early version of her story or of Nota's. She fails as proxy mother to Grotti's daughter, as mistress and as prostitute. She is in part responsible for the death of the child, and so for the childlike, innocent part of herself.

This last point merits some discussion. When Ersilia, in the scene already mentioned, comes round after fainting the stage-directions, and her own words, are as follows: '(*con voce quasi allegra, di stupore quasi bambinesco*) Oh, Dio, sono caduta?' [*MN*, I, 888] [(*in an almost happy voice, of childlike wonder*) Oh God, did I fall?] For a moment she almost returns to the happiness of childhood. Marta Ajala, too, looks back to her happy childhood, and to the moment when she was forced abruptly to become an adult on her marriage to Rocco Pentàgora [*TR* 34-35 and 97]. As Lugnani has shown, for many of the children in Pirandello's work the transition from childhood to adolescence and adulthood is traumatic and often destructive. [16] The most solemn oath Ersilia can swear in her dialogue with Grotti in Act II, is on the soul of the child, but childhood has now become inseparable from her own fall from grace. The image of the child, she says, accompanied her on her return from Smyrna, but abandoned her when she attempted prostitution. So that image has become a nightmare to her, a symbol of shame and disgrace, and in order to redeem it, and herself, she wants, through suicide, is to rejoin the child. To extend the argument a little further, Ersilia's own, inescapable adult sexuality, and the resulting desire men have for her body, are at odds with the child in her, and cause the mind/body split she reveals to Grotti. [17]

So Ersilia does not want, or cannot have, the identities which are associated with her. She becomes a series of negatives, a non-being, fragmented, her language and behaviour hysterical. [18] Chameleon-like, she has to fit in with her surroundings, as is apparent from the beginning of the play where she comes on alone and is then virtually ignored, left standing as Nota and Signora Onoria enjoy what is obviously one in a long series of quarrels. She can only make her presence felt by recourse to pathos and melodrama, by saying 'Sono una povera malata che esce in questo momento dall'ospedale' [MN, I, 869] [I'm a poor sick woman who's just this moment come out of hospital].

Ersilia refers throughout the play to her sense of disorientation, and crisis of consciousness. In Act I, when Nota tells her that he no longer wants her as his fictional heroine but as his companion in a new life, she replies: 'E allora - non quella...non questa - ancora un'altra?' [MN, I, 873] [And so - not that one...not this one - yet another one?]. As we have seen, her claims to selfhood were always slight. After her adultery with Grotti she becomes even more a surface which others can use, and then cast aside, acording to the moment. This surface, as she says, is that of a commodity for others: 'Servire ... obbedire...non poter essere niente ... Un abito di servizio, sciupato, che ogni sera si appende al muro, a un chiodo. Dio, che cosa spaventosa, non sentirsi piú pensata da nessuno. ' [MN, I, 876] [To have to serve ... to obey ... not to be able to be anything ... A threadbare uniform that every night you hang on a nail on the wall. God, what a terrifying thing to feel that no-one is thinking about you any more]. In the play she is frequently urged to loosen her garments, as though we are witnessing a physical as well as a mental strip-tease on stage. The final, prurient detail, which establishes Ersilia as surface comes when we realise that she has no underwear, a situation which is hinted at at the end of Act I but then firmly established by Signora Onoria in Act II.

Vestire gli ignudi is an extreme example of Ibsen's perception that:

> A woman canot be herself in modern society. It is an exclusively
> male society, with laws made by men and with prosecutors and judges
> who assess feminine conduct from a masculine
> standpoint. [19]

However Nora, in *A Doll's House* can leave her husband and family and slam

the door of the house, while Hedda Gabler can find her own version of a

'beautiful' death. Giudice points out that Pirandello detested Ibsen, and that

one reason for this was, perhaps that Pirandello's ideas on women's

independence in society were very conservative. [20] A reading of Pirandello's

article on Feminism confirms this view. [21] Marta Ajala returns to her husband

at the end of *L'esclusa*, although he hates her body which is carrying

Alvignani's child. Mattia Pascal may not know who he is, but he nevertheless

manages to exist in the same town as his wife and her new family, in a

comfortable marginal zone between his library and his own grave. Ersilia Drei

does not have these options, or those of that other governess, Jane Eyre, who

sets out, penniless across the moors only to find family and the financial

independence which enables her to speak to Mr Rochester as an equal.

    Ersilia is not able, as she says at the end of the play, to clothe herself. In

his short story *The Oval Portrait* (1845) Edgar Allan Poe describes how a

painter transfers his young wife, who was:

> ... a maiden of rarest beauty, and not more lovely than full of glee: all
> light and smiles and frolicksome as the young fawn: loving and
> cherishing all things: hating only the Art which was her rival ...[22]

onto his canvas, and in so doing kills her. Ersilia's identity, too, is transferred,

and transformed into whatever the male characters want her to be. Her

presence is continually pushed into the background as the others foreground

themselves, as happens to Irene's statue in Ibsen's *When We Dead Awaken*

(1899). She has been called a 'male construct'. [23] She has also been identified

as the first of those woman who, as Ann Caesar says, are engaged in a far more

fundamental struggle than that of Pirandello's male protagonists, 'that of

establishing for themselves a persona which they can recognize as authentically their own' , and which 'dominates Pirandello's theatre in the ten years from *Vestire gli ignudi* (1922) to *Trovarsi* (1932) ...' [24] Her final dress, which she chooses herself for prostitution or death, is the 'abitino celeste, decente, sciupato un po' dall'uso' [MN, I, 867] [little, sky-blue, respectable dress, a bit worn through use]. This second 'abito sciupato', associated by its colour with the Madonna, is her final working uniform. She becomes, in fact, a threadbare Madonna, which perhaps signals the failure of archetypes to contain her identity. It appears, ultimately, that the play is less concerned with adultery than with adulteration.

FELICITY FIRTH

JULIE DASHWOOD

[1] In English, respectively, The Pleasure of Honesty (1917); The Rules of the Game (1918); As Before, Better Than Before (1919), Tonight We Improvise (1929); As You Desire Me (date of composition uncertain, first performed 1929); Finding Oneself (1932).

[2] In English, respectively, The Excluded Woman (or: The Outcast) (1901) and The Late Mattia Pascal (1904).

[3] T. Tanner, *Adultery and the Novel. Contract and Transgression*, Baltimore and London, The Johns Hopkins University Press, 1979, p. 15.

[4] This text of this letter can now be found in Luigi Pirandello, *Tutti i romanzi*, I, edited and introduced by G. Macchia, with the collaboration of M. Costanzo, Milan, Mondadori, 1973, pp. 881-882.

[5] P. M. Sipala, *Capuana e Pirandello. Storia e testi di una relazione letteraria*, Catania, Bonanno, 1974, p. 28.

[6] G. Debenedetti, 'Una giornata di Pirandello' quoted in Silvana Monti, *Pirandello*, Palermo, Palumbo, 1980, p. 105. [The psychology never goes down to the characters, it never coincides with them; it never becomes their motivation as it is their punishment].

[7] L. Russo, 'Il noviziato letterario di Luigi Pirandello' in *Ritratti e disegni storici*, 4th series, Bari, Laterza, 1953, p. 381

[8] David Lodge, *The Modes of Modern Writing*, London, Edward Arnold, 1977 (paperback edition 1979) p. 40.

[9] Virginia Woolf, 'Modern Fiction' in *Collected Essays*, vol 2, London, The Hogarth press, 1966, p. 106.

[10] N. Borsellino, 'Stratigrafia dell'*Esclusa*' in *Il romanzo di Pirandello*, ed. E. Lauretta, Palermo, Palumbo, 1976, p. 36. In English, 'conscience/consciousness is not enough for me'.

[11] R. Dombroski, *Le totalità dell'artificio: ideologia e forma nel romanzo di Pirandello*, Padua, Liviana, 1978 (chapter on *L'esclusa*).

[12] This is the title of one of the chapters in *Il fu Mattia Pascal*. Literally translated it means 'a bit of fog'.

[13] Quoted in M. Meyer, *Ibsen*, London, Sphere, 1992 (first published in 1967), p. 466.

[14] The play's title is an obvious reference to *Matthew*, 25, 31-46, where clothing or failing to clothe the naked is one reason for salvation or damnation.

[15] Gaspare Giudice makes the point that Pirandello's female characters do not have an autonomous conscience/consciousness; see his *Luigi Pirandello*, Turin, UTET, 1963, p. 232.

[16] Lucio Lugnani, *L'infanzia felice e altri saggi su Pirandello*, Naples, Liguori, 1986, pp. 102-165.

[17] For a full treatment of this theme see Ann Caesar, 'The Branding of Women: Family, Theatre and Female Identity in Pirandello' *Italian Studies*, XLV, 1990, pp. 48-63.

[18] See Maggie Günsberg, 'Hysteria as Theatre: Pirandello's Hysterical Women', *The Yearbook of the Society for Pirandello Studies*, 12, 1992, pp. 32-52.

[19] Quoted in M. Meyer, *Ibsen*, cit., p. 466.

[20] Gaspare Giudice, *Luigi Pirandello*, cit., p. 231.

[21] This article, first published in *La preparazione* in 1909, can now be found in *SPSV*, pp. 1068-1072. There is a very interesting discussion, and translation,

of it in Maggie Günsberg, *Patriarchal Representations. Gender and Discourse in Pirandello's Theatre*, Oxford/Providence, Berg, 1994, pp. 195-207.

[22] Edgar Allan Poe, *Selected Writings*, edited and with an introduction by David Galloway, Harmondsworth, Penguin, 1967, pp. 252-253.

[23] Maggie Günsberg, *Patriarchal Representations*, cit., p. 49.

[24] Ann Caesar, 'The Branding of Women in Pirandello', cit., p. 48.

CHANGING COSTUME, CHANGING IDENTITY:
WOMEN IN THE THEATRE OF PIRANDELLO, BONTEMPELLI AND
WEDEKIND

In the late 19th century the woman question was posed in terms of her
legal and civil rights, but by the 1920s it had become a matter not so much of
what woman wants but of what she is and what she appears to be. Ibsen, Henry
James, Bernard Shaw, Chekhov and Tolstoy created a succession of powerful
women protagonists who combine a sense of their own worth with an
awareness of the futility of their lives. The form taken by their struggle to
escape the constraints of society, to bring an authenticity into their existence,
may well be determined by considerations of gender, but the aspirations that
inform their choices hold true for men as well as women. In the 1920s,
however, the focus changes: we find, on stage at least, that while the practice of
taking woman as protagonist continues, the issues that are addressed as a
consequence are of a very different nature. As the site rather than the
originator of a problem, woman becomes a spectacle to be viewed, a visual
construct, a being who is all surface. What happens in these plays is often
neither intended by her nor willed by her and the questions of guilt or
innocence, right or wrong are no longer foregrounded. This essay will discuss
the representation of women in three European plays. It will suggest that the
readiness of the stage to explore women in terms of spectacle owes much not
only to the underlying unease that accompanied modernism but also to the
increased presence of the visual image in culture, from photography to cinema.

The concentration of female identity on surface and, by extension, costume is the idea informing three related plays - Massimo Bontempelli's *Nostra Dea*, Frank Wedekind's *Der Erdgeist* and *Die Büchse der Pandora* and Luigi Pirandello's *Come tu mi vuoi*. What is striking about these three plays is the extent to which they rely on the visual representation of the woman protagonist for their effect. Appearances replaces psychology as the motivating impulse behind their narratives. As what happens is often neither of the protagonist's volition nor of her management, the plays communicate a sense of aimlessness and hopelessness.

Massimo Bontempelli's *Nostra Dea* [Our Dea] was written in the first two weeks of 1925 for Pirandello's theatre company, the Teatro degli Undici. It was very successfully performed later that year with the then little known actress Marta Abba in the lead role, recruited after her success as Masha in Chekhov's *The Seagull*. Pirandello's meeting with her was to be a turning-point in his own career as playwright, for most of his plays written in the 20s and 30s were specifically for Abba or were ones in which she played the main role. *Nostra Dea* embodies the pornographer's perfect fantasy by taking as protagonist a woman who is all surface. Dea's identities are created by her dressmaker and effected by her maid. Every change of dress is accompanied by a change of identity. To read Dea one must read her wardrobe. The play is a visual materialization at the level of wardrobe of the modernist preoccupation with the dissolution or fragmentation of character. She has no past, no future, she is a living, breathing mannequin, inert and inexpressive. Dea herself is not capable of combining the two sounds needed to articulate 'io' - Italian for 'I' - and she therefore never acquires subjectivity. The plot is determined by the clothes selected for Dea to wear, until the dénouement when the malicious intention to use her as an instrument to inflict the maximum misery on others by dressing her as serpent - venomous, vicious and extremely seductive - is averted when the clothes are literally torn off her back by a man who thereby neutralizes the evil created by women. Reduced to rags, her clothes in shreds, Dea circulates the ballroom begging alms before finally being returned to the state of mannequin. Bontempelli has fun with some well-established literary clichés. The exploited, prostituted and victimised dressmaker of 19th-century fiction becomes a fanatical, almost demonic figure, a 'grande fabbricatrice di divinità' [a great maker of gods], while the mistress-maid relationship is inverted, as Anna the maid ominously comments: 'la signora Dea, la faccio io, due o tre volte al giorno' [it is I who make Madame Dea, two or three times a day].

If the heroine's identity is demoted to a function of costume, her physical reality is similarly displaced when her doctor practices what he calls a 'semeiotica ambientale' [environmental semeiology], which entails visiting his patient's home only in her absence, and making his diagnosis on the basis of 'clues' left in her apartment.

Frank Wedekind's Lulu tragedy is out of chronological step with the other two plays and it has a more complicated history. It is made up of *Erdgeist* [Earth Spirit] and *Die Büchse der Pandora* [Pandora's Box] - two plays that Wedekind worked on intermittently between 1892 and 1913. For censorship reasons, however, they were not permitted a public performance until 1918. The plays reached a much wider audience when in 1929 G.W. Pabst turned them into a film, *Die Büchse der Pandora,* with the American actress Louise Brooks playing the part of Lulu.

Wedekind's heroine Lulu is, like Bontempelli's Dea, a succession of clothes. When *Erdgeist* opens we meet Lulu's Pierrot costume before we meet her, but as one of her admirers notes it is as though her body had been born in the costume.[1] Her skin is indistinguishable from her dress, both are silk. Her 'naturalness' rests in the fact that she is pure artifice: (indeed in an earlier draft of the play Lulu is suspected of dyeing and artificially curling the hair in her armpits).[2] In the course of the two plays the enigmatic Lulu is implicated in the deaths of three husbands, several admirers and the wife of the man who became her third husband. Furthermore there is a strong intimation that she enjoys an incestuous relationship with her father; she has an affair with her husband's son, and among her admirers are a boy whose main preoccupation is that he may be expelled from school, and a lesbian, the Countess Geschwitz, who later, with Pabst's film, was to be the first 'screen lesbian'. Lulu herself embraces death when it comes to her in the figure of Jack the Ripper - the first man in relation to whom she is more desiring than desired and the only man who does not look directly at her. Whenever something unpleasant happens, Lulu changes clothes and her exhibitionist fascination with dress is crucial to her presence as spectacle. Lulu aspires to be what Dea unwittingly is, she simply wishes to be that which others see her as being: 'Ich habe *nie* etwas anders sein wollen also wofür man mich genommen hat' [I've *never* wanted to be anything other than what people take me for].

Pirandello's *Come tu mi vuoi* [As You Desire Me] was published and first performed in 1930. Unlike so much of his theatre, it has no source in any of his stories or novels. When he wrote it, he knew the work of both Pabst and Wedekind. Several years earlier he had intended to direct a Wedekind play (it is not known which), and although it can only be conjectured that he knew Pabst's adaptation, (Pirandello paid an extended visit to Berlin from 1929 to 1930) he was sufficiently impressed by Pabst as a film-maker to recommend him as second choice after Eisenstein (whom he met in Berlin) to make a film version of his story *Acciaio* [Steel] (in the event neither director was available). More compelling evidence of Pirandello's knowledge of the Lulu plays can be found from within *Come tu mi vuoi* where it seems to have escaped critical attention that the first act is a re-working of *Erdgeist*.

The play opens in Berlin in the late 20s where the protagonist L'Ignota [the Unknown Woman] pursues a career as dancer in a night-club. She lives with her lover Salter, but she is desired also by his sexually indeterminate daughter, Mop. Like Dea and Lulu, L'Ignota's identity revolves around appearance and when a photographer 'verifies' that she is Cia, the lost wife of a friend of his in the Veneto, she abandons her dissolute life and accompanies him to Italy.[3] There, dressed in the clothes that Cia wore ten years before when she posed for her portrait, L'Ignota causes some disquiet by looking more like the portrait than Cia ever did. When Salter arrives with a deranged woman from a Viennese lunatic asylum - a woman without speech and without features - who, he claims, is, according to his documentation, Cia, L'Ignota decides to return with her lover to Berlin. The play's reworking of *Erdgeist* is intended primarily as an indictment of social *mores* in Berlin in the 1920s, but the manner in which L'Ignota's identity is constructed shares interesting similarities with both Lulu and Dea. All three young women are presented to us without reliable information about background. Indeed the first index of identity, name and surname, is missing. Naming, a father's prerogative which he later passes on to the husband, is a statement of possession. As they circulate among men, L'Ignota changes name three times, Lulu four times, but the speed and insignificance of the changes mean that none sticks long enough to provide an identity. So depersonalized are the women's names (the name of Dea - 'Goddess' in English - remains constant no matter how many roles she adopts) that they come to represent Woman as a sex rather than individual members of their sex. In the absence of a statement of who they are, the protagonists construct themselves, or are constructed, visually through the dress they wear; it is their 'look' that authenticates their identity.

Theatre was not the only cultural medium of the period to suggest that woman is all surface. A striking aspect of modernism's preoccupation with the indeterminacy of woman's identity is the growing fascination with clothes; dress that can dissemble, conceal and construct the bearer's self. The most startling representations of this preoccupation can be found in Surrealist art; Man Ray, Salvador Dalì and Oscar Dominguez offer their versions of the creation-myth. In Ray's 'The Enigma of Isadore Ducasse' (1920), Dalì's 'Night and Day Clothes of the Body' (1936) and Dominguez's 'Electrosexual Sewing Machine' (1934) it is the sewing-machine that makes woman. In Surrealist images of feminine beauty, clothing and the female body appear to be indissolubly sewn together and frequently, as in the work of Max Ernst and Giorgio de Chirico, the inanimate form of the mannequin replaces woman. Why displace identity on to a woman's wardrobe? Beyond the arts, a new visual semiotics of dress had also come into being, moving the perception of it away from the idea that dress was a means of covering the body (but bearing of course signs of its owner's social status and wealth) towards a concept of dress as an expression or revelation of individual identity. It was not after all so long since women's dress had been a question of bustles, whale-bone stays and tight-lacings, which caused such concern at the turn of the century that the Reform Dress Movement was launched in England to fight the manipulation and distortion of the female body induced by women's clothes. Changes brought about by the technology of the sewing-machine and developments in textiles and fabrics contributed to the changing significance of clothes. Photography made possible the proliferation of fashion plates so that the 'image' or 'look' could be reproduced and made accessible to a wide audience. Gradually the barriers between pure and applied arts began to give; a process both illustrated and advanced by the surge of creativity in Russia in the years immediately following the Revolution. Soon leading artists such as Delaunay, Goncharova and Léger were engaged in costume design both for the stage and for the street.

One area where we can see particularly clearly the assumption that clothes are a manifestation of a core identity is in the cultural representations of androgyny or cross-dressing. The three plays by Bontempelli, Pirandello, and Wedekind all use clothes to raise the question of sexual identity. In the first Act of *Come tu mi vuoi* Pirandello communicates his vision of Berlin in the 20s as a degenerate and reprehensible society by giving Mop, Salter's daughter who competes with her father for L'Ignota's attention, a pair of pyjamas and a masculine haircut. The opening stage-directions describe her face as 'segnata d'un che d'ambiguo che fa ribrezzo' [4] [marked by something ambiguous that makes one shudder]. In *Nostra Dea* when the protagonist is dressed in masculine clothes, her stride lengthens, her physical appetites increase, she knows her own mind; the shy, acquiescent, inviting young woman of the day before has vanished, to her suitor's comical confusion and dismay. Wedekind's representation of Lulu's most constant and loyal suitor, the Countess Geschwitz, is, with her mannish lesbianism, an embodiment of the pioneering sexologist Havelock Ellis's concept of the third sex. In all these examples sexual indeterminacy is attached to a woman's appearance. The anxiety these plays testify to is an expression of widespread unease. Traditionally held views of masculinity and femininity as complementary were being undermined on a number of fronts, from women fighting for emancipation to women replacing men in civic society during the 1914-18 War. The appalling experience of trench warfare itself dealt a serious blow to received notions of masculinity. Emergent theories of the psyche, with their emphasis on the psyche of the unconscious in determining behaviour, also undermined presuppositions about sexual difference. In all this, men, of course, had far more to lose than women. The disquiet so evident in works written by men does not extend to those written by women. When, for example, Virginia Woolf addressed the subject, she produced a witty celebration of androgyny in her novel *Orlando* (1928) where her eponymous hero/ine discovers that her sex and personality change with the clothes she wears.

> Vain trifles as they seem, clothes have, they say, more important offices than merely keeping us warm. They change our view of the world and the world's view of us [...]. There is much to support the view that it is the clothes that wear us and not us them, [...] we may make them take the mould of arm or breast, but clothes mould our hearts, our brains, our tongues to their liking.[5]

Far from the discovery being a source of anxiety, it is accompanied by nothing other than pleasure.

The displacement of identity on to clothes and the continuum between body and dress is developed still further on stage in avant-garde spectacle such as Dadaist performance, where the body becomes a screen constantly imprinting redefinitions and transformations. As early as 1909 the young Kokoschka had caused uproar in Vienna with his staging of his play *Mörder Hoffnung der Frauen* [Murder Hope of Womankind], (a battle between the sexes enacted through progressive mutual mutilation, and culminating in Man's killing of Woman and his departure from a stage red with blood and flames) by covering the actors' bodies in a web of painted lines which traced or represented the network of nerves. Where Dea's dress in Bontempelli's play projects inwards to

manufacture an identity, so erasing the gap between dress and 'self',
Kokoschka's characters' interiority is displaced on to the surface, so they are
just nerves, flesh and blood. Clothes and body, textiles and skin become
indistinguishable.

As character is displaced onto dress, so the body assumes the function of
self-expression or self-revelation. Dance had been largely absent from 19th-
century theatre, but in the period under discussion it returns to the stage, not to
tell a story as in the manner of a masque, but to display the heroine. L'Ignota is
the only professional dancer in our three plays, and we first see her wearing the
costume she designed for the serpentine dances she invents for performance at
the night-club. But Lulu and Dea also dance. Indeed Lulu is only truly alive
when dancing; it is her body's only means of self-assertion. Nietzsche saw dance
as an expression of human liberation, but in the world of our protagonists it is a
morally ambiguous métier associated with display, sexual voyeurism and
seduction. It is always performed in front of a male gaze that pays for the
privilege. In *Come tu mi vuoi* Pirandello brings together dance, drink and
debauchery; in *Erdgeist* the connection between dance, dress and voyeurism is
made when a young avant-garde director is told by his father (who will himself
later put Lulu back into circulation by making her dance in public) that nobody
is going to pay money to see her dance in a raincoat. Lulu is told by Schön that
she will dance before anyone who pays to watch her and later he adds, 'Solang
du noch einen Funken Achtung vor dir selber hast, bist du keine perfekte
Tänzerin!' [6] [As long as you keep a spark of self-respect you can't be a perfect
dancer] The nature of the dance is not specified in these plays - although we are
clearly not talking about classical dance - it is, however, described variously as
'serpentine', convulsive' and 'extravagant'; adjectives that bring to mind the
'uncontrollable' writhings of Charcot's hysterics at La Salpêtrière. The
connection lies in the idea of the body over which the mind has no control, a
reflection on woman as the sex closest to animal and nature. In Wedekind's
play, Lulu is first seen being carried immobile into a circus-ring where the
animal-tamer instructs her as his whip caresses her. What is interesting is that

dance is not simply referred to, but our protagonists are watched by the paying public in the auditorium as they dance by themselves on stage. These are moments which carry no narrative, the only reason for their inclusion is that they focus the spectator's gaze on the dancer.[7]

The dances enacted on stage reflect the influence Isadora Duncan, Loïe Fuller, Maud Allen and others had exercised over traditional classical dance by creating unballetic bodily movements of their own, producing a writing of the female body which was markedly different from the concepts of grace and harmony inherent in classical inscriptions. These dances were shocking not only at the level of performance but also because, as in the case of Isadora Duncan, the dancer herself appeared uncorseted and barefooted. In her book *The Dancer of the Future* Duncan suggested that modern dance freed the female body of social restraints; the contemporary dancer would no longer perform 'in the form of a nymph, nor fairy, nor coquette, but in the form of a woman in her greatest and purest expression'. [8]

Dance and dress, passivity and presence; what is so marked about our three protagonists is that the emphasis falls not on doing but on performing - appearance is everything. In classic realism dress is used as a key to the personality of its wearer, but at the same time, for the device to be effective, the reader or viewer must remain unaware of the extent to which understanding of the protagonist is determined by outer trappings: in these plays dress is foregrounded either to deny any continuity between outer and inner, or to question a concept of interiority. To step into a costume is to step into a role; many of the costumes of Lulu, Dea and l'Ignota are designed to be looked at by a public before whom they perform. When a critic hostile to Pabst's *Lulu* and the performance of its leading actress wrote 'Louise Brooks cannot act. She does not suffer. She does nothing',[9] he inadvertently identified the characteristic Lulu shares with l'Ignota and Dea - impassivity. They are all surface, they do not yield to interpretation.

The primacy of the image in creating an identity is emphasised in both *Erdgeist* and *Come tu mi vuoi* in scenes where the audience is invited to compare the protagonists to their respective portraits in oils. In both cases the portrait was commissioned for private consumption, but where in Wedekind's play its presence simply arouses a voyeuristic pleasure among the male spectators on stage, in Pirandello's play it is used, together with photographs and documents, to authenticate a woman's legal identity and is the subject of discussion among the actors on stage. So important is the heroine's 'look' that it outweighs speech as signifier. This shift in the presentation of the heroine on stage occurred during the time that a new cultural medium had come into being. Silent cinema drew entirely on the reproduction and circulation of images, and it is interesting to speculate briefly on how far theatre was influenced by its younger competitor.

Of the three playwrights Pirandello was most closely involved in cinema, as spectator, writer and theoretician. It was his friend Nino Martoglio who first drew his attention to the new medium when he founded a production company which aimed to adapt for the screen the work of great writers. In 1904 Pirandello wrote a script based on one of his short stories, and although the film was never made, it led to a life-long interest in the medium. When he began work on *Si gira* ... [Shoot!], the first novel to take cinema as its subject, Pirandello asked another friend, who worked in the *Cinestudio* in Rome, to teach him about the technical aspects of film-making.[10] In 1929, after the advent of sound, Pirandello wrote two newspaper articles, 'Contro il film parlato' [Against the speaking cinema] and 'Se il film parlante abolirà il teatro' [Will the talkies kill the theatre?],[11] where he discusses the issues raised by the new technology. Insistent that the discovery of sound must not be used to produce filmed theatre, he argued that the new emphasis on words was mistaken as it detracted from the power of the image: cinema's most fundamental and compelling asset. Narration, he wrote, with some disingenuousness, should be left to the novel, and drama to the theatre, while cinema should hold fast to its own visual language and capitalise on it; 'il cinema dovrebbe trasformarsi in pura visione' [cinema should transform itself into pure vision]. It was, perhaps unexpectedly, the advent of sound that led Pirandello to argue that the threat cinema posed to theatre had been averted. In the days of silent film, he argued, the cinema, defined as 'muta espressione di immagini e linguaggio di apparenze' [mute expression of images and language of appearances][12] had accustomed its huge public to a new language of sight. Theatre, worried by its formidable rival, hastened to turn itself into a theatre of spectacle by studying closely cinematic technique, but now it was the turn of the cinema to seek to emulate, quite misguidedly, the stage, and theatre had nothing further to fear.

If Pirandello is right to argue that the rivalry between cinema and theatre was at its most intense during the years of silent cinema, when theatre had most to lose from an audience accustomed to following narratives through what they saw rather than what they heard, that rivalry may well be expected to have had repercussions on the way in which character was represented. In the introduction to her collection of essays on feminism, semiotics and cinema, Teresa de Lauretis notes that narrative cinema, spoken as well as silent, is the genre in which:

> the representation of woman as spectacle - body to be looked at, place of sexuality and object of desire - so pervasive in our culture, finds its most complex expression and widest circulation.[13]

This is not to suggest that the two media, cinema and theatre, were interchangeable. Where, for example, silent cinema had the possibility of close-up, allowing facial expressions to be a vehicle for self-expression, theatre had the voice whose signifying capacity included tone as well as content. Nor could the signifying techniques developed by the one medium simply be transferred to the other. In the absence of the voice in silent cinema, bodily movements required an exaggerated expressivity to be understood, facilitated by a closeness of range unobtainable in conventional theatre. Nor did the body need to be a constant unity as it did on stage (despite experiments by the Futurists); it could fragment, or parts of the body could be emphasized over others. What screen and stage did share, however, is that both sought to remedy their respective lack, voice in the case of cinema, close-up in the case of theatre, by maximising the potential afforded by dress and bodily movement.

But even if the move towards the representation of woman as image was at least in part an effect of the impact of the cinema on theatre-going audiences at a time when cinema seemed to have much to teach theatre, it is reasonable to assume that the consequences of the shift in attention away from the spoken word to the visual image were not purely technical in character, and that in the shadow of the authority which our culture invests in the word, the redefinition of woman as dramatic spectacle carried an ideological price for woman. The work of Pirandello in particular offers scope for the further exploration of the complex interaction between culture and technology in the aesthetics of modernism.

ANN HALLAMORE CAESAR

[1] Schwarz, 'Der ganzer Körper im Einklang mit dem unmöglichen Kostüm, als wäre er darin zur Welt gekommen:' [Her whole body was as much in harmony with this impossible costume as of she had been born in it], Frank Wedekind, *Erdgeist, Die Büchse der Pandora*, Munich, Willhelm Goldman 1980], pp. 16-17. All references hereafter will be to this edition.

[2] I am grateful to David Midgley for drawing my attention to this detail of Lulu's toilette.

[3] In both *Come tu mi vuoi* and *Erdgeist* the presentation of woman as image is also represented visually through the presence of framed reproductions of Lulu and L'Ignota; portraits or copies that the audience are invited to compare with the 'original' model.

[4] Luigi Pirandello, *Maschere Nude*, I, Milan, Mondadori, 1965 (3rd edition), p. 945.

[5] Virginia Woolf, *Orlando*, London, Grafton, 1985, p. 117

[6] *Erdgeist*, p. 62

[7] Louise Brooks, writing about the making of the film, noted: 'That I was a dancer and Pabst essentially a choreographer came as a surprise to both of us on the first day of shooting'. 'Pabst and Lulu', in Louise Brooks, *Lulu in Hollywood*, London, Hamish Hamilton, 1982, p. 101.

[8] Isadora Duncan, *The Dancer of the Future*, quoted by Elizabeth Dempster, 'Women writing the Body', *Grafts. Feminist cultural criticism*, London, Verso, 1988, p. 38.

[9] Louise Brooks, 'Pabst and Lulu', cit., p19. See also an excellent essay by Thomas Elsaesser, 'Lulu and the Meter Man', *Screen*, July-October, 1983, pp.4-35.

[10] *Si gira* ... was first published in 1916, but a new edition appeared in 1925 with the title *Quaderni di Serafino Gubbio operatore*. (It was translated into English under the title *Shoot!*) Walter Benjamin draws on Pirandello's novel in his essay 'Art in the Age of Mechanical Reproduction', *Illuminations*, London, Fontana, 1973, pp.219-53.

[11] 'Contro il film parlato', *Corriere della Sera* Milan, 19 April 1920. 'Se il film parlante abolirà il teatro', *Anglo-American Newspaper Service*, London-New York, June 1919. Both articles can be found in Francesco Càllari, *Pirandello e il cinema*, Venice, Marsilio, 1991, pp.118-20 and pp.120-25

[12] L. Pirandello, 'Se il film parlante abolirà il teatro', cit., p.122.

[13] Teresa de Lauretis, *Alice Doesn't. Feminism, Semiotics, Cinema*, London, Macmillan, 1984, p.4.

'ORA CHE TUTTO ERA FINITO...'
THEME AND DIALOGUE IN *BELLAVITA* AND *TUTTO PER BENE*

In a subtle and stimulating essay on 'L'interiezione nel dialogo di Pirandello' [Interjection in Pirandello's Dialogue], Giovanni Nencioni characterizes Pirandello's dialogue as follows:

> 'Un costrutto lanciato da un personaggio, e interrotto da un altro, può esser raccolto e proseguito da un terzo e concluso da un quarto, così da passare mnemonicamente e formalmente integro, ma non monotono, attraverso più bocche, con una struttura che, una volta impostata, persegue ostinatamente, sopra ogni intoppo, il proprio sviluppo. Viceversa la stessa voce, svolgendo un unico tema e magari un unico costrutto, può modularlo e variarlo sì da apparire plurima.'[1] [A construction launched by one character and interrupted by another can be picked up and continued by a third and concluded by a fourth, so that in passes mnemonically and formally complete, but not monotonous, through a number of mouths, with a structure which, once established, pursues its development obstinately over every obstacle. Conversely one voice treating a single topic and even a single construction can modulate and vary it so as to appear multiple].

I should like to examine the link between the dialogue form and certain themes, in two of Pirandello's plays, the one-act *Bellavita* (1928) and *Tutto per bene* [All for the Best] (1920).

The particular slant given to the triangle situation constitutes the link, although in Pirandello no two plays present a problem from exactly the same viewpoint. Take for example the identity of Signora Ponza in *Così è (se vi pare)* [Right You Are (If You Think So)]and of l'Ignota in *Come tu mi vuoi*

[As You Desire Me]: in the first the mystery is elaborated through the eyes of the townspeople, in the second through the eyes of the protagonist. In both *Bellavita* and *Tutto per bene* the death of a woman has as its legacy the continuing relationship between the husband and the lover, and the questioned paternity of the offspring. In *Bellavita*, however, the husband had been aware of the wife's affair, which had lasted ten years and which had made him the laughing stock of the town; but as he had accepted it for so long, he now expects the lover to continue his show of friendship for him and for his son. It is the lover's (Denora's) intolerance of the relationship, now that he sees no more reason for it, and his desire to send the boy (Michelino) to the best boarding school in Naples, that make Bellavita spring to life in defence of his position as a father, and decide to take revenge the only way he can, by continuing in his obsequious reverence for his rival.

In *Tutto per bene* instead the husband, contrary to what everyone else thought, had been unaware of his wife's infidelity and of the real paternity of his daughter, and only discovered the situation following the marriage of the daughter, after his wife had been dead for sixteen years. Here too, the lover, Salvo Manfroni, cannot see why the husband, Lori, wants to continue with the charade once the daughter, Palma, has left the paternal home. In *Bellavita*, it is the death of the wife that causes a crisis in the relationship between the two men, whilst in *Tutto per bene* it is the marriage of the daughter. It is a crisis in the sense that the relationship becomes intolerable to the lover (and in *Tutto per bene* to the 'daughter' also), and is clung to instead by the husband - in the case of Bellavita with a final twist, in the case of Lori until his position is inadvertently made explicit to him. 'Ora che tutto era finito...' [Now that it was all over] are words that Lori utters, summing up the aspect of the two plays which I am highlighting.

1. Antagonists versus protagonists

Let us look first at the two antagonists, the notary Denora and Senator Manfroni, both social superiors to the café-owner Bellavita and the civil servant Lori, respectively. In what way does their attitude to the protagonists affect their behaviour, and more relevantly for this study, their mode of expression, when they are with third parties? They are presented in very different ways. Denora has been driven by his exasperation to seek the help of a lawyer friend, Contento, and as he waits to see him he manifests his animosity against Bellavita to Signora Contento. Salvo Manfroni instead seems loftily oblivious of Lori's existence, except when actually face to face with this irritant, so that, unlike in *Bellavita*, the relationship between the two men in *Tutto per bene* is only revealed when they are both present. It is therefore on Denora that I shall concentrate in this section.

As Denora is shown into the waiting room he gives vent to his obsession even in the presence of the clerk, interrupting the explanation that Signora Contento is coming to keep him company: '*Lo Scrivano*. Sí, perché ha detto... *Denora* ...che vuole ridere anche lei alle mie spalle, ho capito!' [*MN*, II, 587] [*Lo Scrivano*. Yes, because she said - *Denora*. ... that she wants to laugh behind my back as well, I know!]. After Signora Contento's arrival, followed by a brief appearance on the part of her husband, who has come to check that Denora is being well looked after, the conversation between the three of them is full of questions and exclamations, as Contento cannot believe Denora is so suspicious. '*Contento*. Un sospetto? Che sospetto? *La Sig. Contento*. Che vogliamo farci beffe di lui, anche noi! *Contento*. Io? Beffe?' [*MN*, II, 588] [*Contento*. A suspicion? What suspicion? *Mrs Contento*. That we want to make a fool of him as well. *Contento*. Me? Do a thing like that?].

Denora justifies his interpretation by observing himself from the outside and finding his situation ridiculous; the speech in which he explains this consists of repetitions, exclamations, interrogatives, and suspensions which are going to be the hallmark of a style of discourse which expresses an untenable situation.

> *Denora*. Perché è naturale! naturale! Vi pare che non lo capisca?
> La cosa spaventosa è questa, che lo vedo da me il ridicolo della
> mia situazione; e mi metterei a ridere anch'io, vi giuro, di
> qualunque altro - fosse pure mio fratello - a cui fosse capitato
> questo stesso mio caso! Ora, che io debba soffrirne, mentre ne

riderei come tutti ne ridono, è cosa... è cosa che mi sta facendo
impazzire, ecco: impazzire!
[*MN*, II, 588-9]
Denora. Because its natural! natural! Do you think I don't
understand? The terrible thing is this, that I see myself how
ridiculous my situation is; and I promise you I'd start laughing
myself at anyone else - even if he were my brother - whom the
same thing had happened to! Now, the fact that I have to suffer
from it, while I would laugh at it just as everyone is laughing, is
something that's driving me mad, that's it: mad!]

The features I have mentioned, although particularly conspicuous in
passages like these, are to be found in the whole play, and contribute to its
emotional, excited, almost breathless pace. Especially striking is the frequency
of repetitions. I counted about eighty in the fifteen pages which make up this
short text. They are mostly emphatic repetitions which do not add to the
semantic content of the sentence, but rather reinforce its emotive character:
they belong not to the referential function of the message, but rather to
functions of expression and appeal: 'lo deve in gran parte a me! a me!'; 'Perché
è naturale! è naturale!'; 'ho schifo, schifo', etc. ['he owes it mostly to me! to
me!'; 'Because its natural! its natural!'; 'I loathe, really loathe'].

To return to the opening encounter, Denora is momentarily calmed by
Contento's reassurance that he is there to help him and by the proof of
solidarity manifested in the lawyer's reference to Bellavita as 'quella pittima'
[that bore], but as Contento leaves, Denora's concern comes to the fore again
and he reminds him: 'il miglior collegio di Napoli: diteglielo pure!' [*MN*, II,
589] [the best boarding school in Naples, please tell him that]. This 'diteglielo
pure!' represents Denora's technique for trying to resolve the situation: he does
not want a confrontation with Bellavita, he wants the lawyer to speak for him
and reduce to the minimum the contacts between them. In *Tutto per bene*
Manfroni too wants to rid himself of Lori's presence, but he expects this to
happen automatically after Palma's marriage and he appears with the social
assurance of one who does not depend on others.

Denora instead is relieved to unburden himself to Signora Contento once
his confidence has been restored: he talks of the boy Michelino, who he claims

is his; she joins in with her memories of Bellavita's wife and the flourishing pastry-shop,[2] and he follows with his grief at his lover's death, which he was not even allowed to mourn in peace, without the unwelcome attentions of Bellavita.

His speeches and exchanges are occasionally objective and calm: 'Non è solo il padre, signora mia, a non poterlo sapere con certezza, neanche la madre può mai sapere di certo se il proprio figlio appartiene al marito o all'amante' [*MN*, II, 589] [It isn't just the father, dear lady, who can't be absolutely sure, even the mother can never be quite sure whether her son is her husband's or her lover's] and 'quando non vogliamo sapere una cosa - si fa presto - fingiamo di non saperla. - E se la finzione è più per noi stessi che per gli altri, creda pure, è proprio, proprio come non si sapesse' [*MN*, II, 590] [when we don't want to know something - its easy - we pretend not to know. - And if the pretence is more for ourselves than for others, believe me, it is really, really as though we didn't know]. But more often they are subjective and passionate. He has no-one to live for, except Michelino: 'Sono pronto a tutto: adozione, testamento per assicurargli l'eredità. Non ho nessuno' [*MN*, II, 590] [I'm ready for anything, adoption, a will to make sure he inherits. I have no-one]. He wants to rid himself of Bellavita: 'Voglio liberarmi di lui, del padre, a qualunque costo!' [*MN*, II, 590] [I want to rid myself of him, of the father, at any cost]; it is unbelievable that he cannot be tempted with money: 'Inaudito! inaudito! E doveva toccare proprio a me di aver da fare con un marito di quella specie!' [*MN*, II, 590]. [Unheard of! unheard of! And it had to be me who had to deal with a husband like that!]. Bellavita was grateful to Denora for his defence of him with his wife (socially of a higher standing) who accused him of tactlessness with their clients: 'Certe scenate! - ora capirà, presa l'abitudine d'andare con gli amici in quel caffè - pacifico come sono sempre stato - ne soffrivo. Mi provai a rimettere la pace, e...' [*MN*, II, 591] [What rows! - now you will understand, once I'd acquired the habit of going to that café with my friends - peace-loving as I've always been - I suffered because of them. I tried to restore the peace, and ...]

Denora's longest and most agitated speeches are his re-evocation of Bellavita's reactions after his wife's death. One speech culminates in 'l'odio per questo! perché non me la lascia piangere da solo, come vorrei! Lei capisce, signora, che ho schifo, schifo a piangerla insieme con lui?' [*MN*, II, 590] [the hatred I feel for him! because he doesn't let me mourn her alone, as I'd like! Do you understand, signora, that I loathe, really loathe mourning for her with him?]. He still remembers the disgust of Bellavita's embrace: 'L'ho ancora qua, vivo, nelle dita il ribrezzo di quelle sua braccia magre sotto la stoffa pelosa dell'abito nero ritinto, quando feci per strapparmi dalla violenza con cui volevano aggrapparmisi al collo!' [*MN*, II, 592] [I still feel, alive, in my fingers the disgust for those thin arms under the hairy cloth of his black dyed suit, when I tore myself from the violence with which they wanted to cling to my neck]. This is reminiscent of the deathbed scene between Lori and Salvo, re-interpreted by Lori now that he knows the truth: 'Ma di scatto allora si levò, e com'io, convulso, gli tendevo le mani per abbracciarlo, mi respinse, mi respinse con rabbia, a spintoni nel petto' [*MN*, I, 1155] [But he then got up abruptly, and as I, agitated, stretched out my hands to embrace him, he pushed me back, pushed me back angrily, shoving me violently in the chest]. Denora's final words to Signora Contento, on hearing that Bellavita has arrived to see the lawyer, are: 'L'ammazzerei! L'ammazzerei!' [*MN*, II, 592] {I'd kill him! I'd kill him!]. We are thus left with the impression of a disturbed, resentful and excitable individual, whose vindictiveness would appear more conventionally appropriate in the wronged husband rather than in the lover. In fact we shall see later that Lori in his susceptibilities and his distress has elements in common with Denora as well as with Bellavita.

2. *The protagonists' loss of illusion*

When Bellavita is in conversation with the intermediary, Contento, we see the relationship from a different point of view. The husband is dazed and bewildered. Like Denora, he too sees himself from the outside: 'Come se un altro mi avesse preso per le braccia e messo a sedere accanto a un tavolino, come un fantoccio' [*MN*, II, 594] [as though someone else had taken me by the arms and sat me down at a table like a tailor's dummy], and he feels as if the flies, which have now taken over in his café, are buzzing around inside his head. He describes his situation in two seven-line speeches which reveal his confusion and his grief, but the rhythm of conversation changes the moment Michelino is mentioned. Bellavita cannot understand why Denora needs a third party, and a lawyer at that, to make a proposal for Michelino. Contento tries to calm him:

> *Contento*. Non v'allarmate, non v'allarmate prima di sapere di
>
> che cosa voglio parlarvi!
> *Bellavita*. Ma sissignore che m'allarmo! M'allarmo perché, se
> il signor Notajo è ricorso a lei...
> *Contento*. ...ma io sono anche amico vostro...
> *Bellavita*. Grazie. signor avvocato - che amico, no! - troppo
> onore - lei m'è padrone! - Ma vede? io... io ecco - appassisco
> appassisco...[*MN*, II, 595]
> [*Contento*. Don't be alarmed, don't be alarmed before you know
> what I want to talk to you about!
> *Bellavita*. But I am alarmed! I'm alarmed because, if the notary
> came to see you ...
> *Contento*. ... but I'm your friend as well ...
> *Bellavita*. Thank you, Mr Lawyer - but not a friend! - you do
> me too much honour - you're way above me! - But you see? I - I
> - that's it - I'm fading - fading ...]

When Contento finally manages to tell him that the proposal is to send Michelino to school in Naples, Bellavita responds with a series of incredulous questions: 'Il ragazzo? a Napoli? [...] E perché? [...] A Napoli?' [The boy? to Naples? [...] Why? [...] To Naples?]. The idea of separating himself from Michelino is unthinkable: 'Io? Ma che dice? Io, dal ragazzo? [...] Separarmi? Signor avvocato, che dice? [...] Ma scusi, perché? [...] Ma il ragazzo qua studia; va bene a scuola; e il Notajo lo sa! Mandarlo a Napoli? E io? Ah, ma dunque non vuol più tener conto di me il signor Notajo?' [*MN*, II, 596] [Me? What are you saying? Me and the boy? [...] Separated from him? What are you saying, Mr Lawyer? [...] Why, please? [...] But the boy's studying here; he's doing well at school; and the notary knows it! Send him to Naples? Oh, so the notary no longer wants to take me into account?]. Bellavita's disturbed amazement at the suggestion expresses itself in this series of interrogatives; it is his first reaction as he tries to understand this threatening new situation.

Let us now look at the equivalent episode in *Tutto per bene*, up to Lori's first reaction to the truth which comes to him not through an intermediary chosen by Salvo, but inadvertently from Palma, who in the penumbra greets him as 'Papà', mistaking him for Salvo.

Lori takes his entrance returning home after the wedding, to find two unwelcome visitors, la Barbetti and Carletto. La Barbetti is Palma's grandmother and Carletto her step-uncle. They were unknown to the family as Lori's wife, Silvia, had rejected her mother when the latter abandoned her much loved father, the scientist Bernardo Agliani. Lori feels indignation that these two intruders should be welcomed by Palma, with no thought of how her mother would have felt. After a few brief exchanges ('Tu capisci, Palma, che se tua madre fosse qua...' [*MN*, I, 1118]) [You understand, Palma, that if your mother were here ...], Lori voices his disapproval, the stronger as the visitors have brought a present and promised to do even more for Palma.

> *Lori (non riuscendo più a contenersi).*Tuo nonno, Bernardo Agliani, restituì a costei tutti i suoi denari, anche quelli della dote, che appartenevano a tua madre; e tua madre ne fu felicissima, e preferì, rimasta orfana, guadagnarsi il pane, insegnando. Ma fai, fai, prendi pure: turbo la tua festa, e non ho più neanche il diritto di parlare, come t'ha detto la signora...
> [*MN*, I, 1119]
> [*Lori (no longer able to contain himself)*. Your grandfather, Bernardo Agliani, gave her back all her money, even that of her dowry, which belonged to your mother; and your mother was very happy at this, and when he died she preferred to earn her living by teaching. But go ahead, go ahead, take it: I'm spoiling your party, and I no longer have the right to speak out, as the signora has told you ...].

At this point, Salvo Manfroni and Marchese Flavio Gualdi, Palma's husband, make their entrance and Lori fades out of the conversation as they engage with

Palma and the visitors. Here there is an example of turn loss. Lori wants to
speak, but he misses his opportunity.[3] Palma suggests the whole episode should
be taken lightly: 'quando si sta per andar via...', to which Falvio agrees: 'Ma sí,
per me, figurati!', and la Barbetti triumphs: '(*con sincerità*) Ecco, già, come
dicevo io!' It is only now that Lori manages to intervene: '(*ferito dalle ultime
parole di Palma*) Potevo non volerlo anche per te, mentre ti stacchi da questa
casa...' [*MN*, I, 1120-1121]. ['when you're about to go away'; 'Yes, as far as I'm
concerned'; '(*with sincerity*) Yes, it's as I told you'; '(*hurt by Palma's last words*)
I could have not wanted it for you as well, as you go away from this house ...'].
Lori feels out of his depth, his statements now reveal pain and incomprehension
at his brusque treatment by his daughter and their benefactor, Salvo Manfroni,
who had provided her with a husband and dowry. First there is a dialogue with
Salvo who tries to suggest to Lori the inappropriateness of his position;
thinking that Lori knows the situation, he has a brief exchange with him at
cross purposes, which allows both of them to continue with their illusions.

> *Lori.* Posso ritrarmi da qualunque sentimento! Da questo, no!
> no! perché non vivo d'altro, tu lo sai!
> *Salvo (concitato, quasi tra sé)* È incredibile! incredibile!
> > *Poi, aggressivo, rapidamente:*
> Va bene; persisti in codesta fissazione; ma accorgiti almeno
> della pena che fai a chi ti vede intestato cosí, e vorrebbe cacciarti
> dal ridicolo in cui ti metti da te stesso!
> *Lori.* Dal ridicolo? Ti pare ridicolo?
> *Salvo.* Ma sí, caro mio, perché esageri, esageri maledettamente! E
> giusto ora che Palma si libera e ti libera, santo Dio, potevi farne a
> meno! [*MN*, I, 1122]
> [*Lori.* I can put all feelings to one side! But not this one! no!
> because it's all I live for, and you know it!
> *Salvo. (angrily, almost to himself).* It's incredible! incredible!
> > *(Then, aggressive, quickly)*
> All right; you're carrying on with your obsession; but at least realize
> the distress you're causing to those who see you being so obstinate and
> want to try to stop you making yourself ridiculous!
> *Lori* Ridiculous? You think it's ridiculous?
> *Salvo.* Of course, my dear fellow, because what you're doing is so
> damned exaggerated! And right now when Palma's freeing herself
> and you, good God, you could behave differently!]

With Palma too, there is the same talking at cross purposes:

> *Lori.* [...] una lunga sofferenza che tu - (non dirmi di no, perché
> è chiaro) - non hai, non hai indovinato, non hai supposto, e non
> supponi ancora in me.
> *Palma.* Ma chi te lo dice, Dio mio?
> *Lori.* Ecco. Il tono stesso con cui me lo domandi.
> *Palma.* No, scusa, questo tono è appunto perché la conosco, e la
> conosco bene, codesta tua sofferenza, su cui è edificata, vuoi
> dirmi questo? la mia fortuna! Oh! e vuoi che non lo sappia,
> scusa?
> *Lori.* Saperlo, non dovrebbe voler dire il fastidio che ne mostri.
> *Palma.* Ma non è fastidio; è che proprio non vedo piú la ragione,
> scusa, per cui vuoi ricordarmela anche adesso, quando ha già
> finito di pesar tanto, credi, su te, su me, su tutti... [*MN*, I, 1127-
> 1128].
> [*Lori* [...] I've suffered so long and you - (don't say no to me,
> because it's clear) - you've never, never seen it, never imagined,
> and still don't imagine I suffer.
> *Palma.* But who says so, for heaven's sake?
> *Lori.* That does. The very tone of voice in which you ask me.
> *Palma.* No, you're wrong, I'm speaking like this precisely
> because I know, and I know well, your suffering on which my
> good fortune, is this what you're telling me? is built. Oh, and
> you expect me not to know, do you?
> *Lori.* Knowing shouldn't mean that it annoys you so much.
> *Palma.* I'm not annoyed; it's just that I no longer see why,
> forgive me, you want to remind me of it even now, when believe
> me it has already stopped being such a burden, on you, on me,
> on everyone ...]

Lori's later conversations, when he visits Palma in her new home, are
similar to the ones on her wedding day. In a dialogue with Salvo, who tries
again to tell him of the inappropriateness of his behaviour, he responds with
brief, pained rejoinders: '*Salvo (non potendone piú)*. Ma è tutto un modo di
agire, il tuo, abbi pazienza, anche di fronte a me... *Lori (stupito)*. Il mio?' [*MN*,
I, 1143] *Salvo (out of patience)*. But it's your whole way of behaving, for
goodness' sake, even with me ... *Lori (astonished)*. My way of behaving?]
Salvo tells him there is no reason why he should not come to see Palma: 'Vieni,
ma con un'aria, con un tono piú conveniente, ormai, che renda anche agli altri
piú agevole il trattare con te... *Lori*. Ma mi sembra che io...' [*MN*, I, 1143]

[Come, but behave and speak in a more suitable way, now, so that it's easier for other people to deal with you ... *Lori.* But I think that I ...] To Salvo's suggestion that Lori should stop expecting so much and change his ways: 'E perciò ti dico di smettere, di cambiare, come sono cambiate le condizioni...' Lori reacts uncomprehendingly: 'E come potrei cambiare?' [*MN*, I, 1143] ['And so I'm telling you to stop it and to change, just as circumstances have changed'; 'And how could I change?']

At this point there is an interruption and Lori is eventually left alone with Signorina Cei, Palma's companion. Apart from the instance when Lori tries to assert himself over la Barbetti's visit and is explicit in his denunciation of her, there is one other occasion, before the revelation, when he is again explicit. It is in this encounter with Signorina Cei, who realizes he knows about Salvo Manfroni's plagiarism of Bernardo Agliani's scientific papers and asks him why he kept quiet. Lori tells her openly of the effect this discovery had on him: 'Lei non sa che cosa è stata per me la scoperta di quegli appunti... non solo perché ha offeso in me, offuscato tutto a un tratto la stima, l'ammirazione infinita che avevo per lui; no, no, non per questo soltanto' [*MN*, I, 1146] [You don't know what the discovery of those notes meant to me ... not only because straight away it harmed and clouded the respect, the boundless admiration I had for him; no, no, it wasn't just that.] The other reason he gives is a more personal one, again clearly stated. He knew he should not have kept silent; his ill-treatment at the hands of Salvo and Palma, he felt, was fitting punishment for his cowardice at not revealing the truth.

Parallel to Bellavita's immediate reaction, in the form of anguished questions, to the suggestion that Michelino be taken from him and educated in Naples, is Lori's reaction to the revelation that Palma is Salvo's daughter; the revelation is more terrible for Lori in that it implied infidelity on the part of an adored wife, an infidelity which instead Bellavita had lived with consciously for ten years. After the mistaken appellation, Palma is brutally frank: 'Tu sai bene che mio padre è lui, e che io non devo chiamare così altri che lui' [*MN*, I, 1150] [You know very well that he's my father, and that he is the only one I have to call that]. This sets off a sequence of horrified questions from Lori: 'Lui - tuo padre?... Che... che dici? [...] Che dici, che dici? Chi te l'ha detto, lui? [...] T'ha detto che tu sei sua figlia?' [*MN*, I, 1150] [Him - your father? ... What ... what are you saying? [...] Who told you, him? [...] He told you that you're his daughter?]. Palma insists: 'E che tu sai tutto!' [*MN*, I, 1150] [And that you know everything!]. This again occasions a series of anguished interrogatives, exclamations, repetitions and suspensions, four syntactic traits which, as we have already seen in the case of Denora, Pirandello combines in speeches which are particularly fraught: 'Io? [...] T'ha detto che io so? Oh Dio... Oh Dio... Ah che cosa!...[4] Come t'ha detto? dimmi come t'ha detto! [...] Voglio saperlo! voglio saperlo!' [*MN*, I, 1150] [Me? [...] He told you I knew? Oh, God ... Oh, God ... What a terrible thing! [...] What did he tell you? Tell me what he told you! [...] I want to know! I want to know]. The exchange inevitably shifts to the question of the mother. Lori claims: 'Non so nulla! Ti disse che tua madre...? Parla! Parla! [...] Che lei... di'? di'? [...] Ti disse che fu la sua amante?' [*MN*, I, 1150] [I don't know anything! Did he say that your mother ... ? Speak up! Speak up! [...] That she ... well? well? [...] He told you that she was his lover?] Palma, who in the course of this conversation has gradually come to realise that Lori knew nothing, now wants to avoid wounding him and lamely answers: 'Ma no...', which occasions an outburst from Lori, longer than his previous speeches, but like them constituted of questions, exclamations, repetitions and suspensions: 'No? Come no? Se ti disse che sei sua figlia! [...] Oh Dio... oh Dio... Possibile? Possibile?... Lei!... Non è possibile! No! Egli ha mentito... ha mentito... ha mentito... perché... perché non... non è possibile... che lei...' [*MN*, I, 1150] [No? How can it be no? If he told you you're his daughter! [...] Oh, God ... Oh, God ... Is it possible? Is it possible? ... Her! ... It isn't possible! No! He's been lying ... lying ... lying ... because ... because it isn't ... it isn't possible ... that she ...]. Here again it can be observed that these traits are particularly evident in the passage we are discussing, but they appear also in other sections of the play which are less emotionally charged. For instance, the opening scene with the exchange between la Barbetti and Carletto consists almost exclusively of interrogatives and exclamations, with frequent use of suspension dots. These may of course have different functions indicating either a sentence left unfinished by the speaker,[5] as in: 'Ma introdurci cosí... [MN, I, 1107] [But to come in like this ...] or an interruption, as in: 'con l'ajuto di tuo cognato... *Carletto (con uno scatto)*. Ma che cognato, per carità!' [MN, I, 1108] [with the help of your brother-in-law ... *Carletto (angrily)*. What brother-in-law, for heaven's sake!]. It is noticeable that in the fragmented syntax of excited exchanges between Palma and Lori at the end of Act II, the dots indicate suspensions (the inability of the speakers to complete their sentences under the stress of emotions and revelations they cannot come to terms with) rather than interruptions. The interruptions in the first part, with la Barbetti and Carletto, seem to correspond to the realm of petty family contrasts, whereas the suspensions in the dialogue between Palma and Lori are indicative of an emotionally tense situation in which both participants are united in the distress of their new knowledge.

3. *Coming to terms with reality*

After the first moments of shock have passed for both Bellavita and Lori, there is an attempt to take more rational stock of the situation and to work out a strategy for the future. In the case of Bellavita it is a strategy he devises for himself - he has no allies; in the case of Lori, it is a strategy suggested by Palma, who now realises how he has been wronged. In the dialogue with Bellavita, the lawyer tries to point out to him, as Salvo had done with Lori, that his behaviour was no longer appropriate. It is this advice which gives Bellavita the inspiration of how he should proceed. The first part of this conversation is conducted in brief statements and questions. Contento has mentioned the excess of 'remissione' shown by Bellavita, who fails to understand him: 'Remissione? [...] Che vuol dire remissione, scusi? Non capisco' [MN, II, 598] [I'm remissive? [...] What does remissive mean, please? I don't understand.]. When he has grasped that it is his respect for Denora which is considered ridiculous, at first he is incredulous: 'Lui che per piú di dieci anni mi ha reso lo zimbello di tutto il paese, ora teme il ridicolo. - Lui!' [*MN*, II, 599] [This man who for more than ten years has made me the laughing-stock of the whole town is now afraid of ridicule. - Him!] His speeches now get longer, he is regaining his self-confidence as he glimpses the possibility of revenge. He agrees not to go and see Denora any more, either alone or with the boy, 'ma quanto a rispettarlo, eh! quanto a rispettarlo - mi dispiace - ma non posso farne a meno, glielo dica' [*MN*, II, 599] [but as for respecting him. ah! as for respecting him - I'm sorry - but I can't help doing that, tell him.] It is Contento's turn to be bewildered: 'Come sarebbe a dire?', to which Bellavita replies: 'Eh, rispettarlo. Me lo può forse proibire? L'ho sempre rispettato, quando il rispetto poteva costarmi avvilimento e mortificazione; e vuole che ora, proprio ora, cosí d'un tratto, non lo rispetti più? Non è possibile, signor avvocato! - Per forza, sempre, lo rispetterò: glielo dica' [*MN*, II, 599] ['What does that mean?'; 'Ah, respect him. Can he perhaps forbid me to do that? I've always respected him, when respect could bring me humiliation and mortification; and now, of all times, just like that, he wants me not to respect him any longer? It isn't possible, Mr Lawyer! - I shall necessarily, always, respect him: tell him that.] In these last two exchanges of Bellavita's, the element which had at first disturbed him, the fact that he was being spoken to by an intermediary, is now seized on to make his point: 'glielo dica', he emphasises. Contento is beginning to get the message: 'Ah come allora, per dispetto?'. Bellavita this time is explicit: "No, che dispetto! Mi scusi: me l'insegna lui, ora, il mezzo di vendicarmi, e vuole che io non me ne approfitti?' [*MN*, II, 599] ['Well, then, out of spite?'; 'No, not spite! Look: he is now showing me the way to take my revenge, and you want me not to take advantage of it?']. At this point the antagonist Denora bursts in.

Let us see how the parallel section is treated in *Tutto per bene*, up to the appearance of Salvo Manfroni. Lori goes over episodes in his life which should have alerted him to the reality which he has just learnt from Palma. There are two particularly long and important speeches, both of over three hundred words. One reconstructs his first unhappy year of marriage and then his wife's repentance and the subsequent harmony of their life together. [6] The second re-evokes the deathbed scene already mentioned, where Salvo's aggressiveness had been interpreted by Lori as guilt for his responsibility for Silvia's death, as she had caught a chill when Salvo had accompanied her and the three year old Palma to a circus. The first speech still reveals Lori's agitation. It is full of that expressive combination of interrogatives, suspensions, exclamations and repetitions:

> Questo? io? potevo saper questo e sopportare d'esser trattato
> cosí? e che lui... Ah Dio ... fu certo allora ... Sí, sí ... Dovette
> essere allora ... Sí ... L'insegnamento ... voleva riprendere
> l'insegnamento ... [...] Ma già! Ma ecco ... ecco perché lui,
> quando fu Ministro, prese me ... E io abbagliato, abbagliato da
> due glorie, da quella del padre, dal prestigio di lui, mio capo
> supremo, mio padrone, non vidi nulla! non vidi nulla!' [*MN*, I,
> 1151]
> [This? me? could I have known this and have borne to be treated like
> that? and that he ... Oh, God ... it was certainly then ... Yes, yes ... It
> had to be then ... Yes ... teaching ... she wanted to start teaching again
> ... [...] But of course! But that's ... that's why he, when he was a
> Minister, took me on ... And I was dazzled, dazzled by two glories, by
> that of her father, and by his prestige, my supreme boss, my master, I
> saw nothing! I saw nothing!]

The intervening exchanges are briefer, but there are several rejoinders by Lori of over a hundred words, in which he tries to come to terms with the contempt Salvo Manfroni and Palma must have felt for him if they thought he had been the complaisant husband out of self-interest, and in which he also goes over the misunderstandings which had resulted from their different expectations. These speeches oscillate between the disjointed: 'E dove sono stato io? ... Come sono stato? ... Oh Dio! Ma allora non sono stato mai nella vita, io...' [*MN*, I, 1153] [And where have I been? ... What sort of person have I been? ... Oh, God! But then, me, I've never really been part of life ...], and the well argued: 'In una illusione ho vissuto senza nessun sostegno! perché voi tutti me li avete sempre tolti, tolti, perché vi parevano inutili, e mi lasciavate con scherno, con disprezzo appoggiare a quella morta per la rappresentazione

esagerata della mia commedia' [*MN*, I, 1153] [I've lived in an illusion without
any support! because all of you have always taken my support away, away from
me, because it seemed pointless to you, and with derision and contempt you let
me lean on that dead woman, over-doing my comedy.]

When we get to the second long speech, his relationship with Palma is
already in the process of changing, as she kneels before him, concerned about
his welfare, and he is able to give a very coherent account of the deathbed
scene; but as he ends his account, his desire for revenge comes to the fore and
he swears that Salvo will pay for the tears he made him shed. The conversation
with Palma closes on an excited note, as Lori wants to escape and think about
his revenge. Palma tries to stop him: 'Ma assurdo, dopo tanto tempo, scusa ...
Dove vai? *Lori (come un pazzo).* Non lo so... *Palma.* Rimani ancora qua. *Lori.*
No ... no ... [*MN*, I, 1156] [But it's absurd, isn't it, after all this time ... Where
are you going? *Lori (like a madman).* I don't know ... *Palma.* Stay here a bit
longer. *Lori.* No ... no ...] His destination is in fact Salvo Manfroni's house,
where he awaits his return and compulsively starts talking to Salvo's
manservant of long standing, whom he questions about his master's affairs in
the past, as if wishing to humiliate himself totally. He imagines the women
who were received by Salvo:

> Signorette maritate di fresco ... E quando fu ministro, poi,
> giovani mogli di impiegati...
> > *Notando che il cameriere si turba. aggiunge subito
> > furbescamente:*
> Fui suo capo di gabinetto, e lo so ... Posti di fiducia! Non
> s'ottengono, caro mio, se non a costo di passare sotto certe
> forche...
> *Fa le corna, pallido e ridente. e gliele mostra. Il cameriere lo
> guarda sbigottito.*
> [*MN*, I, 1160]
> > [Young newly-married ladies ... And when he was a Minister, then,
> > the young wives of employees ..
> > *Seeing that the manservant is disturbed, he adds at once, slyly:*
> I was the head of his office, and I know ... Positions of trust! You
> don't get them, dear man, unless you're prepared to suffer for them ...
> *He makes the sign for cuckoldry, pale and laughing, and shows it to
> the manservant. The manservant looks at him dumbfounded.*]

The manservant is taken aback even further when the description becomes more personal: 'Chi sa quante volte se la sarà stretta qua, lui, cosí, e baciata, eh?' [*MN*, I, 1161] [Who knows how many times he held her in his arms here, like that, and kissed her, eh?]. Lori has worked himself into a state which will make him unrecognisable to Salvo when he enters, just as Bellavita has gained strength to stand up to Denora.

4. *Effect of revelation and public resolution*

The opening exchange between Denora and Bellavita reveals their social relationship: to Denora's outburst, using the familiar *tu*: 'Ah tu vuoi dunque vendicarti cosí?', Bellavita replies with courtesy: 'Io no, signor Notajo!' [*MN*, II, 600] ['Ah, so you want to taake your revenge in that way?'; 'Not me, Mr Notary'], but his courtesy has now become a weapon. The more Denora insists Bellavita must give up his respect, the more Bellavita claims it is impossible, until Denora, driven to exasperation, loses all self-control: '(*fremendo*). Ti prendo a calci, sai, Bellavita!' [*MN*, II, 600] [(*trembling with rage*). I'll kick you, you know, Bellavita] which provokes encouragement and gratitude from the future recipient: 'Forza! Calci! E lo ringrazierò, pubblicamente!' [*MN*, II, 600] ['Go on! Let him kick me! And I'll thank him publicly].

Although the lawyer has been present, the conversation is carried on as a duologue, with Contento limiting himself to restraining Denora physically and uttering the words: "No, per carità! Che fate, Notajo!' [*MN*, II, 600] [No, for goodness' sake! What are you doing, Notary!]. The uproar has however attracted the attention of the other clients waiting, who enter the room to see what is happening. Bellavita now has a larger audience with whom he wants to share his new-found confidence, which he expresses in a series of chilling exclamations: 'Ah che sollievo, signori miei! Posso ridere! posso ridere! Ho pianto tanto! Ora posso ridere! Ridere e far ridere tutti con me del pianto che ho fatto finora per questo ingrato! Ah, che sollievo!' [*MN*, II, 601] [Ah what a relief. I can laugh! I can laugh! I've cried so much! Now I can laugh! Laugh and make everyone laugh with me at the tears I've wept up to now for this ungrateful wretch! Ah, what a relief!]. He loses all inhibitions and turns to another cuckold, il signor Giorgino, to whose horror, but to the amusement of everyone else, he spells out his remedy: 'Cervo! cervo come me! Ma non ne faccia caso, ché non è niente! Si vuole vendicare? - Veneri, veneri, si metta a venerare, a incensare davanti a tutti l'amante di sua moglie' [*MN*, I, 601] [Horned! horned like me! But pay no attention, because it's nothing! Do you want revenge? - Worship, worship, start worshipping, flattering your wife's lover in front of everyone]. He bows and raises his hat repeatedly to Denora, who rushes out whilst Bellavita has the last word. He is going to dress in black and shadow Denora wherever he goes; the final image is one of juxtaposition: 'Prosegue; proseguo. Lui il corpo, ed io l'ombra! L'ombra del suo rimorso!' [*MN*, I, 602] [He moves; I follow. He's the body, and I'm the shadow! The shadow of his remorse!].

The pattern which we have observed at the close of *Bellavita*, with the conversation between protagonist and antagonist, extended at the finale to more characters, is also found in the third act of *Tutto per bene*. At first Lori and Salvo are alone together, and the new Lori asserts himself at the start of this encounter by refusing to shake Salvo's hand and informing him that he has two things to tell him. Seeing Lori assert himself in this way causes Salvo to comment: 'Io non ti riconosco piú', to which comes the reply: 'Eh sfido! Sono un altro, da tre ore!' [*MN*, I, 1162] ['I don't recognise you any longer'; 'I'm sure! I've been a different man for three hours']. Whereas formerly their conversation had been allusive and ambiguous, it now becomes explicit, and on the part of Lori, harsh - he explains he knew nothing: 'Nulla. Né che mia moglie fosse stata la tua amante, né che Palma fosse tua figlia ...' [*MN*, I, 1162] {Nothing! Neither that my wife had been your lover, nor that Palma was your daughter ...]. Whereas formerly Lori had said very little in Salvo's presence, he is now eloquent. He makes a speech of over two hundred words, in which he re-examines the knowledge gained in the last three hours. He uses rhetorical devices, addressing himself:

Com'hai potuto credere che un deputato che non ti conosceva, diventando ministro, prendesse te, umile segretario di ministero, e solo perché avevi sposato la figlia di un suo maestro, ti mettesse a capo del suo gabinetto? e poi, morta la moglie, s'affezionasse tanto alla tua bambina, e te la crescesse come sua, e le trovasse marito, costituendole una vistosissima dote? [*MN*, I, 1162].

[How could you believe that a member of Parliament, who didn't know you, when he became a Minister would take you, a Minister's humble secretary, and simply because you had married the daughter of a teacher of his would make you head of his office? and then, when your wife was dead, would show such affection for your daughter, and bring her up like his, and find her a husband, giving her an enormous dowry?]

He then switches from addressing himself to addressing Salvo: 'Credetti all'onestà di quella donna, capisci? [...] Credetti nella tua venerazione per il tuo maestro, nonostante che poi ebbi la prova che, altro che venerazione, la tua!' [*MN*, I, 1162]. [I believed in the virtue of that woman, you see? [...] I believed in your veneration for your teacher, even though I later had the proof that it was anything but veneration]. This is the second fact that Lori wants to tell Salvo, that he was aware of the plagiarism. This revelation, which changes the relationship between the two men further, leaving Salvo clearly in the inferior position, is interrupted by the telephone ringing, after another rhetorical speech by Lori, in which he talks about his naiveté being assailed by the thorns of this discovery ('la mia ingenuità come in un covo di spine, di spine che la punsero da tutte le parti, a sangue' [*MN*, I, 1163]).

Again Lori asserts himself in the quick exchange which follows. He knows it is Palma on the phone, and requests that she and her husband come over, so that the four of them can decide what to do: '*Lori*. Voglio che c'intendiamo bene, tutti e quattro. *Salvo*. Ma su che? Se siamo già intesi! *Lori*. No. Per l'avvenire. Dobbiamo stabilire tante cose. *Salvo*. Lo faremo domani, se mai! *Lori*. Ora! ora!' [*MN*, I, 1163] *[Lori*. I want the four of us to understand each other properly. *Salvo*. But about what, if we're already in agreement! *Lori*. No, for the future. We have to decide on so much. *Salvo*. We'll do it tomorrow, if we have to! *Lori*. Now! now!]. While they are waiting for Palma and Flavio to arrive, Lori insists on finding out how the affair started, and pursues every point, wounding himself and even more Salvo, who tries to cut him short (*'Per troncare* [...] Smetti, ti prego! [...] non so che gusto provi [...] Basta, basta ora, ti prego!' [*MN*, I, 1165] [*To cut things short* [...] Please stop! [...] I don't know why you're doing it [...] That's enough, now, please!]). Lori now sees the situation clearly and wants to have his revenge: 'Oh! t'odiò, t'odiò, quando ritornò a me! S'accorse che a te era più cara la tua ambizione, e t'odiò!'. Salvo does not even try to contradict him: 'Ma sí, lo so bene...' - anything to bring the conversation to an end. But Lori stresses: 'Per me comincia adesso!' [*MN*, I, 1165] ['Oh, she hated you, she hated you, when she came back to me! She knew that your ambition was dearer to you, and she hated you!'; 'Well yes, I know that'; 'for me it's starting now!'].

Whereas in previous conversations Salvo had tried to silence Lori, because he was irritated by what seemed to him inappropriate considerations, but he had felt secure in his superiority, now he tries to silence him because he senses that the conversation can only show him up in a worse light. On the one occasion he tries to reassert himself, he does in fact condemn himself further. He vaunts, although hesitatingly, his social position: 'Ma... non so, io... io potrei fare ancora qualcosa per te...' Lori lunges out at him, physically and verbally: 'Tu? Meriteresti d'essere ucciso ora, per questo che hai detto!' [*MN*, I, 1166] ['But ... I don't know, I ... I could still do something for you ... ' ; 'You? You deserve to be killed now, for what you have just said'.]

By the time Palma and Flavio arrive, Lori is master of the situation and leads the conversation in the direction he chooses. He acts as puppet master, claiming he is Palma's real father and getting them all to agree. In terms of turn taking, whereas in the past when there was more than one person present he missed his turn, he now takes the lead, and first involves in conversation Palma, who is ready to recognise him as her father. He does not have to be commanding to be listened to, even in his torment he can now impose himself. To her he refers to the 'comedy' he has been playing, which took them all in; to Salvo, who expresses some relief ('E dunque basta, via...') [*MN*, I, 1169] [So that's it, come on ...], he talks about the consequences of pretence and how he would like to escape from himself. His speeches are about a hundred words long, as opposed to the five or six word exchanges of the others, who are nonplussed by the situation. Lori however still has his strongest card to play, the accusation of plagiarism in front of all three of them. Here the statement is unequivocal and brief: 'Un ladro! Un ladro! [...] È un ladro, perché ha rubato a Bernardo Agliani!' [*MN*, I, 1170] [A thief! A thief! [...] He's a thief because he stole from Bernardo Agliani]. The dialogue with Salvo, who at first tries both to laugh off the accusation, and to claim that no-one would believe Lori rather than him, is composed of rapid, brief exchanges: '*Lori.* Ti smarrisci... *Salvo.* No! *Lori.* Ti sei fatto pallido. E ora arrossisci! [*MN*, I, 1171] [*Lori.* You're confused ... *Salvo.* No! *Lori.* You went pale. And now you're blushing!].

Lori decides that revenge is despicable, all that matters is that Palma should believe him. Having ascertained this, he is ready to leave. At this point Palma intervenes. She and Flavio show solidarity for Lori, whilst Salvo is left out of their considerations completely, and no longer takes part in the conversation. Palma's suggestion is that the relationship which before had been an illusion, should now become true: she will be Lori's real daughter. Now it is Palma who takes command: her statements are decisive and persuasive, whilst Lori is disorientated: '*Palma.* Anche tu! anche tu! lo crederai anche tu, per forza! *Lori.* Io?... come?... [...] *Palma.* No! Nessuna commedia! Il mio affetto vero, ti dico! *Flavio.* Sí, certo ... Sarà cosi... *Lori (a Flavio).* Tutto per bene?...' [*MN*, I, 1174] [*Palma.* You too! you too! you'll have to believe it as well! *Lori.* Me? ... how ? ... [...] *Palma.* No! No play-acting! I telll you my affection is real! *Flavio.* Yes, certainly ... That's how it will be ... *Lori (to Flavio).* All for the best? ...] A dazed Lori is led off at the end, taking leave of Manfroni with a gesture of the hand and a slight bow, turning to Palma with the final words of the play: 'Tutto per bene...' .

The last exchanges of the two plays are indicative of the different outcomes: Bellavita is determined in his solitary revenge; he has found strength in himself and has nothing to lose from the new situation. Lori is dependent on others for his new position. He has lived an illusion for so long, that the temptation to make it real is very strong, but for this he needs others, and confidence in himself is not sufficient. The final gesture of dismissal, the bow, also has different connotations: for Bellavita it is the prelude to a last vindictive outburst, whereas for Lori it is the silent enactment of the ambivalent ('Tutto per bene') resolution.

ANNA LAURA LEPSCHY

NOTES

1 G. Nencioni, *Tra grammatica e retorica. Da Dante a Pirandello*, Turin, Einaudi, 1983, p. 212.

2 The focalization for these memories is instead from the point of view of Bellavita in the corresponding short story *L'ombra del rimorso* (1914) [*NA*, I, 1130-1].

3 For turn taking categories with reference to Pirandello, see M. Günsberg's chapter 'Reconstructing the Family: the Power of Speech in *Six Characters in Search of an Author*', in her book *Patriarchal Representation: Gender and Discourse in Pirandello*, Oxford, Berg, 1994.

4 For these and other interjections, see the article by G. Nencioni, 'L'interiezione nel dialogo di Pirandello', in *Tra grammatica e retorica*, cit., pp. 210-53. Here it is a case of 'l'esclamazione che, sorgendo su quanto l'emittente ha finito di dire, esprime la sua autoreazione emotiva (*interiezione reattiva*, anziché *incitativa*, la chiama infatti Karcevskij ['Introduction à l'étude de l'interjection', *Cahiers Ferdinand de Saussure*, vol. I (1941), pp. 57-75]), p. 232. See also M. L. Altieri Biagi, *La lingua in scena*, Bologna, Zanichelli, 1980, p. 93: 'Se [Pirandello] vi inserisce *interiezioni, intercalari*, è per mimare l'affanno di un ragionamento che non segue le scansioni sintattiche della logica abituale, ma procede a tentoni, con le segmentazioni, le pause, le inversioni (le anticipazioni, le posticipazioni) di un'*idea* che si fa sentimento [...]'.

5 On the function of silence in Pirandello (together with other interesting linguistic observations), see M. A. Grignani, 'Il farsi e il disfarsi del linguaggio: retorica del discorso e del silenzio', in E. Lauretta (ed.), *La persona nell'opera di Luigi Pirandello*, Milan, Mursia, 1990, pp. 175-89.

⁶ This is part of the narrative in the short story *Tutto per bene*, (1906), *NA*, I, p.347 ff.

ORCHESTRATING THE INCONGRUITIES;
SEI PERSONAGGI IN CERCA D'AUTORE

1. Genesis

The genesis of *Sei personaggi in cerca d'autore*, according to a letter dated 23 July 1917 which Pirandello wrote to his son, Stefano, can be traced back to the first World War. In this letter Pirandello gives the title of the work, and speaks of a 'romanzo da fare' [novel to be written] based on the author's rejection of the characters who haunt him with their terrible drama. In the Mondadori edition of Pirandello's *Saggi, poesie, scritti vari* the relevant passage appears in a footnote to an undated fragment published by Corrado Alvaro in 1934. This fragment is mostly concerned with a description of the state of mind in which a man (later to be the Father in the play) sets out for the brothel of a certain 'Signora Pace'. There are also some allusions to the characters who, after being created by the author, pursue him acting out some of the scenes of the novel 'cosí come dovrebbero essere' [*SPSV*, 1256-1258] [just as they should be].

These two documents refer precisely to the genesis of the work, conceived of as a novel, and allow us to date it back to at least five years before Pirandello wrote the text of his play, very rapidly, in 1921. [1] Critics have also often referred to two short stories, *La tragedia di un personaggio* (1911) [The Tragedy of a Character] and *Colloquii coi personaggi* (1915) [Interviews with Characters], as precursors of *Sei personaggi*.

In my opinion we should make a clear distinction between the relevance of the short stories on the one hand and the letter and fragment on the other. In general, the short stories illustrate Pirandello's conception of the artistic birth of the characters as a 'living and eternal reality' which, once generated by the artist's creative mind acquires an autonomous existence of its own and so, to some extent, is independent of the author himself. This is the theme of the 'interviews' with the characters created by the author's imagination, which is an allegorical representation of Pirandello's conception of art, repeated both in the 1921 text of the play and the 1925 *Preface*. [2]

The two short stories do not appear to have played a particularly significant role in the genesis of *Sei personaggi*, except in as much as they show us that the text with which Pirandello began his revolution of theatre is in perfect accord with a notion of art which he had been developing and writing about for a long time. It is an aesthetic formula (whose origins have been amply studied [3]) which increasingly becomes thematic, part of the author's poetic and triggers off a process of self-consciousness of the text. In other words, it leads to a metaliterary discourse in line with a general tendency which has been shown to be part of the modernist trend. Moreover the germs of this theory have been found by Macchia in *Il fu Mattia Pascal* [4] [The Late Mattia Pascal] (1904) and linked via a single thread to *La tragedia di un personaggio*, the *Colloquii coi personaggi* and *Sei personaggi* itself. Macchia finds the matrix of Pirandello's idea in theosophical sources of the early twentieth century. We could, if we wish, go back even further to the essay *L'azione parlata* (1899) [Spoken Action], where Pirandello already expresses the essence of his aesthetic belief that: 'Dalle pagine scritte del dramma i personaggi, per prodigio d'arte, dovrebbero uscire, staccarsi vivi, semoventi' [*SPSV*, 1015] [The characters should emerge from the printed page through the prodigy of art, step out alive in their own right]; that if the characters created by a playwright are really 'characters', and not:

> ... manichini, ciascuno di essi avrà un particolar modo d'esprimersi, per cui, alla lettura, un lavoro drammatico dovrebbe risultare come scritto da tanti e non dal suo autore, come composto [...] dai singoli personaggi, nel fuoco dell'azione, e non dal suo autore. [*SPSV*, 1017]

[... puppets, each of them will have a particular mode of expression, so that on reading a play it should seem to have been written by many people and not by its author, as though composed [...] by the characters in the heat of the action, and not by its author.]

At this point it could be said that some small part of what Dr Fileno says in *La tragedia di un personaggio*, whose context is still the problem of the birth and autonomy of the character, ends up in almost identical form in the speeches of the Father in *Sei personaggi*. We know, however, that when writing his works Pirandello frequently used a collage technique which allowed him, years later, to re-use whole passages from his previous works. Critics have already cited countless examples of this. Relevant to the present argument is the fact that, for example, a passage from the *Colloquii coi personaggi* can be found in very similar form and with an identical content in the surreal short story *Di sera, un geranio* (1934). [5] In addition, in the fragment of a novel relevant to *Sei personaggi* the state of erotic excitement of the character who prepares to enter the brothel is described in a way almost identical to that of the young, newly-wed husband who prepares to consumate his marriage in the short story *Un cavallo nella luna* (1907). [6]

This is, therefore, a technique of composition which Pirandello had already used widely, so we cannot argue that one work is directly derived from another. Because of this the apparent 'loan' of Dr Fileno's words to the Father in *Sei personaggi* has little relevance to the precise problem of the genesis of the play.

Our conclusion must be that the only sure basis for our considerations is that Pirandello had the idea for *Sei personaggi* in 1917, and at that time thought of writing a novel whose story was based on a conflict between actants generated by the author's imagination and rejected by the author. We know also, as is shown by the very short fragment we have, that Pirandello did try for some time to write this novel, but was unable to do so until, all of a sudden, he was inspired to write a play rather than a novel

2. *Novel versus play.*

In the *Preface* to *Sei personaggi* which he added to the 1925 edition of the play Pirandello does not completely disavow the narrative matrix of the work. What he does though, with hindsight of course, is to add the genre of comedy to the works that his imagination dictates. He says that his imagination delights in bringing home the most discontented people in the world for him to write short stories, novels and plays about, but a little further on he adds that the initial intention of his imagination in bringing him the six characters was so that he would use them the subject for a magnificent novel. [7] Up to this time he had spoken only of short stories and novels, and even in the *Preface* he writes of characters who by some prodigy have stepped out of the pages of the book they were in - not bothering to say that this book does not exist because it has not actually been written -and who then insist that they should be brought to life through art. The way out of the problem, says Pirandello, came to him all of a sudden when he hit on the idea of writing a play based on the case of an author who refuses to let a some of his characters live. He adds that they have already detached themselves from him, have their own life, have acquired speech and movement and so have already by their own efforts in struggling against him become dramatic characters, which can move and speak by themselves.

The link with the ideas put forward years earlier in *L'azione parlata* is clear, but the sudden passage from characters in a novel to dramatic characters, mediated by the author's rejection of them, reads more like a verification than a convincing explanation. This is even more so because, as we know from the letter he wrote to his son in 1917, the six characters were thought of even then as characters rejected by their author, and their novel as a 'novel to be written'. So we should go further into the reasons for their conversion into characters for a play, and why the novel was not written during those years but, or so it seems, continued to obsess the mind of the author.

The causes of this long and difficult gestation have been linked to the serious personal difficulties which Pirandello had during those years. [8] On the one hand, according to Vicentini, the madness of Pirandello's wife, Antonietta, and her unjust accusations that her husband harboured incestuous desires for their daughter contributed to the thematic nucleus of *Sei personaggi*. [9] On the other the trauma of the outbreak of war, the departure of his son Stefano for the front and Stefano's subsequent imprisonment distracted Pirandello from his writing. He now saw narrative writing, in particular, as a arduous task, irrelevant to what was happening in the world and to his own personal vicissitudes. In an interview for *Le Temps* Pirandello spoke of the impossibility of writing not just novels but also short stories, and said that his preoccupations at this time could not be expressed in the forms he had used up to then.

These are the years in which Pirandello alternates between the reservations, doubts and theoretical objections which lead him to consider abandoning the writing of plays and intensive writing for the theatre. As Vicentini has shown, this situation applies up to and including the writing of *Sei personaggi*, so that the play which starts Pirandello's revolution of theatre was also intended to represent his theatrical swan-song. [10]

To these very interesting and well-founded arguments others could be added which are particularly relevant to *Sei personaggi*. In 1915 Pirandello had published his novel *Si gira!* [Shoot!], and he continued to work on it , although making only minor modifications, for the Treves edition of 1916. At the same time he began what was to prove the very lengthy task of writing his last novel, *Uno, nessuno e centomila* [One, No-one and a Hundred Thousand], and some chapters of the second book of this novel appeared again in 1915 in the review *Sapientia*. As we know from StefanoPirandello's *Preface* to the edition of the novel, which was published in serial form in the *Fiera letteraria* between 1925 and 1926, Pirandello continued to work on this text even when he was fully engaged in writing plays, as he considered it to be the work which best represented his thinking:

> T'hanno sforzato spesso le necessità della vita, e le tue stesse intime di creatore, a divagarti da questo lavoro> Ma ad esso sempre col desiderio tendevi. Raggiungerlo, ritrovarlo non appena conclusa una

fatica, è stato per quindici anni lo scopo che ti ha fatto lavorare con tanta alacrità. Rifugio tormentoso. Anche evitato, talvolta, e temuto, lo so. Forse non avresti scritto qualcuna delle tue commedie, se non ci fosse stato in attesa sul tuo tavolino il manoscritto incompiuto di *Uno, nessuno e centomila.* [11]

[The necessities of life and your own personal needs as a creative writer have often compelled you to put this work to one side. But it was always in your thoughts. To be able to go back to it, to find it again as soon as you had finished a hard task has been the aim which has made you work with such alacrity for fifteen years. An unquiet refuge. Even one, I know, you avoided and at times feared. Perhaps you would not have written some of your plays if the unfinished manuscript of *Uno, nesuno e centomila* had not been waiting for you on your desk.]

So although, also in 1917, Pirandello wrote *Cosí è (se vi pare)* [Right You Are (If You Think So)], which contains many elements, thematic and otherwise, which prelude *Sei personaggi*, he did not at all stop writing narrative works in that period; and indeed he had some major plans for this genre.

In this case it does not seem entirely strange that in those same years he thought of *Sei personaggi* as a novel. But if the author shows immediately that he wants to reject the 'story' that torments his c.haracters, his reasons could also apply to the story itself, as he conceived it. I think we could say that Pirandello, as a writer of narrative, is closely linked to the model of the novel centred on the fundamental theme of the 'search for meaning'. Even when this search, as in *Si gira!* and even more in *Uno, nessuno e centomila,* has a markedly negative outcome, it nevertheless gives his narrative work its form. This is so much so that even the metaliterary implications of these works, that is their self-conscious level, concern the problem of the role of novel-writing. It is a role which oscillates between that of *pharmacos* (*Si gira!*) and the reduction to silence (*Uno, nessuno e centomila*) and to the vanification of writing itself. In the latter novel the function of writing dissolves at the moment when Vitangelo Moscarda is forced to ascertain that there is no longer any meaning to seek for.

For the novel to express the search for meaning, it must be polyphonic and dialogic. This is what Bakhtin has taught us, insisting that the dialogic governs the construction of meaning both in the intrinsic relationship of the speaking subject with what others say and in the direct relationship with the 'comprehension of reply'. [12] The novel , that is, should represent a plurality of points of view in a dialectical relationship. The 'story' of the six characters, from what we know of it through the text of the play and from what Pirandello himself says in the *Preface*, is polyphonic in the sense that all the characters have their own mode of expression in artistic terms. But it is not dialogic as the different points of view do not so much interact as clash with each other without any possibility of mediation. As Gioanola has rightly said, in *Sei personaggi* Pirandello has represented the condition of the Family as the prison of the individual at its most absolute, as a sort of tightly-closed circle which it is impossible to leave. The non-dialectical situation of the pure pathos of the binding fetters of family relationships makes the 'psychological drama' impossible to perform. [13]

In a story so conceived the narrative discourse of events is substantially static, lacking that essential dialectic on which the search for meaning in the novel is based. It appears, therefore, inevitable that onto the closed circle of the characters should be superimposed the other vicious circle out of the author's refusal to give artistic life to the work. It is, in reality, a refusal which does not become apparent 'all of a sudden' but is there right from the first moment of the work's conception. Such a situation, when writing a novel, could have generated a metaliterary process which did not deal with the search for meaning, as we have tried to clarify it, and psychologism (of which there is a clear trace in the fragment we have). This process might possibly have focalized on a 'game' with the characters, rather like Queneau in *Icare envolé* , or Calvino, or moving closer to Pirandello like Bontempelli in *La vita intensa* [The Intense Life] and *La vita operosa* [The Active Life]. Pirandello was not yet ready for this type of narrative, in my opinion, if only because he had to finish *Uno, nessuno e centomila* which is also, in a way, a final reckoning of accounts with his typology of the novel.

In our view, therefore, the reasons which prevent *Sei personaggi* from becoming a novel are the same as those which make it impossible for the characters to act their story in the theatre. We shall deal later with this aspect of the play; what we should note now is that in the text of the play as well the 'story' of the characters retains its basic characteristic of a novel *manqué*.

When in the play the Father and the Stepdaughter clash in front of the Producer as they explain what they did the Father, at a certain point, asks the Producer to impose a bit of order so that he can make due explanation. The Stepdaughter bursts out with the cry: "Qui non si narra! Qui non si narra!" [*MN*, I, 87] [We're not telling a story here! We're not telling a story here!], and the Father replies: 'Ma io non narro! voglio spiegargli. [*MN*, I, 87] [I'm not telling a story! I want to explain to him]. But in fact the Characters' demand to be allowed to 'live' their story runs counter first and foremost to the fact that it can only be told, not acted. This is not so much because the author's rejection prevents them from acting themselves as because the 'story' in itself is a sequence of facts, comments and psychological situations which, as they stand, cannot be acted out on stage.

When the facts are put yet again the Producer interrupts, saying: 'Ma tutto questo è racconto' [*MN*, I, 91] [But all this is a story]. The Father and the Son then move on to discuss the opposition between reality and fiction, but what the Producer wanted to indicate was that the stuff of their drama is narrative, and not suited to the theatre. Moreover, as the Director himself observes, because it is narrative it does not satisfy the criteria of unity of place, time and action which are necessary for performance. It is difficult, therefore, to understand why he thought he could 'cavarne un bel dramma' [*MN*, I, 97]˙ [get a good play] from a subject which in all offers only one sequence which could perhaps be rendered on stage, that is, the scene at Madama Pace's. We should be quite clear that even the final scene in the garden has no dialogue, and so it can be narrated, explained and commented on but not made into theatre. So we might ask ourselves, provocatively, just what is in the script, written with mutual agreement, which the Director gives to the Prompter, saying: 'Guardi: questa è la traccia delle scene, atto per atto' [*MN*, I, 101] [Look: this is the outline of the scenes, Act by Act].

The six characters are and remain the actants of a novel which is intrinsically impossible or, if you prefer, of a novel *manqué*. Looking at it another way, putting them into a play alters the structural modalities of the work, as we shall see. It also coincides with and gives artistic voice to the theoretical problems and doubts about theatre which beset Pirandello in the same years in which his work for the theatre was winning increasing acclaim.

All this is linked to the theme of 'rejection', which we shall now consider.

3. Rejection

We have established that the rejection does not occur 'all of a sudden' but is inherent to the idea of *Sei personaggi*. What most probably does emerge all of a sudden is the connection between the author's rejection and the prospect of writing a play rather than a novel. In his *Preface* Pirandello declares that his refusal to write the 'story' of his characters springs from the fact that it was impossible to find in it 'un particolar senso della vita' [*MN*, I, 58] [a particular sense of life] which would give the creatures of his imagination 'un valore universale' [*MN*, I, 58] [universal significance]. This universal significance is found on a metaliterary plane, as the rejection of the 'tabloid news item' - as we might call it - of the tragedy of incest gives way to the existential awareness of the 'inganno della comprensione reciproca' [*MN*, I, 60] [delusion of mutual understanding] and the ensuing game of role-playing. The rejection is, therefore, a strategy of radical estrangement by the author, who removes his 'theological' word from the text. [14] So there is no organizing point of view, no axiological principle (in the sense of a conception of the world which imposes itself on the other conceptions and structures the work's ideologeme). This absence of a dominating point of view means that the characters are abandoned to their own conflicts. The author refuses to narrate, that is to explain, their conflicts, and this leads to the chaos of the different points of view which are held.

As Lone Klem has said:

> ... ognuno dei personaggi vuole il proprio dramma, perché non ne hanno nessuno in comune, e non è possibile scegliere un punto di vista, ugualmente rappresentativo per tutti i personaggi e per ogni aspetto del conflitto. [15]
> [... each of the characters wants his or her own drama, because they do not have one in common, and it is not possible to choose a point of view which is equally representative for all the characters and for every aspect of the conflict.]

From the state of conflict, which made the dialogic formulation of the projected novel impossible in the first place, comes the impossibility of dialogue. In theatrical terms this generates a situation centred on the game of role-playing, on the struggle to dominate the argument and on the obsessive verbalization, by the Father and the Stepdaughter, of their inner drama.

So when Pirandello declares that, having rejected the drama of the six characters he has nevertheless 'accolto l'essere rifiutando la ragion d'essere' [*MN*, I, 62] [accepted their being while rejecting their reason for being], this means that their 'reason for being' shifts from 'fact' to 'comment'. Letting them go 'dove son soliti d'andare i personaggi drammatici per aver vita: su un palcoscenico' [*MN*, I, 60] [where dramatic characters usually go to live: on a stage] means a theatrical exploitation of verbal (not dialogic but 'dialogized') and instinctual chaos at the expense of the 'story'. The only form for this chaos is dramatic, and indeed, at the moment when the Producer underlines the fact that the story cannot be staged the Father takes up the threads of the argument declaring: 'Il dramma viene adesso, signore! Nuovo, complesso.' [*MN*, I, 91] [The play comes now, sir! New, complex.]. This play will be the drama of mutual incomprehension which emerges from the commentary kept up by the Father and the Stepdaughter as they cut in on each other.

The metatheatrical implications of Pirandello's gesture in avoiding the task of fully realizing the characters are immediately apparent and necessarily alter his original conception of the work. We should consider first the explanation of the motives, in part conflicting, which the Father and the Stepdaughter put forward for that gesture. The Father declares: 'Ma ora forse indovino anche perché il nostro autore, che ci vide vivi cosí, non volle poi comporci per la scena. Non voglio far offesa ai suoi attori. Dio me ne guardi! Ma penso che a vedermi adesso rappresentato ... - non so da chi... ' [*MN*, I, 104] [But perhaps I can begin to see as well why our author, who saw us alive like this, didn't then want to write us into a play. I don't want to insult your actors. God forbid! But I think that seeing myself acted ...- I don't know who by ...]. The Stepdaughter, however, believes that: 'fu piuttosto, signore, per avvilimento o per sdegno del teatro, cosí come il pubblico solitamente lo vede e lo vuole...' [*MN*, I, 128] [it was really out of discouragement or disgust with the theatre, as the public usually sees and wants theatre to be ...]. The Father alludes to Pirandello's well-known theoretical aversion to the theatre, which was guilty of betraying the living and spontaneous reality of the artistic creation through performance. [16] The Stepdaughter in a way historicises the problem and links Pirandello's gesture to aversion to the traditional bourgeois theatre. In fact the two sets of explanations refer to two different conceptual orders.

The first of these presupposes the idea that theatre as such is incapable of capturing the absolute pathos of tragedy because performance - which is repetition through the conventional acting of roles - denaturizes the unique and unrepeatable nature of tragedy. [17] But this is a false problem since the impossibility of tragedy is already sited in reality and comes from the fundamental inauthenticity of living. Tragedy originates in an absolute conflict, and in Pirandello's universe there is no conflict which is not relative, or which is not susceptible of becoming so humoristically. So what is always shown is doubling, pretence and compromise.

But what Pirandello speaks of is a theatre of 'necessity', by which he means that when the play is put on the stage it must retain the immediacy and uniqueness which it derives, at the moment of creation, from the free flow of vital movement which is incarnated in the character.

What is challenged, above all, is the representational pact based on the 'as if' of mimetic art. Pirandello envisages a different stage, able to capture - in a sense very like that later formulated by Artaud in *The Theatre and Its Double* - the profound, unique and unrepeatable meaning of dramatic 'necessity'. All this he explains in his *Preface* when he speaks of the appearance of Madama Pace. He says that this scene represents his imagination caught in the act of creation, and that the birth of the creature in the imagination is necessary 'in misteriosa organica correlazione con tutta la vita dell'opera' [*MN*, I, 67] [in mysterious and organic correlation to the whole life of the play]. The urgency and immediacy of this event are underlined by the surrounding incongruities on the stage: the irreconcilable presence of the Mother, the whispered dialogue which cannot be heard, and so on. In spite of this, or perhaps because of this, Madama Pace's appearance is indispensable. It will occur every time, at the moment it should occur, magically evoked by the objects and states of mind, like a unique and unrepeatable fact, against all mimetic logic and all codified rules. So the drama, the vendetta, is accomplished but on another stage, or rather a stage which belongs to another theatre, already in prospect in the cruelty and identity of theatre and life.

This is one of the most profound changes in Pirandello's revolution of the theatre. It lies in the moment when the author declares himself absent (as a preordained logos) but is, in effect, very much present as the mind which before our very eyes brings to life the creatures of the imagination. In so doing Pirandello replaces the stage with another one which is concerned not only with the imagination but also with the deepest laws and needs of the psyche. This stage, which opens out onto the theme of incest, the link between victim and executioner, onto feelings of guilt and the preconcious guilt of others, establishes the necessity of what must happen beyond mimetic rules and the obvious relationship of cause and effect.

We are now in a position to consider another aspect of rejection: the absence of the audience. The six characters come to the theatre at a time given over to rehearsal, that is, at a time when there is no audience. This generates a series of textual signals which indicate that the audience, too, is rejected, or at least considered absent. Acts are replaced by accidental intervals (when the curtain is lowered by mistake) or by pauses which are part of the improvisation of the play (the Father and the Producer go off to plan the script). Then there are also the many times when the Producer goes into the auditorium to observe the scenic effects, the coming and going of the characters between the auditorium and the stage, the bare stage itself, the way in which theatrical tricks are exposed as such. It is as if the audience had been expelled from the theatre and so displaced from its usual role. Only with an apparent final incongruity does Pirandello have the curtain brought down, as it should be, at the end of the play. This is perhaps a tardy recognition of the audience's presence, which at the same time acknowledges that we, the public, are there but gives us a different role as witnesses of a unique event. We are rejected as an audience during the process of deciding whether or not what was happening on stage could be included within the traditional confines of mimetic art. We are then admitted as witnesses after the deaths of the Young Boy and the Little Girl have sanctioned what has been represented as real.

It is here, overall, that we find the keystone of the revolution set in motion by Pirandello in *Sei personaggi*. It is a revolution which goes beyond Pirandello's theatre, as arguably his subsequent works do not take the implications which abound in this 'play to be made' to their final consequences. The problem of the inability to represent tragic pathos because the author is missing interests Pirandello only as a pretext, indeed, I would say, as a pre-text, in the sense that it precedes the text and generates it tangentially, via a deliberate fracture, as a different text.

The author's search is one for a passage from action to words, as the mediating element between the tragic material and the dramatic form but also as axiological overdetermination of this material. He moves towards tragic unity and the cathartic sublime. But while he is doing all this, through the fracture a different word escapes laterally, and before being written it is individual spoken action, subjective, fragmentary and at the same time transgressive and tragic without catharsis. Pirandello is the author of this second text, because he did not want to, or could not, be the author of a novel or play centred on the most classic of tragic themes: incest. Indeed, he shows an irony towards this theme which implies an awareness that modern tragedy does not exist, and that in its place is the drama of the fragmentation of consciousness, of doubling, and of the loss of unity of the self. In Sartre's *Huis clos*, for example, this will more clearly become the inferno of relationships with others.

Let us now come to the other side of the matter, and look at the reasons the Stepdaughter gives for the rejection, citing the state of contemporary theatre. Rejection, and the consequent search for an author, shift the terms of the 'interview' with the characters towards a problematic dialogue with an 'other' who is the physical representative on stage of the potential author of the play 'to be made'. Pirandello could hypothetically have presented another playwright and given him the role of interlocutor of the characters, just as Dr Fileno turns to Pirandello himself as though to a second author capable of writing his story afresh, with greater efficacy and understanding. But while Dr Fileno's story has in fact been written and Pirandello, in the short story, has the upper hand in refusing to rewrite it, the story of the six characters has still to be written. So another playwright would have been a kind of specular double, with the same problem that Pirandello resolved by refusing to write the play. This would, in practice, have produced a fairly meaningless system of chinese boxes. So once more the shift from novel to play proves very productive, as it enables Pirandello to slide from writing to saying, and so to highlight the theme of theatre with all its implications.

So the characters address not a real author but a producer. He cannot, because he does not have the means, translate the characters' drama into written words except by putting it on stage and then transcribing what happens on stage into a script. The script, should, therefore, faithfully reflect the content of the drama exactly as the characters have it within themselves, that is, exactly as Pirandello conceived of them but then refused to write about them. The fact is, however, that the necessary mediation of performance naturally triggers off a discussion of the representational stereotypes in vogue in the contemporary theatre. These are seen to be are based on codes inadequate to express on stage the theme that an individual's reality coincides with his or her mask.

This puts the actors, and the Producer himself, on trial. The former are guilty of robbing the characters of their essential drama by the way they act; the latter is accused by the Stepdaughter of wanting a 'pasticcetto romantico' [*MN*, I, 118] [a romantic little sob-story] suitable for his audience. The audience, in turn, is directly put on trial by the author's declaration of scorn at the way it backs this kind of theatre, and it is doubly punished for its tastes: firstly because it is considered absent (almost expunged from the theatre) and secondly because the kind of performance it so much wants to see does not take place.

If we look at the motives for rejection given by the Father and the Stepdaughter we have a stratification of reasons of a general theoretical nature (concerning theatre as such) and of a concrete, historical nature (about the possibility of theatre and public taste). On this basis Pirandello seems, *tout court*, to decree the death of the theatre, given the multiple and incurable fractures between text and performance.

In my opinion all this is still pre-text, as the text does in fact exist, and it exists and is performed precisely because of the contradictions which generate it. This proves that Pirandello, as a man of the theatre, is in no way disposed to draw the final conclusions of what he is saying.

At this point we should return once more to the six characters as a living text, where the vital act which creates the character metaphorically and in reality precedes the written word. The only way to act the text is to live the events each time, as though they were happening for the first time (as the

Mother says: 'No, avviene ora, avviene sempre! Il mio strazio non è finto,
signore! Io sono viva e presente, sempre, in ogni momento del mio strazio,
che si rinnova, vivo e presente sempre.' [*MN*, I, 121] [No, it's happening now!
it's happening all the time! My torment isn't made up! I'm alive and present ,
always, in every moment of my torment, which is renewed, alive and present,
always] and not by repeating or re-performing a part. The immanent reason
for being of a character is his or her part, and playing the part means
representing the intrinsic 'necessity' of that 'eternal moment' the Father speaks
of, in which theatre and life, the ephemeral and the permanent, the mask and
subjective truth come together.

Pirandello's intuition seems laden with contradictions, and these are
voiced later in *Questa sera si recita a soggetto* when, after Mommina's illness,
the comic actor says to Hinkfuss: 'Noi siamo qua per recitare, parti scritte,
imparate a memoria. Non pretenderà mica che ogni sera uno di noi ci lasci la
pelle!' [*MN*, I, 311] [We're here to act, written parts, learnt by heart. You can't
be wanting one of us to drop dead every evening!]. Once more the idea of a
new theare is implied, prefiguring to some extent the experimental tendencies
in theatre after Pirandello, from the Surrealists to Artaud to Grotowski, for
example, often based on the paradox of a theatre where theory and practice are
out of step.

But let us return to the conflict between characters and actors. When he
characterizes the two groups Pirandello seems, significantly, to hesitate. In the
stage directions he recommends that the six characters should be physically
separated from the actors. The characters should appear not as phantasms but
as figures of created reality, and so he advises the use of masks which express
the immutability of their characters. We should note that the part of the stage-
directions relating to the use of masks was added by Pirandello in the 1925
edition of the play. But he did not do away with the minute descriptions of the
characters, present from the 1921 edition onwards, which come shortly
afterwards and which read almost like a disavowal of his advice. The Father,
for example:

...sarà sulla cinquantina: stempiato, ma non calvo, fulvo di pelo, con
baffetti folti quasi acchiocciolati attorno alla bocca ancor fresca,
aperta spesso a un sorriso incerto e vano. Pallido, segnatamente
nell'ampia fronte; occhi azzurri, ovati, lucidissimi e arguti... [MN, I,
77]

[*is about fifty: thinning at the temples, but not bald, reddish hair, with*
a hick moustache almost coiling around his mouth which is still fresh
and often open in an uncertain, empty smile. He is pale, especially
his wide forehead; and has oval blue eyes, very bright and piercing].

It is clear that the author is caught between the idea of submitting the six
characters to a process of figural abstraction which firmly expresses their
nature as 'created' realities and a characterisation which is realistic even in its
smallest details and corresponds to the character's subjectivity and inner
drama. This is the opposite of the Producer and actors, who in their clothes
and gestures reveal the stereotyped signs of belonging to 'theatre people'. A
prime example of this (and another variant added after the first edition) is the
Leading Lady, who comes on stage 'tutta vestita di bianco, con un cappellone
spavaldo in capo e un grazioso cagnolino tra le braccia' [*MN*, I, 73] [dressed all
in white, with a huge, dashing hat and a pretty little dog in her arms]..

Pirandello's first requirement is to distinguish clearly between those
acting a part and those living one, and so the fixity of the mask emphasizes the
immutability of the created form.. It also prevents the rapidly changing
mimicry and gestures of the character who becomes agitated in the grip of his
drama, against the pretensions of those who apply stereotyped models of
acting.

This ambiguity, at another point in the play, is transferred to the
Producer who at one point thinks the actors are amateur actors, insisting to the
Father: 'Eh via, lei deve aver recitato!' [*MN*, I, 97] [Come on, you must have
acted]. In his reply the Father refers to the theatricality of life, showing the

split which exists between the two groups and their respective concepts of theatre: 'Ma no, signore: quel tanto che ciascuno recita nella parte che si è assegnata, o che gli altri gli hanno assegnato nella vita.' [*MN*, I, 97] [Not at all: just the acting everybody does in the part we give ourselves, or which other people give us]. But soon afterwards, when the characters themselves remonstrate, rejecting the actors' performance, the Producer exclaims: 'Non s'imagineranno mica di saper recitare loro! Fanno ridere ...' [*MN*, I, 102] [You don't imagine you can act, do you? You're being ridiculous ...]. Whether this is a defence of his profession or an incongruity there is almost an identification of the two groups, which is then denied but is also underlined by the moments of admiration which the characters' apparent acting arouses in the actors.

We might, therefore, remember that in *I giganti della montagna* (unfinished) [The Mountain Giants], when Cotrone receives Ilse's company in the villa della Scalogna, he says to his Scalognati: 'anche loro sono press'a poco della nostra stessa famiglia' [*MN*, II, 1316] [they too are almost of the same family as us]. So here, too, there is a recognition of the near-identity between those who perform in theatre and those who live theatre as a necessity. It is a near-identity which Pirandello shrank from as a matrix of confusion for the audience of *Sei personaggi*, but which he allows in the last of his Myth Plays. The difference between the two works is that, while the six characters live the performance of their drama as a tragic necessity, the Scalognati (who are also characters without an author, but are their own authors) live it on a ludic plane.

In the final analysis the dissension between acting a part and living it, which in *Sei personaggi* seems to lead to an insoluble conflict, was instead the presage of a new kind of theatre. Pirandello resolves this conflict when he succeeds in conceiving of a theatre which openly declares its identity with life. However this is no longer in the tragic context of the game of role-playing and of subjective masks as the prison of the individual, but rather as a liberating game and an instrument of personal authenticity. In *Sei personaggi* Pirandello speaks largely in terms of negatives and this work is the *pars destruens*, necessarily founded on a system of opposites and ambiguities, preluding a new kind of theatre which he never succeeded completely in defining. It is not, therefore, by chance that the six characters make their appearance on a stage where *Il giuoco delle parti* [The Rules of the Game, or The Game of Role-Playing], his final word on the theatre of the grotesque, is being rehearsed. The grotesque emphasizes and denounces the falsity of bourgeois life, but by this time has been accepted and part of the reassuring game of theatrical performance. Pirandello wants to ge beyond and abolish all that had become static, tranquillizing and recognisable.

4. Deconstructing the theatre

At the beginning of *Sei personaggi* the stage is empty, dark and bare. This is, therefore, no longer the *locus* where, when the curtain rises, a simulacrum of reality is in place, ready for mimetic illusion, inviting the public to immediate identification. It is, instead, a space open to a potentially infinite number of transformations. The presence of the stage-hand nailing pieces of wood together, and the disorderly entrance of the actors, underline the polyvalent and chaotic aspect of the stage. The arrival of the Producer and the brilliant white light which floods the stage at his orders then impose a conventional order which starts the rehearsal of *Il giuoco delle parti.*

The producer follows the reading of the script and with words and gestures divides the stage space in a virtual way, making it clear that the stage is a fiction which must be prepared for the future spectators at the performance.

So the pact which underlies the mimetic illusion is broken, and the audience is to some extent ready for the struggle which will shortly begin for the possession and definition of the stage space.

The arrival of the characters from the auditorium, announced by the usher, is the structural opposite of the arrival of the actors from the stage door. This creates a split and ambiguity between the two groups, Pirandello recommends in the stage directions should remain separate both spatially and through special lighting effects, and he adds:

> *I* Personaggi *non dovranno infatti apparire come* fantasmi *ma come* realtà create, *costruzioni della fantasia immutabili; e dunque più reali e consistenti della volubile naturalità degli Attori.* [MN, I, 76]
> [*The* Characters *must not in fact seem to be* phantasms *but* created realities, *immutable constructions of the imagination and so more real and consistent than the volatile, natural actors*].

Beginning with this differentiation the stage space remains as though symbolically divided. For the actors it is the space of theatrical performance, with all the emblems of representational fiction; for the characters it is the place necessary to complete an existential drama which is consecrated as lived reality.

As the play proceeds this generates movements of attraction and repulsion between the two groups. The most significant moments are:

A. Attraction.

1. The actors draw close to the Stepdaughter who sings and dances: '*attratti da un fascino strano, si moveranno verso lei e leveranno appena le mani quasi a ghermirla*' [MN, I, 82] [*drawn by a strange fascination, they move towards her and raise their hands a little as though to grab her*]. She slips away from them and '*quando gli Attori scoppieranno in applausi, resterà, alla riprensione del Capocomico, come astratta e lontana*' [MN, I, 82] [*when the Actors burst into applause and the Producer remonstrates with them she stands looking as though abstracted and lost in thought*].

2. The Mother faints from anguish and the actors rush to help her.

3. The Mother rebels against Madama Pace and the actors intervene to hold her back.

4. The actors approach the Mother and the Son in the garden scene to study their parts, and are driven back.

5. The Young Boy, after his death, is carried behind the white cloth. Only the actors return to the stage.

B. Separation and moving away.

1. The Producer and the characters go off across the stage to plan the script; the actors remain on stage *'come storditi'* [<u>MN</u>, I, 99] [*as though stunned*].

2. The Producer makes the actors leave the scene in Madama Pace's back room before the characters start to 'rehearse' the scene.

3. When Madama Pace appears, the actors and the Producer run from the stage screaming with terror, rushing down the stairs as if making for the main aisle.

4. The Mother's cry during the scene with Madama Pace makes the producer recoil.

5. At the beginning of 'Act III' the actors and characters sit in two lines on opposite sides of the stage.

6. At the end of the play the actors leave the stage; the characters appear as shadows projected onto the backcloth. When they appear the Producer rushes in terror from the stage.

The movements of the actors towards the characters are determined by interest in their theatrical potential or by emotional participation in the tragic pathos of their story. There are corresponding signs of approval, scorn, horror, pity and hilarity whenever the characters claim they are beings which are 'more true' than 'those who live and wear clothes' showing the contradiction between their drama and the kind of theatre in which they want it to be set.

In practice Pirandello gives the actors the role of the (absent) public as is shown by their emotional participation in the plot, and at the same time uses them as a critical instance opposing the identification of theatre and life. Rather than being helpers at the rehearsal they become, instead, adversaries.

The reality of the characters which takes shape on the stage has its most intense and significant moment in the appearance of Madama Pace, which expels the actors from the stage. This episode is doubled in the finale, when the presence of the characters behind the back-cloth terrorizes the Producer and puts him to flight. Both moments show the impossibility of reconciling the conventional theatre of the actors and the created reality which longs to take over the theatrical space.

We should add to the movements we have listed the six times when the Producer moves between stage and auditorium. When he leaves the stage this shows the need to look at the stage effects from the point of view of the audience. When he returns to the stage he imposes order and organizes the rehearsal as a pseudo-demiurge in the absence of the author.

All this creates an ambiguity which invests the stage, where there is a clash between the characters' theatre, seen as immutable and superior to reality, and the conventional, mimetic theatre of the actors. The status of the stage space changes continually, as is shown by the explicit use of stage tricks by the Producer which alternates with the characters' spontaneous creation of life on the stage. The status of the set and lighting also becomes ambiguous: the lighting is mentioned or asked for by the Producer to create illusory effects, but at times the lights are 'mysterious', marking the alterity of the real actants in the rehearsal. Objects are set out in a summary fashion according to the requirements of the moment, and bear only a fleeting resemblance to the real objects. They can, however, acquire a magic and evocative power which leads to the appearance of Madama Pace, while the backcloth which represents the sky in the garden scene becomes the screen onto which the phantasmatic shadows of the characters are projected.

This dialectic between fiction and reality invests the stage and deconstructs it, destabilizing its function as the recaptacle of mimetic art. Madama Pace's appearance introduces a third element. With her, the stage becomes the place where the imagination is caught in the act of creation, and so a place which expresses all the potential of the imagination. So the kind of theatre understood by the actors is rejected, as Pirandello alludes to another stage which is that of the spiritual gestation which led to the characters' 'book'.

The stage, for the characters, is a necessary element for living out their story. It also sends them back to another place and another time which predate or follow the finished act of creation. For the Son, for example, this place coincides with an 'elsewhere' which removes from him the obligation to take part in the action. The mysterious force which prevents him from going down the steps into the auditorium makes the stage into a prison which is the double of the prison of the family in which the play in enclosed. The Stepdaughter alludes to an 'elsewhere' which will be the place of her flight from the family, as becomes apparent when she abandons the group at the end of the play and runs away across the auditorium and foyer. The presence of the characters on stage refers to a life 'other' than that narrated and acted, and which is already being lived or has already 'happened' while we watch the 'play to be made'. It is a life which does not come within the orbit of what happens on stage, but from there the characters have come into the stage space out of necessity, as they are in search of an author.

As we see, the deconstruction of the stage space is total. Pirandello's initial gesture of rejection grafts the plot of a novel onto a play, turning it into dramatic metacomment. But Pirandello has not so much wanted, or been able, to define what that other stage capable of accommodating a new kind of theatre would be like. Rather, he completely deconstructs the mimetic stage, presenting it as rhe space where illusion, imagination and real life converge and clash.

How does this convergence, and conflict, come about?

Pirandello chooses not to write the novel, and so not to complete the semiotic orchestration of the story, and as we have seen gives different reasons for his choice from the original ones, although these are generally in line with the rejection of the characters. From this moment the characters feel authorized, and at the same time compelled, to plead their case y becoming their own authors and inviting the Producer to write a text of their drama. This proves to be an impossible task.

There are other, more profound, reasons than the ones we have given for this impossibility. Free from (or deprived of) a logos which installs itself in the text as an ordering and axiological principle, the characters live out in drama the split between the dramatic essence of the events of which they are the protagonists and the subjective interpretaion of those events. More than what actually happens, what counts is the way events were perceived by each of them. The result is that the temptation to 'narrate' or 'live' the event on the stage comes constantly into conflict with the subjective comment. Each of the characters, but especially the Father and the Stepdaughter, interprets the facts according to a different psychological state and so in a different way, and attributes to the other an inner truth which the other does not recognize, and rejects.

So the performance continually shifts from the events to comment on the events, and this triggers off a conflict between a naturalist story and a psychological story which becomes radicalized and interrupts the action on the stage. In addition, Pirandello wanted his characters to be fixed rigidly, as is shown when he advises that they should wear fixed masks. His characters should be fixed:

> nell'espressione del proprio sentimento fondamentale, che è il rimorso per il Padre, la vendetta per la Figliastra, lo sdegno per il Figlio, il dolore per la Madre [...] [MN, I, 76]
> [each in the expression of his or her basic feeling, which is remorse for the Father, revenge for the Stepdaughter, contempt for the Son and sorrow for the Mother.]

By doing this Pirandello seems to go beyond psychological drama, denying it any possible dialectical essence, even in a humoristic sense. If we now return to what was said earlier about the intrinsic lack of the dialogic in the text we could argue that the dialogue in fact breaks up into fragments of monologue. Each character uses these fragments to try to take over the dialogue, to snatch it away from the others, in order to give free reign to the narration of his or her own phantasms. The point of view shifts continuously, without producing any mediation. So the Father has to try again and again to put together a coherent nexus which the Producer can understand. In this way, however, the characters' desire for performance, which is choral in nature and which leads them into the theatre, clashes with the subjective, which cannot be performed. As the producer says, in the end this jeopardizes and annuls the theatrical potential of the drama:

> Non può stare che un personaggio venga, cosí, troppo avanti, e sopraffaccia gli altri, invadendo la scena. Bisogna contener tutti in un quadro armonico e rappresentare quel che è rappresentabile! Lo so bene anch'io che ciascuno ha tutta una sua vita dentro e che vorrebbe metterla fuori. Ma il difficile è appunto questo: farne venir fuori quel tanto che è necessario, in rapporto con gli altri; e pure in quel poco fare intendere tutta l'altra vita che resta dentro! Ah, comodo, se ogni personaggio potesse in un bel monologo, o... senz'altro ... in una conferenza venire a scodellare davanti al pubblico tutto quel che gli bolle in pentola. [*MN*, I,119].
> [One character can't come too much to the forefront like this and take over, upstaging the others. They have all got to be contained in a harmonious picture and act what can be acted! I know very well, too, that everyone has a whole inner life they want to bring out. But this is precisely the problem: how to bring out that bit which is necessary in relation to the others, and yet in that little bit reveal all the rest of the life which stays inside! It would be a fine thing if everyone could have a lengthy monologue or ... certainly ... a lecture and come and dole out to the audience everything that's brewing inside].

In *Sei personaggi*, in the final analysis, Pirandello has superimposed a theatre which is open to the instinctual and to compulsive verbal aggression on naturalist theatre based on the event and its mimesis (which he rejects from the outset). The representational pact which the producer alludes to is, therfore, broken first and foremost by the characters themselves.

In his *Preface* Pirandello says that the real theatrical 'reason for being' of his rejected characters, what gives their drama its 'universal sense', is:

> ... nella concitazione della lotta disperata che ciascuno fa contro l'altro e tutti contro il Capocomico e gli attori che non li comprendono.
> Senza volerlo, senza saperlo, nella ressa dell'animo esagitato, ciascun d'essi, per difendersi dalle accuse dell'altro, esprime come sua viva passione e suo tormento quelli che per tanti anni sono stati i travagli del mio spirito: l'inganno della comprensione reciproca fondato irrimediabilmente sulla vuota astrazione delle parole; la molteplice personalità d'ognuno secondo tutte le possibilità d'essere

che si trovano in ciascuno di noi; e infine il tragico conflitto
immanente tra la vita che di continuo si muove e cambia e la forma
che la fissa, immutabile. [*MN*, I, 60].
[... in the frenzy of the desperate battle waged by each one against the
others and by all of the against the Producer and the actors who do not
understand them.

Unintentionally, inadvertently, each one of them, defending himself
in a state of considerable mental agitation against the recriminations
of the others, shows himself to be tormented by the same fierce
sources of suffering that have racked my own spirit for years: the
delusion of mutual understanding hopelessly based on the hollow
abstraction of words; the multiple nature of every human personality,
given all the possible ways of being inherent in each one of us; and
finally the tragic built-in conflict between ever-moving, ever-
changing life, and the immutability of form which fixes it]. [18]

and later on he adds:

... ma che questa sia una ragion d'essere, che sia diventata, per essi
che già avevano una vita propria, la vera funzione necessaria e
sufficiente per esistere, neanche possono sospettare. [*MN*, I, 62]
[... but that this might be a reason for being, that it might have
become, for them who already had their own life, the true, essential
and sufficient reason for their existence, is something they cannot
even suspect].

However, in one of his verbal clashes with the Stepdaughter, urged on by

the Producer, who wants 'facts' not 'discussions', the Father first declares: 'un

fatto è come un sacco: vuoto non si regge. Perché si regga, bisogna prima farci

entrar dentro la ragione e i sentimenti che lo han determinato' [*MN*, I, 93] [a

fact is like a sack: it won't stand up when its empty. For it to stand up, you

first have to put inside it the motives and feelings that determined it]. Then,

becoming to some extent the author's spokesman, he declares: 'Il dramma per

me è tutto qui, signore: nella coscienza che ho, che ciascuno di noi - veda - si

crede

'uno' ma non è vero: è 'tanti', signore, 'tanti', secondo tutte le possibilità

d'essere che sono in noi [*MN*, I, 94] [The drama for me is right here: in my

awareness I have that each one of us - you see - thinks we are 'one' person, but it isn't true: each one of us is 'many' different people according to all the possibilities of being that are in us].

So he puts forward the same reasons as the author, which are also those at the real heart of the matter. They prevent the story from being performed, unless it were to take place as the repetition of an event in the 'theological' stage, which would necessarily mean writing the text. This leads to a negative circularity which always returns to its origins and to the absence of the author.

The producer and the actors are called upon by the characters to fill this gap, and they appeal to the theatre canon and to respect for codified rules. Their refusal to improvise stresses the need for a text, but what the Father recognizes as the essential drama of the characters - 'reason and feelings' - , and hence the conflict between the different reasons and subjective feelings, cannot be made into a text within the conventions of mimetic theatre.

There is, therefore, one circle which closes inside the other in a linked series of negatives. This throws the referentiality of mimesis in traditional theatre definitively into crisis, and also shows that theatre cannot represent the split and fragmented inner being of modern man.

The impossibility of tragedy takes us back once more to the need for a new kind of theatre. In *Sei personaggi* this theatre is not defined, and perhaps it lies beyond Pirandello's own intuitive and cognitive abilities. It is, however, potentially present in and beyond the author's gesture of rejection. *Sei personaggi* is a play in which everything hangs admirably together because nothing hangs together any longer. It is a perfect and calculated orchestration of incongruities which are at once the value and the limit of the play, but which open out a whole series of ideas which are as surely prolific as they are undetermined for the theatre of the future.

CORRADO DONATI

¹ See Orio Vergani's account, now in G. Davico Bonino (ed.), *La 'prima' dei 'Sei personaggi in cerca d'autore'*, Turin, Editrice Tirrenia Stampatori, 1983, pp. 57-62. Some new and very interesting accounts regarding Pirandello's masterpiece have been published recently in F. Taviani, *'Sei personaggi*, due interviste in una al primo padre', in *Teatro e storia*, VII, 1992, No. 2, pp. 295-328.

² For a more detailed analysis of the allegorical mechanisms in *Sei personaggi* see R.Luperini, 'L'atto del significare allegorico nei *Sei personaggi* e in *Enrico IV*', *Rivista di studi pirandelliani*, IX, 1991, Nos 6-7, pp. 9-19.

³ See in particular C. Vicentini, *L'estetica di Pirandello*, Milan, Mursia, 2nd ed., 1985; R. Scrivano, *La vocazione contesa*, Rome, Bulzoni, 1987.

⁴ G. Macchia, *Pirandello o la stanza della tortura*, Milan, Mondadori, 1981, p. 57.

⁵ The two passages in question are: 'Perché la vita, cosí dura com'è, cosí terra com'è, vuole se stessa lì e non altrove, ancora e sempre uguale. E vorrà anche il cielo, per tante cose; ma, sopra tutto, creda, per dare respiro a questa terra' [*Colloquii coi personaggi*]; 'Ah come la vita è di terra, e non vuol cielo, se non per dare respiro alla terra' [*Di sera, un geranio*].

⁶ The two passages are: '[the young husband] guardava qua e là coi piccoli occhi neri, lustri, da pazzo, e non intendeva più nulla, e non mangiava e non beveva e diventava di punto in punto più pavonazzo, quasi nero' [*Un cavallo nella luna*]; 'E allora, a poco a poco, gli occhi, già lustri, gli s'indurivano; e mentre su le tempie egli diventava paonazzo, quasi nero nelle grosse orecchie ronzanti [...]' [*Fragment of novel*].

⁷ A translation of Pirandello's preface, by Felicity Firth, can be found in Luigi Pirandello, *Collected Plays*. Vol. 2, ed. Robert Rietty, London and New York, John Calder, Riverrun Press, 1988, xi-xxv.
The résumés of the sections of the *Preface* referred to in this essay are based largely on this translation.

⁸ See especially C. Vicentini, 'Sei personaggi in cerca d'autore. Il testo' in AA.VV., *Testo e messa in scena di Pirandello*, Florence, La Nuova Italia, 1986, pp. 49-62.

⁹ Pirandello seems to deny this possibility indirectly when he says in the *Preface* that the Father's mental anguish springs from causes that have nothing to with the drama of his own personal experience. However, he is also defending himself against accusations of autobiographic writing.

[10] C. Vicentini, 'Sei personaggi in cerca d'autore', cit., p. 50.

[11] S. Pirandello, *Prefazione all'opera di mio padre* in L. Pirandello, *Tutti i romanzi,* vol. II, ed M. Costanzo, Milan, Mondadori, ser. I Meridiani, 1973, pp. 1058-1059.

[12] M. Bakhtin, *Esthétique et Théorie du Roman,* trans. D. Olivier, Paris, Gallimard, 1978.

[13] E. Gioanola, *Pirandello la follia,* Genoa, Il Melangolo, 1983, p. 269.

[14] I am using the term in the meaning given to it by J. Derrida in his *Prefazione* to Antonin Artaud, *Il teatro e il suo doppio,* Turin, Einaudi, 1978, xi: 'The stage is theological as long as it remains dominated by speech, by the desire to speak, by the plan of a primary logos which does not belong to the theatrical *locus* and directs it from a distance'.

[15] L. Klem, 'Umorismo in atto. Accenni ad una interpretazione integrale dei *Sei personaggi in cerca d'autore*' in AA.VV. *Il teatro nel teatro di Pirandello,* Agrigento, Centro Nazionale di Studi Pirandelliani, 1977, p. 42.

[16] See his essay *Illustratori, attori, traduttori* [Illustrators, actors and translators; C. Vicentini has given an excellent reconstruction of Pirandello's theoretical position; see especially his *Pirandello. Il disagio del teatro,* Venice, Marsilio, 1993, esp. pp. 53-72.

[17] On the theme of the 'tragic' in Pirandello see G. Bárberi Squarotti, ' 'I *Sei personaggi* e la distruzione del testo teatrale', in *Le sorti del tragico,* Ravenna, Longo, 1978.

[18] Translation by Felicity Firth, in *Pirandello. Collected Plays,* cit., xvi.

A TRIBUTE TO THE MAGIC OF THEATRE:
QUESTA SERA SI RECITA A SOGGETTO

The summer of 1928 marked a major break in Pirandello's career as man
of the theatre. On August 15 his company, the Teatro d'Arte, gave its last
performance at the summer resort of Viareggio. Pirandello had spent three and
a half years of intensive activity as its director. The company's achievements
had been many: it had presented a varied and ambitious repertoire (fifteen
world premières and nine Italian premières of foreign plays), given its leading
actress, Marta Abba, the opportunity to develop her talent, expanded the range
of stagecraft by introducing innovatory lighting, and produced a high standard
of acting based on careful attention to the text. During this period Pirandello
had travelled extensively with his company in Europe and South America, and
through the prestige he gained revived hopes of an Italian national theatre. But
he was finally defeated by some of the problems he had set out to solve:
competition for playing places and funding, and so the company had to
disband.[1]

Pirandello was sixty and had no long term plans. He accepted an
invitation from a cinema company to go to Berlin to make a film of *Sei
personaggi in cerca d'autore* [Six Characters in Search of an Author]. He had
thought of a six month visit: in fact, he stayed for over two years before
transferring to Paris. In the spring of 1929 he paid a short visit to London,
again in connection with making a film of *Sei personaggi*. This project failed
because of problems with British censorship, but while in London Pirandello

saw his first 'talkies' (the first 'talkie' *The Jazz Singer* had been released in 1927.) By the spring of 1929 Pirandello had completed the text of *Questa sera si recita a soggetto* [Tonight We Improvise] which received its première in Könisberg on January 25 the following year. By November of the same year he had published his views on the talking film.

An understanding of *Questa sera si recita a soggetto* is enhanced by an understanding of the contexts within which it was written and produced. These are, as the above brief biography indicates, the invention of the 'talkies' and Pirandello's responses to them; his intensive and extensive knowledge of the mechanics of theatre, a result of his years as playwright attending rehearsals and, more importantly, his years as director of the Teatro d'Arte; and the impact made on him of German theatre and theories of directing.

Pirandello and film

Pirandello's initial negative reaction to the 'talkies' - he described them in a letter home as 'monstrous' - is often taken as an indication of his antagonism to film in general.[2] But this is a misconception.

Pirandello's acquaintance with the film world began very early in his career, in 1896 in fact, and he held carefully considered views on the art which he developed over time.[3] Marcel L'Herbier's version of *Il Fu Mattia Pascal* [The Late Mattia Pascal] constituted an important moment in the history of Pirandello's relationship with film. As a *cinéaste* L'Herbier was among the European avant-garde who were offering an alternative approach to film from that offered by Hollywood. Pirandello's comments at the time, and his later article 'Se il film parlante abolirà il teatro' (1929), need to be seen in the light of the ongoing debate between a populist, commercial approach to film, as exemplified by Hollywood, and film seen as an art form. By 1924 Pirandello knew where he stood, not least because of negative experiences with Hollywood (it had been suggested that *Henry IV* should end happily with the marriage of 'Henry' and Matilde).[4]

There are two issues here: Pirandello's developing attitude to film and the impact that the growth of this art and industry was to have on his attitude to theatre. On the former Pirandello expressed his views in 1924 to an interviewer on *Les Nouvelles Littéraires*: film had special qualities that differentiated it from any other art form; the cinema could more easily and more completely than any other means of expression make thought visible; it made no sense to remain aloof from a means of expression which offered the possibility of doing things that neither narrative nor theatre could do, that is, put into images [*rendere sensibili*] dream, memory, hallucination, madness and the doubling of personality.[5] In the essay of 1929 these thoughts were further developed: in words that almost echo those of the *cinéastes* he stressed the need to keep the two genres, theatre and cinema, separate and to develop them as individual art forms. Coining the word 'cinemelografia' he described film as an evocative art that should explore the intermingling of image and music. Linear narrative could have an inhibiting effect on a form which is the 'muta espressione di immagini e linguaggio di apparenze' [the silent expression of images and the language of appearances]. Likewise the talking character, an image with a disembodied voice, was a travesty of theatre. In attempting to imitate theatre with characters who use dialogue, film could only produce a mechanical copy of something that is living and vibrant. If cinema suffered from attempting to imitate theatre, so theatre was on the wrong track in appropriating cinematic techniques. This had led to repertoires that stressed visual effects over and above dramatic power, and had made certain directors strive to create 'uno spettacolo per gli occhi' [a spectacle for the eyes] by gradually darkening the stage and creating another scene from the blackout to the sound of music ('oscurando gradatamente la scena e facendone sorgere un'altra dal buio momentaneo con accompagnamento di suoni').[6]

What Pirandello has to say in 'Se il film parlante abolirà il teatro' seems a far remove from the interview he gave in Paris in 1925 called 'En confidence' where he reiterated the ideas criticising theatrical performance that he had expressed in 1908. All performance, he had then stated, was a travesty of the playwright's writing, all acting was artifice that was quite unable to translate on to the stage the image held in the writer's mind. Theatre was therefore an 'impossible art'. It was symptomatic of Pirandello's concern for theatre as he experienced it in the late twenties that he did not indulge in provocative ideas concerning it and kept provocation in the later essay to the area of cinema. It is also the case that Pirandello later revised his ideas on cinema and accepted the talking film as a viable medium.[7]

Pirandello's experience in the theatre

Pirandello gave the interview 'En Confidence' when he was on his first European tour with his company, the Teatro d'Arte. It was clear from the opening night of the theatre in Rome in April 1925 that one of Pirandello's aims was to bring Italian theatre (in the form of his theatre) up to date with respect to technical innovation, particularly lighting. Corrado Alvaro, who reviewed the opening night for *Il Risorgimento*, noticed with approval that the footlights had been abolished and commented favourably on the use of front of house and on stage spots in five colours which plunged the stage into pools of colour, allowing for amazing effects of proximity and distance.[8] In planning the reconstruction of the Odescalchi theatre Pirandello had been insistent on giving it a sophisticated lighting system with an understage control box; and during the period of preparing the plays for performance ample time was given to lighting rehearsals. The presence of advanced and modern lighting probably influenced the revised ending to *Sei personaggi in cerca d'autore* with its projection of the shadows of the Characters on the cyclorama. The play that marked Marta Abba's debut, Bontempelli's *Nostra Dea* [Our Dea] contained a scene where frenetic dancing was lit by green and yellow spots; these varied according to the psychological moments of the play and led Silvio D'Amico to comment that it constituted the finest Futurist scene he had ever seen. In Marinetti's own play, *Vulcano* [Volcano], presented the following year, Prampolini created the effect of the volcano with a show of lights and projected huge shadows of the shepherds on to the wall behind. Other scenic effects included the earthquake effected by Marchi at the end of *La nuova colonia* [The New Colony]. In the last moments of the play the earth trembles, shaken by the earthquake, and the island and all its people are swallowed up by the sea. Only La Spera remains, sitting on one raised piece of land holding her baby, a symbol of the redemptive power of motherhood. Marchi, the play's designer, hit on the ingenious idea of using a vast piece of heavy cloth as a stage carpet with which he and a number of stage hands, dressed as islanders, enveloped the stage and actors at the appropriate moment, giving the impression that a huge wave had engulfed the whole scene.[9]

That Marchi chose this method of conveying the impression of an earthquake is indicative of theatrical conditions in Italy at the time. It was both ingenious and effective, but it used old technology. Whereas in France and Germany theatres were becoming increasingly well equipped and, in Germany in particular, had incorporated the new technologies into theatre making, such as the revolving stage, Italy's theatre was still to a large extent living in the nineteenth century. Pirandello was fortunate in the quality of his actors, but even they, gifted and conscientious as they were, baulked at the time and energy given to effects. Much of Pirandello's time was taken in retraining his actors, to look carefully at what they were saying but also in what now seem such basic considerations as wearing the appropriate costumes. Even Ruggeri, as guest artist, needed to be persuaded when he played Henry IV to wear the costume especially designed for the production rather than his customary black, in which, he claimed, he had gained many a success.[10] Actors of the time were used to playing in makeshift sets which they ignored, and had to be taught how to act with more substantial materials. An indication of the state of affairs can be seen in a rough copy of a letter that Guido Salvini, one of Pirandello's designers and coproducers, drafted when about to hand in his notice: he told Pirandello that he had sixteen canvas sets, twelve paper ones, 800 square metres of materials and drapes and indicated that this was far more than any other theatre company in Italy.[11]

The Theatre Scene in Germany

Pirandello had done much to bring his Italian company to a European standard of theatrical expertise. How far there was still to go was brought home to him when he took up temporary residence in Berlin, at a time when Berlin might be said to be Europe's theatre capital. In fact, Pirandello's two years in Berlin coincided with a crisis point in German theatre. He was there during some of the last years of the Weimar Republic (1919-1933); more specifically, the Wall Street slump (24 October 1929) came midway in his stay. The beginning of his stay, then, was during the tail end of what is sometimes referred to as 'the golden twenties' (1925-8); the rest during the end of the economic boom when drastic economies had to be made in all sectors of German life, a period that can be characterised in terms of politicisation and polarisation in its theatre as in other aspects of cultural and social life. Even more specifically, the writing of *Questa sera si recita a soggetto* was completed within the years of the 'golden twenties', its presentation, first in Könisberg then in Berlin, outside them. This fact alone will have had something to do with its reception (see below).

Pirandello's reputation in Berlin as a playwright had begun with Max Reinhardt's production of *Sei personaggi in cerca d'autore* in December of 1924 at the Die Komödie theatre in Berlin. This had been followed by productions of seven other plays in 1925 and 1926, which had constituted a brief period of Pirandello mania. Though by 1928 enthusiasm for Pirandello's theatre had abated he could still both attract and command some attention: a table was kept every night for him at the Romanisches Café, where he was always surrounded by theatre directors, foreign journalists and his own regular friends. Anton Giulio Bragaglia, who was in Berlin at the same time, recalled how interested Pirandello was in the varied kinds of people who frequented the cafés, how he was fascinated by transvestites, went to cabarets and theatre and generally enjoyed the night life of Berlin.[12]

What Pirandello was witnessing in Berlin in the late twenties was a theatre scene which was unique in Europe. Various factors contributed to this distinction. Perhaps the most important was the assumption built into the German consciousness that theatre, along with other arts, was not a luxury or entertainment but part of the educational process of self improvement and therefore social improvement: in one German word, *Bildung*, which John Willett has nicely described as 'the intangible equipment of a well-ordered life'.[13] From this stem other factors: municipal and governmental subsidy; the recognition that all art is art, that it is not necessary to make distinctions between 'high' and 'low' culture. The Volksbühne [People's Stage] Movement from the 1890s had opened up theatre to a new audience and was unique in Europe, and the effects of this lasted well into the twentieth century. The movement was strong enough to build its own theatre in 1914, and survived until it was taken over by the Nazis. But perhaps the greatest difference Pirandello would have noticed between theatre in Berlin and theatre in Rome was its sheer virtuosity. While he had been persuading his leading actor to wear the costume appropriate to the set design in his production of *Enrico IV*, directors such as Max Reinhardt and Leopold Jessner were devising vast extravaganzas which afforded scenic displays hitherto unparalleled and required a discipline from actors and stage staff unimagined in Italy. The economic boom coming from the stabilisation of the mark in the mid twenties attracted investment from both within Germany and outside: American state short term loans under the Dawes plan and private American investment contributed to Germany's temporary wellbeing and had its effect on theatre.

There were a few new theatre buildings, but the most notable improvements were to the theatre apparatus in existing buildings. The growing success of the two major electrical firms, Siemens and AEG, had its spin off in the major refurbishment of theatre lighting systems: arc lights were replaced by high power bulbs, and film projection was added or improved in most theatres. Other improvements included revolves and lifts. In a number of theatres the raked stage was abolished. And this new equipment brought with it new roles in the theatre: the age of the director, European-wide, had its centre in Berlin. Whereas in Italy there was no word for this person until the thirties, and in

1929 Pirandello was using the word *régisseur* in his essay on the talkies, the function of the stage director was a major talking point in Berlin's cultural circles in the twenties.

An important factor in the modernisation of theatre was the ideological impulse that lay behind it. Going hand in hand with the concept of *Bildung* was the prevailing notion that culture was a social act and that innovations in culture were central to the well organised life. Innovative theatre was not a fringe or shoestring operation. This also meant that innovations, progress in other spheres of life, needed to be integrated into culture. Technical innovations were not simply mechanisms with which to create effects or modify the ways a stage could be organised; they were an expression of theatre's entry into history, of its ability to adapt to new social forces in the integration of the new products and new technologies. In order to say meaningful things to contemporary audiences theatre needed to use the means at society's disposal. It followed from this that technical invention and machinery tended to become central to theatrical production.[14] This also meant that although Germany had some very fine actors during this period of its theatre history, for instance, Max Pallenberg, Emil Jannings, Elisabeth Bergner (from Austria), Lucie Höflich and Agnes Straub, German theatre was better known for its directors and scenic invention than for its actors.

The role of the director was, therefore, crucial to German theatre. The argument concerning theatre direction and the role of the director was focused on the concepts of 'production' and 'reproduction': was it the director's task to reproduce what the writer had written, or was it to produce a work of art inspired by the writer's text? In his *Der Regisseur*, Leopold Jessner claimed that what the writer had written was the director's material in the same way as reality was the writer's material; that the stage had its own laws which were determining factors of the director's work; and that the director had to unravel the writer's text into parts which would constitute the stage work. It was this process of unravelling and analysis that constituted both the director's freedom and his work. It was how the director transformed the written play into a stage performance.[15]

It is also the case that the European director was crucial to the development of Pirandello's career as a dramatist and man of the theatre. It was Pitoëff's memorable production of *Sei personaggi in cerca d'autore* which, though not the first production of a Pirandello play in Paris, was the one that excited the Parisian theatre going public and promoted his work in France; and it was Max Reinhardt's production in Berlin in December 1924 that promoted interest in Pirandello's plays in Germany. Writing to his daughter Lietta from Paris in the April of 1923 on the occasion of Pitoëff's production, Pirandello claimed excitedly: 'Sono veramente arrivato al colmo della mia carriera letteraria.' [I've really arrived at the peak of my literary career].[16] It was these two major European productions that not only prepared the ground for the visits of the Teatro d'Arte in 1925 but also account for the presence of Pirandello as creative influence, particularly in France.

Questa sera si recita a soggetto
(a) *'Leonora, addio!'*

As its title indicates, *Questa sera si recita a soggetto* is a meta-text about improvisation; the story on which the theatrical company in the play works is one of Pirandello's own, *'Leonora, addio!'* ['Leonora, Farewell!']. In this story, a group of young Italian officers stationed in a town on the south coast of Sicily spend their spare time with don Palmiro, his Neapolitan wife donna Ignazia and their four daughters Mommina, Totina, Dorina and Memè. By convincing them that this is how people behave on the mainland, the officers take various liberties with the young women, and the family gains a reputation in the town for loose living. They are noisy visitors to the theatre and when this is shut create their own versions of opera at home with improvised costumes and make up - the young women dressing up as men if the need arises. Among this group of young officers is one Sicilian, Rico Verri, who takes a fancy to Mommina, the eldest of the four daughters. Knowing that her father is a spendthrift, that they haven't two beans to rub together, Mommina encourages Rico Verri's attentions. As he becomes seriously attached to her his attitude changes: no more dressing up, no more theatre. His jealousy breaks forth one evening ending up with a lot of noise, hurled chairs, broken glass and three duels. The result: Rico Verri promises to marry Mommina after his term of duty is completed. Mommina is warned against accepting his offer, as Rico's father was a jealous and miserly man whose wife died of a broken heart, but she has romanticised her prospective husband into duel-fighting opera characters, Raul, Hernani and don Alvaro, and goes ahead with the marriage. Rico takes Mommina away to the highest point of the little town, imprisons her in a house overlooking the African sea where the doors are kept locked, the windows barred and shuttered; all except one where she stands for hours, at first on her own, then with her two little daughters gazing out at the sea, the sailing ships and the countryside. Rico Verri's obsessive desire to possess has taken a terrifying and irremediable form: he is jealous of the past, of the embraces the frivolous young men have given her, of what cannot be eradicated. He goes out for much of the day, allows no one into the house, and Mommina becomes fatter and more slatternly; until one day, inspired by a theatre bill for Verdi's *La forza del destino* [The Force of Destiny] she finds in his pocket, her passion for the theatre takes possession of her and she begins to sing opera to her children: *La forza del destino* one night, *Les Huguenots* the next and finally *Il trovatore* on the third, taking all the parts, from beginning to end. When Rico Verri returns he finds the two little girls, hands in their laps, wide-eyed and open-mouthed, waiting for the show to continue. Mommina is dead.

The story first published in the *Corriere della sera*, 6 November 1910 [17] is a powerful and haunting presentation of an obsessively insistent theme in Pirandello's writing. Rico Verri is possessed by the same obsession as his father and inflicts upon his wife the results of his passion. Mommina is possessed by the very memories he wants to eradicate in her. But it is also a story about other favourite preoccupations of Pirandello's: the nature of reality and the borderline between art and life.

(b) Prologue

In the play, this story holds a place a place similar to that of the six characters in *Sei personaggi in cerca d'autore*: it is the inner drama around which the debate on the nature of theatre is conducted. The play itself begins with members of the audience (that is, characters written into the text) expressing their restlessness as the lights go down but the curtain does not go up. After the gong has sounded for the second time (a recent German innovation) the strange figure of Dr. Hinkfuss [18] erupts into the auditorium and comes onto the stage. Amidst various interruptions from the audience he explains what is going to happen: the audience is to have the privilege of experiencing a piece of theatre improvised on a short story by Pirandello called *'Leonora, addio!'*, which will be all of his making. In part 1, which acts as a prologue, Hinkfuss tries to introduce the actors to the audience but meets with his first problem. The actors, who have been preparing themselves for their roles, no longer want to be known as actors but as characters; already art has begun to take over and the characters are living their parts. Hinkfuss interprets their reluctance as rebellion, and tries to save face with the audience by pretending that their rebellion is a planned part of the performance. Tensions are beginning to show; the actors as a group resent Hinkfuss who treats them as material for his experiment, as if, they say, they were puppets; and quarrels arise between the actors themselves; the Leading Lady, for instance, (who is playing Mommina) has prepared her lines in advance while the leading man, (Rico Verri), has worked his way into the part so that he can react in character with a spontaneous response. After the presentation scene Hinkfuss allows a five minute interval.

From this prologue it can be seen that possession, control and conflict are the three major motifs of the play. Hinkfuss has a potential disruption on his hands in the restless and unruly audience. The situation Pirandello has set up here is similar to that of a futurist evening; the way the situation develops, however, can be termed an inversion of futurist theatre. Rather than taking conflict from the theatre out into the streets, Pirandello constructs a carefully controlled evening where no member of the real audience has the opportunity to speak, let alone throw tomatoes, and lets it be known that the stage is the privileged place of theatre.[19] Hinkfuss also has a conflict on hand with his actors, who later in the play will rebel against his autocratic procedures and turn him out of his theatre. In the prologue the actors are already squabbling amongst themselves; as the evening progresses their disagreements will fade before the more overriding objective of ridding themselves of their importunate director and living their lives as the characters. Both within the story they use for their theatrical activity and within that activity itself control and possession figure prominently: Verri is possessed by jealousy and tries to control his wife, Mommina, who is in turn possessed by operatic stories. The actors are possessed by their parts to the extent that these take over their lives. And Hinkfuss's mania for scenic effect leads him to try to control his actors as if they were part of the mechanics of theatre.

(c) Hinkfuss's scenic effects and 'Tonfilm'.

In his public utterances, Pirandello gave priority to this last concern. Hinkfuss is not, as the Berlin audiences mistakenly thought, a parody of Reinhardt, to whom Pirandello dedicated the German text of this new play with fulsome gratitude for his production of Sei personaggi in cerca d'autore in 1924; rather he represents more generally what Pirandello saw as the excesses of German scenic direction. His presence as described in the text (but not presumably representable - three feet high, with a shock of hair, and fingers that look like hairy caterpillars), his demeanour and his autocratic language all point to the comic portrayal of a man obsessed, who maniacally piles one scenic effect upon another. He begins with a Sicilian religious procession, meticulously described in the text, which enters through the auditorium at the beginning of part 2; follows this with a presentation on stage of a cabaret where Sampognetta, Mommina's father, meets the Singer, sets up an opera on stage with projection and gramophone, then as his pièce de résistance, creates an airfield on stage

when most of the audience are out of the auditorium, only to dismantle it when
the audience returns. Here Pirandello had hit on a way of affording his
audience enormous pleasure in the virtuosity of Hinkfuss's achievements while
at the same time satirising his high jinks as excessive and irrelevant display.
Pirandello believed that technique, carried to its maximum perfection and
unrelated to text, was beginning to destroy theatre ['la tecnica portata alla sua
massima perfezione, sta finendo coll'uccidere il teatro']. His new play, he
declared in an interview, was to be a reaction to this tendency.[20]

Pirandello's concern for the survival of theatre as he understood it is
evident at this stage of his life. After all, his own company had failed due to
financial pressures, part of which were due to putting money into scenic effects.
The use of words such as 'abolire' {to abolish] in the title of his article on film
and 'uccidere' [to kill] in the above pronouncement mark the strength of his
reactions - or over-reactions. Writing *Questa sera si recita a soggetto*
Pirandello envisaged theatre attacked on two interconnected fronts: cinema and
technique. His counter attack is a parodic deconstruction of both. Hinkfuss is
not destroyed, however, in the process; he is chastened, put in his place.
Banished by the very people he is subjecting, who forget their individual
differences and form a group to force him to leave the theatre, it is he who
provides the lighting effects for the scenes the actors improvise on their own.
The talking film gets shorter shrift. In reconstructing a scene where the family
go to the opera, Hinkfuss arranges for the opera they are to see, *La forza del
destino* or *Il trovatore*, to be reproduced by scenic projection on to a white wall
on the stage synchronised with a gramophone on stage and turning to the
audience, he informs them 'Tonfilm' - the German word for talkies. [21]

(d) Actors and acting

From early days Pirandello conceived of drama as the interplay of characters:
'Non il dramma fa le persone; ma queste, il dramma [....] Con esse e in esse
nascerà l'idea del dramma.' [The play does not make people; it is people who
make the play.... The idea of the play will be born with them and in them].[22]

Hence the most important element of theatre is the actor. Pirandello clung to this belief during the period of avantgarde experimentalism, when Gordon Craig was was putting forward theories of the *über marionette*, when the Futurists were creating puppet drama, symbolists were using the human form to create mood and, in Italy, D'Annunzio was creating poetic dramas with statuesque speaking figures. His condemnation of the actor as ineffectual mask, as artifice, stemmed from an unrealistic disappointment that the actor could not *be* the character. [23] To express the impossible magic of theatre Pirandello repeatedly used an image in a poem by Heine called 'Geoffrey Rudèl und Melisande von Tripoli', where the characters woven into a tapestry come down from the wall at night time, alive and real. [24] In the absence of this magic, we have to content ourselves with make-believe. It is actors, Pirandello came to understand after years of work with them (for one of whom he had a very special regard), who had the capacity to make believe. It was they who could guarantee the survival of theatre.

The two most important scenes of *Questa sera si recita a soggetto* in this respect are the those which form the climaxes of the play: the death of Sampognetta and the creation of the scene with Mommina leading to her death. The first occurs in the middle of the third part of the play when the wounded Sampognetta is accompanied home by the singer and a client at the cabaret. The Comic Actor is a problem for the rest of the cast at this point because instead of responding to their speeches with one of his own he just smiles. This causes the dialogue to slacken, and when asked by one of characters struggling to keep the improvisation going why he is smiling, the Comic Actor comes out of his part to say that he is smiling because he is happy to see how much better his colleagues are at improvising than he is. He cannot get the mood right, he explains, because no one responded to his cue and he has not had the training to do a death from cold - he is a comic actor, he is at pains to stress. Why don't they just cut the build-up to his death? He lies down on the sofa and declares 'I'm dead!'

Hinkfuss butts in at this point saying that that will not do and the scene, it seems, is lost. But in justifying himself to Hinkfuss the Comic Actor describes how he had constructed the scene, explaining his character and his reactions to members of the family and to Hinkfuss, working himself into the situation to the extent that he defends himself as if he were being contradicted; inserting the actions, smearing blood on his face from his wounds; momentarily slipping out of the description to ask his colleagues if he's got it right; trying out his last fluttering whistle for which he was known and finally with one arm around The Singer's neck and the other around that of the client he lets his head drop and falls to the ground. The Singer cries out 'Oh God, he's dead, he's dead!' and Mommina throws herself on to her father crying 'Papà, papà mio, papà mio ...' [*MN*, I, 287] [Daddy, daddy, daddy ...] and bursting into real tears in which she is joined by the other actresses. Hinkfuss expresses his delight.

Through Sampognetta's speech we see that what makes a theatrical moment is the input not only from the character who is playing the part, but also from those who contribute to the scene. It is the Singer's cry and Mommina's tears that create Sampognetta's death. But it is also the Comic Actor's ability to create in the audience's mind if not in is own, by the words he uses, the impression of his death. The moment is created by concentration and co-operation. This is ensemble acting at its best, when actors help one another to create the required effect. The other actors' concentration, Sampognetta's carefully thought out character sketch and strategy, and his description all help prepare for the moment when narrative becomes drama. Grammatically this is shown in the speech through the movement from the imperfect 'dovevo parlare...dovevo dire queste cose' to the use of the infinitive dependent on but separate from these verbs: ' - e atterrirvi e farvi piangere - ma piangere davvero - col fiato che non trovo piú, appuntando le labbra cosí - *si prova a formare un fischio che non viene: fhhh. fhhh* - per fare la mia ultima fischiatina; e ecco - *chiama e sé l'Avventore del Cabaret*: - vieni qua anche tu - *gli si appende al collo con l'altro braccio*: cosí - tra voi due - ma piú accosto a te, bella mia - chinare il capo - come fanno presto gli uccellini - e morire' [and terrify you and make you cry - really cry - and I can't find the breath any more - as I try to shape my lips -_ *he tries to whistle. but he can't; "fhhh, fhhh"* to whistle my last song; and then, there - *calling the customer from the cabaret to him*: - come here. You too - *he places his other arm around the customer's neck* - like that - between the two of you - but closer to you, my dear - bow my head - and - quickly, as little birds do - die.] [25] It is as if the actors invoke the theatrical moment by preparing for it through their words and concentration. As Claudio Vicentini puts it, when the actor is performing he seeks 'non tanto di "rappresentare" il personaggio, quanto di "attirarlo" ' [not so much to "represent" the character as to "attract" him]. The function of the actor is not now, as it had been before for Pirandello, to reproduce faithfully the image of the character as conceived in the author's mind, but rather to evoke the character's presence so as to invest the stage with its power.[26] Acting here has more to do with magic than with mimesis. *Questa sera si recita a soggetto*, on this analysis, articulates a stage of Pirandello's thinking about acting that will lead to his final play *I giganti della montagna* [The Mountain Giants].

Something similar occurs later in the same part of *Questa sera si recita a soggetto* when the actors prepare for Mommina and Verri's scene after they have chased Hinkfuss from the theatre. The actors build the scene together. No longer are they squabbling about cue lines, lost opportunities, failing dialogue. The desire to be the characters they have spent time working out takes hold of them; but more importantly, the sense of being a group, of having a joint responsibility to create the scene, propels them. The Character Actress tells her daughter to sit down on the chair a stage hand has brought and, bit by bit, she with the actresses playing Totina, Dorina and Nenè help the Leading Actress become Mommina. Nenè goes off to get make-up, a mirror and a dress; together they make up the Leading Actress to look old, with bags under her eyes, grey on her hair which they dishevel because Verri does not like her to comb her hair; they take the red from her lips, put lines at the corners, arrange her dress to droop at the shoulders. As they do so the lines Pirandello has given them cut into one another, not as interruptions but as parts of long sentences shared by the actresses. There is one pause in the build up when Nenè returns with the makeup box, to take breath, as it were; then a longer sentence begins to form through the collaborative process until the actresses fade into the darkness on stage and Mommina, still referred to in the text as the Leading Actress, knocks her head against the walls to indicate her prison. Each time she touches a wall it is lit sharply from above. After the scene with Verri, where all the actors are referred to in the text by their character names, and the scene when Mommina sings opera to her children, the Leading Actress has become so involved in her part that at Mommina's death she faints. By the end of this scene acting is not seen as action, something that a person does, nor as magic invoked by the actor magician, but as possession. At this point it becomes clearer why Pirandello has selected *'Leonora, addio!'* from among his many short stories for the improvisation: Mommina possessed by opera parallels the actress possessed by Mommina.

It is worth noting that both the climax scenes in this play involve death and are interrupted by Hinkfuss. Death calls for heightened emotion and Pirandello is interested in demonstrating what theatre can do with words, presence and an audience. But death is also the demarcation line between life and theatre. An actor can eat a real meal on stage but he must not die. If he does he is no longer acting. Only acting that is 'lived' is authentic; but lived acting asks too much of actors; it might indeed cost them their lives. Experiment is needed to explore the boundaries of theatre but theatre is also an institution, acting a profession, and some form of protective boundary is required. That protective boundary Pirandello saw as the text, whether author or actor made.[27]

Hinkfuss's interruptions are essential to Pirandello's point. In a letter to his former colleague, Guido Salvini, who was preparing the Italian production of the play Pirandello made it clear that there was not to be an interval after Sampognetta's death, and that Mommina's death must not be the end of the play. Salvini, it seems, was tempted to make of Mommina's death the play's final emotive climax. In the first case, Pirandello explained, it would have been unrealistic of the actors to rebel after the interval, they would have left during it; in the second, it was vitally important that the message of the necessity for some kind of script was clearly heard. [28] In both cases the audience is not to be left, as they are at the end of the second version of *Sei personaggi in cerca d'autore*, inside the emotive illusion of theatre. That illusion must be seen to have been created by the actors through their collaborative work.

Reception

The first two productions of this play took place in Germany; the first in Königsberg, directed by Hans Carl Muller, in January, 1930; the second in Berlin, directed by Gustav Hartung in May of the same year. Pirandello was delighted with the Königsberg production and a letter he wrote to Guido Salvini contains an excited description of the evening. [29] Hartung had taken some liberties with the text which won Pirandello's approval: he had put all the interval scenes which Pirandello had stipulated should be played in various parts of the theatre (the foyer etc.) into the auditorium. This meant that the audience could both participate in the individual group scenes and watch Hinkfuss create his airfield. Pirandello recommended this alteration to Salvini. The Berlin production was quite another story. A review by Herbert Jhering, Berlin's most respected theatre critic, described the fiasco and contributed to the play's poor reception.[30] A number of Berliners mistakenly thought that the opinionated, obstreperous Hinkfuss was e parody of 'their' director Reinhardt and took objection to this. They also found, as did Jhering, the arguments about direction and acting out of touch with current thinking. What was new to Pirandello, fascinated as he was by the German theatrical scene, was already history to Berliners. Pirandello wrote the play during the tail end of the period when the role of the director was under discussion, but by time the it was produced the effects of the Wall Street collapse were already being felt and a different form of theatre was on its way in. That Pirandello was out of sympathy with this can be seen from remarks he made to an interviewer when

asked about his opinions of German dramatists: Pirandello said he liked Georg
Kaiser, Ferdinand Bruckner and a play by Angermayer but added 'Ma se mi è
concessa una critica, devo dire che i nuovi esiti dell'arte drammatica non mi
piacciono molto. Intendo gli esiti che portano al dramma di tendenza. La
tendenza mortifica l'arte' [If I may make a criticism, I'd say that I don't like the
recent wave in theatre. I mean the recent plays that are part of the current
trend. Trends do damage to art]. [31] Here Pirandello is referring to the political
tendency of contemporary German theatre. Most other cities would have been
excited by Pirandello's play - the far away Königsberg genuinely was, Turin
was when Salvini produced the play there in 1930 and Berlin would probably
have been so a year or two earlier; Paris received the play well when Pitoëff
staged it in 1935 and the Living Theatre's production in 1959 was deemed
memorable; [32] but the political atmosphere in Berlin in the early thirties, with
its increasing polarisation of left and right, was not conducive to the
appreciation of an introspective play about the nature of theatre. The first night
audience was unsympathetic to Pirandello's argument, and had neither the
patience nor the inclination to wait for the moving tribute to acting that occurs
in the last part of the play. This, in any case, would have been understood in
Berlin as a denigration of theatre direction, considered a major national
product.

Conclusion

Claudio Vicentini rightly describes *Questa sera si recita a soggetto* as an
historically important play. It is, he says, 'uno dei piú preziosi documenti della
coscienza dell'avanguardia teatrale europea alla fine degli anni venti' [one of
the most precious documents of the consciousness of the avantgarde theatre of
Europe at the end of the twenties]. [33] It combines in one text both the
experience of the avantgarde and a simultaneous critique of it; both a tribute to
the magic of theatre and a consciousness that it is theatre, neither life nor
magic. Theoretically Hinkfuss's activities are excessive; experientially they are
vitally necessary not to the actors' improvisation of *'Leonora, addio!'* but to

Pirandello's play. The procession, the cabaret, the airfield, they too are part of the magic of the evening, and Sampognetta's and Mommina's deaths gain in power from being different from Hinkfuss's extravaganzas. It is regrettable that there have been so few opportunities to see this fascinating and crucial text for, of all Pirandello's plays, this tribute to the theatre needs to be experienced in the theatre.

JENNIFER LORCH

[1] Details of Pirandello's career as theatre director are in A. D'Amico and A. Tinterri, *Pirandello capocomico*, Palermo, Sellerio 1987; see also S Bassnett and J. Lorch, *Luigi Pirandello in the Theatre: a Documentary Record*, Switzerland etc., Harwood Academic Publishers, 1993), pp.87-150.

[2] See G. Giudice, *Luigi Pirandello*, Turin, UTET, 1963, pp. 510-520.

[3] Pirandello was invited by Ugo Ojetti to see the twelve shorts by Louis Lumière at the Studio Fotografico Le Lieure in Rome in March 1896; see F. Càllari, *Pirandello e il cinema*, Venice, Marsilio, 1991, p. 17. Càllari provides a detailed account of all aspects of Pirandello's involvement with film.

[4]. For the development of Pirandello's thought on the cinema, particularly in relation to the *cinéastes* and contemporary debate, see the excellent article, J. Stone, 'Cinéastes Texts', *The Yearbook of the British Pirandello Society*, no.3, 1983, pp. 45-66.

[5] F. Càllari, *Pirandello e il cinema*, cit., p. 10.

[6] L. Pirandello, 'Se il film parlante abolirà il teatro' [*SPSV*, 1030-36]; for an English translation, see S. Bassnett and J. Lorch, *Luigi Pirandello in the Theatre*, cit., pp. 153-7.

[7] 'En confidence' in *Le Temps*, 20 July, 1925. For the notion of theatre as an 'impossible art' see C. Vicentini, 'Pirandello and the problem of Theatre as an Impossible Art', *The Yearbook of the British Pirandello Society*, No. 4, 1984, pp. 1-20. Pirandello first expressed his doubts concerning the efficacy of scenic representation in 'Nell'arte e nella vita. Vignette e scene' in *Il momento*, 1 June 1905, now in Sara Zappulla Muscarà, *Pirandello in guanti gialli*, Caltanissetta-Rome, 1983, pp. 265-271. His ideas are elaborated in the better known and more susbstantial *Illustratori, attori e traduttori* [*SPSV*, 209-224]. For an English translation, S. Bassnett and J. Lorch, *Luigi Pirandello in the Theatre*, cit., pp.23-34. For Pirandello's revision of his ideas on the talking film see F.

Càllari, *Pirandello e il cinema*, cit. pp. 74-7. As early as May of 1930, when *Questa sera si recita a soggetto* was running in Berlin, Pirandello wrote the following to Marta Abba: 'Bisogna orientarsi verso una nuova espressione d'arte: il film parlato. Ero contrario; mi sono ricreduto' [We must move towards a new artistic expression: the talking film. I was against it: I've now changed my mind]. See F. Càllari, *Pirandello e il cinema*, cit., p. 10.

8   C. Alvaro, *Cronache e scritti teatrali*, ed. A. Barbina, Rome, 1976. pp. 76-86; for an English translation, see S. Bassnett and J. Lorch, *Luigi Pirandello in the Theatre* (op. cit.), pp. 104-8.

9   See sections on the plays mentioned in A. D'Amico and A. Tinterri, *Pirandello capocomico*, cit.; C. Vicentini, *Pirandello, Il disagio del teatro*, Venice, Marsilio, 1993, pp. 122-4.

10   See C. Vicentini, *Pirandello. Il disagio del teatro*, cit., p. 125-6.

11   The autograph of this rough copy (it is not known whether a fair copy was actually sent to Pirandello) is in the Museo dell'Attore, Genoa; for the full text in English translation, see S. Bassnett and J. Lorch, *Luigi Pirandello in the Theatre*, cit., pp. 129-130.

12   See M. Cometa, *Il teatro di Pirandello in Germania*, Palermo, Novecento, 1986, pp. 30-221 for details of German productions of Pirandello's plays and pp. 285-317 for information concerning Pirandello's stay in Berlin and the German productions of *Questa sera si recita a soggetto*.

13   See John Willett, *The Theatre of the Weimar Republic*, New York/London, 1988, p. 206. This section on 'the Theatre Scene in Germany' is indebted to John Willett's lucid and detailed account, especially chapters 4, 7 and 10.

14   See C. Vicentini, *Pirandello. Il disagio del teatro* , cit., p. 128.

15   See G. Corsinovi, '*Questa sera si recita a soggetto:* il testo. Tra progettazione vitalistica e partitura musicale', in R. Alonge et al., *Testo e messa in scena in Pirandello*, Rome, La Nuova Italia Scientifica, 1986, pp. 105-132, especially pp. 115-121; and G. Corsinovi, '*Questa sera si recita a soggetto*: dalla "rappresentazione" allo "spettacolo", dalla "riproduzione" alla "creazione scenica" ', in *Le due trilogie pirandelliane*, ed. J. C. Barnes and S. Milioto, Palermo, Palumbo, 1992, pp. 63-70.

16   M. L. Aguirre D'Amico, *Vivere con Pirandello*, Milan, Mondadori, 1989, p. 124.

17   *'Leonora, addio!'* was later collected into the the volume *Il viaggio*, vol. 12 of *Novelle per un anno*, Bemporad, Florence, 1928.

[18] Hinckefuss was the name of Pirandello's landlord in Hitzigstrasse, Berlin from 15 December 1928 to 15 February, 1929; see G. Giudice, *Luigi Pirandello*, cit., p. 501, n. 1.

[19]. See C. Vicentini, 'La trilogia pirandelliana del teatro nel teatro e le proposte della teatralità futurista', *The Yearbook of the British Pirandello Society*, no. 3, 1983, pp. 15-32; more recently, Professor Vicentini has further refined his argument in his important *Pirandello. Il disagio del teatro*, cit., pp. 141-151

[20] See the interview with Corrado Alvaro in *L'Italia letteraria*, 14 April, 1929, now in M. Cometa. *Il teatro di Pirandello in Germania*, cit., p. 29.

[21] See C. Vicentini, *Pirandello. Il disagio del teatro*, cit., p. 183.

[22] *L'azione parlata* (1899) in L. Pirandello, *SPSV*, cit., p. 1061; for an English translation of this essay, see S. Bassnett and J. Lorch, *Luigi Pirandello in the Theatre*, cit., pp. 20-23.

[23] *Illustratori, attori e traduttori*, cit., pp. 215, 218. See note 7 for English translation.

[24] Heine's poem in his collection *Romancero*, 1851. See Hal Draper (tr.), *The Complete Poems of Heinrich Heine*, Boston, 1982, for an English version.

[25] *Questa sera si recita e soggetto* in L. Pirandello, *MN*, I, Milan, Mondadori, 1962, pp. 286-7; for English translation, see *Tonight We Improvise and 'Leonore, Addio'*, tr. and ed. J. Douglas Campbell and Leonard G. Sbrocchi, *Biblioteca di Quaderni d'italianistica*, vol. 3, 1987, pp. 86-7.

[26] See C. Vicentini, Pirandello. *Il disagio del teatro*, cit., p. 175.

[27] See Pirandello's explanation of the end of the play in a letter to Guido Salvini, dated 30.3.1930, held in Museo dell'Attore, Genoa. For an English translation see S. Bassnett and J. Lorch, *Pirandello in the Theatre*, cit., p. 163: 'The actors cannot do this every evening. At an enormous cost of effort and energy, they can do it for one evening. The actors must have a part to play. And so the dramatist is needed to provide it for them. This is what is really expressed, but perhaps in too condensed a way, implicit rather than clearly stated'. At this point Pirandello rewrites the last few lines of the play to clarify it for Salvini.

[28] As above, p.162.

[29] As above, pp. 160-62.

[30] Jhering's review is now in H. Jhering *Von Reinhardt bis Brecht, III. 1930-32*, Berlin, Aufbau-Verlag, 1961; for an English translation see S. Bassnett and J. Lorch, *Pirandello in the theatre*, cit., pp. 165-6.

[31] See M. Cometa, *Il teatro di Pirandello in Germania*, cit., p. 294

[32] For descriptions of some of these productions and accompanying slides, see F. Firth, *Pirandello in Performance*, Cambridge and Alexandria, VA, Chadwyck-Healey, 1990.

[33] See. C. Vicentini, *Pirandello. Il disagio del teatro*, cit., p.139.

Bibliography of works on Pirandello cited.

Aguirre D'Amico, M. L., *Vivere con Pirandello*, Milan Mondadori, 1989.

Artioli, U., *L'officina segreta di Pirandello*, Bari, Laterza, 1989.

Alberti, C., *Il teatro dei pupi e lo spettacolo popolare siciliano*, Milan, Mursia, 1977.

Alonge, R., *Pirandello tra realismo e mistificazione*, Naples, Guida, 1972.

Alonge, R., *Missiroli. I giganti della montagna*, Turin, Multimmagini, 1980.

Alonge, R., 'Pirandello, l'attore, il regista' in AA. VV., *Pirandello e il teatro del suo tempo*, Palermo, Palumbo, 1985, pp.

Alonge, R., *Teatro e spettacolo nel secondo Ottocento*, Bari, Laterza, 1993 (2nd ed.).

Alvaro, C., *Cronache e scritti teatrali*, ed. A. Barbina, Rome, Abete, 1976.

Altieri Biagi, M. L., *La lingua in scena*, Bologna, Zanichelli, 1980.

Angelini, F., *Teatro e spettacolo nel primo Novecento*, Bari, Laterza, 1988.

Angelini, F., *Serafino e la tigre: Pirandello tra scrittura teatro e cinema*, Venice, Marsilio, 1990.

AA. VV., *Il teatro nel teatro di Pirandello*, Agrigento, Edizioni del Centro Nazionale di Studi Pirandelliani, 1977.

AA. VV., *Pirandello saggista*, Palermo, Palumbo, 1982.

AA. VV., *Pirandello e il teatro del suo tempo*, Palermo, Palumbo, 1983.

AA. VV., *Pirandello e la cultura del suo tempo*, Agrigento, Edizioni del Centro Nazionale di Studi Pirandelliani, 1983.

AA. VV., *Teatro e messa in scena di Pirandello*, Rome, La Nuova Italia Scientifica, 1986.

AA. VV., *Pirandello e D'Annunzio*, Palermo, Palumbo, 1989.

AA. VV., *La persona nell'opera di Luigi Pirandello*, Milan, Mursia, 1990.

AA. VV., *Pirandello e l'oltre*, Milan, Mursia, 1991.

AA. VV., *Pirandello e la politica*, Milan, Mursia, 1992.

AA. VV. , *Pirandello e il teatro*, Milan, Mursia, 1993.

Bárberi Squarotti, G., *Le sorti del tragico*, Ravenna, Longo, 1978.

Barnes, J. C., Milioto, S., (eds), *Le due trilogie pirandelliane*, Palermo, Palumbo, 1992.

Bassnett, S., Lorch, J. (eds), *Luigi Pirandello in the Theatre*, Switzerland etc., Harwood Academic Publishers, 1993.

Bassnett, S., 'Female Masks: Luigi Pirandello's Plays for Women' in B. Docherty (ed.), *Twentieth-Century European Drama*, London, MacMillan, 1994, pp. 13-25.

Bassnett-McGuire, S., *Luigi Pirandello*, London, MacMillan, 1983.

Bentley, E., *The Pirandello Commentaries*, Evanston, Illinois, Northwestern University Press, 1986.

Bloom, H. (ed.), *Luigi Pirandello*, New York, Chelsea Hine, 1989.

Bragaglia, L., *Carteggio Pirandello-Ruggeri*, Fano, Biblioteca Comunale Federiciana, 1987.

Brustein, R 'Luigi Pirandello' in *The Theatre of Revolt*, London, Methuen, 1965, pp. 279-317.

286

Caesar, A., 'The Branding of Women: Family, Theatre and Female Identity in Pirandello' in *Italian Studies*, XLV, 1990, pp. 48-63.

Càllari, F., *Pirandello e il cinema*, Venice, Marsilio, 1991.

Cardillo, M., *Tra le quinte del cinematografo: cinema, cultura e società in Italia. 1900-1937*, Bari, Dedalo, 1987.

Cometa, M., *Il Teatro di Pirandello in Germania*, Palermo, Novecento, 1985.

Corsinovi, G., *Pirandello e l'espressionismo: analogie culturali e anticipazioni espressive nella prima narrativa*, Genoa, Tilgher, 1979.

Croce, B., *La letteratura italiana*, vol. 4, Bari, Laterza, 1963.

D'Amico, A., Tinterri, A., *Pirandello capocomico. La compagnia del Teatro d'Arte di Roma, 1925-1928*, Palermo, Sellerio, 1987.

D'Amico, S. (ed.), *Storia del teatro italiano*, Milan, Bompiani, 1936.

Dashwood, J. R., Everson, J. E., *Writers and Performers in Italian Drama from the Time of Dante to Pirandello*, Lewiston, Queenston, Lampeter, The Edwin Mellen Press, 1991.

Davico Bonino (ed.), *La 'prima' dei 'Sei personaggi in cerca d'autore'*, Turin, Editrice Tirrenia Stampatori, 1983.

De Felice, F., *Storia del teatro siciliano*, Catania, Giannotta, 1956.

DiGaetani, J. L., (ed.), *A Companion to Pirandello Studies*, New York, Westport, Connecticut, London, Greenwood Press, 1991.

Dombroski, R., *Le totalità dell'artificio: ideologia e forma nel romanzo di Pirandello*, Padua, Liviana, 1978.

Firth, F., *Pirandello in Performance*, Cambridge and Alexandria, VA, Chadwyck-Healey, 1990.

Gioanola, E., *Pirandello la follia*, Genoa, Il Melangolo, 1983.

Giovanelli, P. D. (ed.), *Pirandello poeta*, Florence, Vallecchi, 1981.

Giudice, G., *Luigi Pirandello*, Turin, UTET, 1963

Granatella, L. (ed.), *L'ultimo Pirandello*, Brescia, Comune di Brescia, 1988.

Guercio, *Sicily, the Garden of the Mediterranean: the Country and its People*, London, Faber, 1938.

Günsberg, M., 'Hysteria as Theatre: Pirandello's Hysterical Women' in *The Yearbook of the Society for Pirandello Studies*, 12, 1992, pp. 32-52.

Günsberg, M., *Patriarchal Representations. Gender and Discourse in Pirandello's Theatre*, Oxford/Providence, Berg, 1994.

Krysinski, W., *Il paradigma inquieto. Pirandello e lo spazio comparativo della modernità*, trans. C. Donati, Rome, Edizioni Scientifiche Italiane, 1988.

Lauretta, E., (ed.), *I Miti di Pirandello*, Palermo, Palumbo, 1975.

Lauretta, E., (ed.), *Il romanzo di Pirandello*, s.l., Palumbo, 1976.

Leone de Castris, A., *Storia di Pirandello*, Bari, Laterza, 1971 (revised ed.).

Lepschy, A. L., 'The treatment of antefact in Pirandello's theatre' in *The Yearbook of the British Pirandello Society*, 8 & 9, 1988-1989, pp. 68-90.

Lepschy, A. L., 'The Treatment of the Antefact in Pirandello's Theatre in the Theatre Trilogy', in J. R. Dashwood and J. E.Everson (eds), *Writers and Performers in Italian Drama from the Time of Dante to Pirandello*, Lewiston, Queenston, Lampeter, The Edwin Mellen Press, 1991.

Lorch, J., 'Philip Stone; Pirandellian Actor' in *The Yearbook of the British Pirandello Society*, 1, 1981, pp. 19-25.

Lugnani, L., *L'infanzia felice e altri saggi su Pirandello*, Naples, Liguori, 1986.

Luperini, R., 'L'atto del significare allegorico nei *Sei personaggi* e in *Enrico IV*, in *Rivista di studi pirandelliani*, IX, 1991, Nos 6-7, pp. 9-19.

Luperini, R., *Introduzione a Pirandello*, Rome-Bari, Laterza, 1992.

Macchia, G., *Pirandello o la stanza della tortura*, Milan, Mondadori, 1981.

McFarlane. J, 'Neo-modernist Drama: Yeats and Pirandello' in M. Bradbury, J. McFarlane (eds) *Modernism. A Guide to European Literature. 1890-1930*, London, Penguin, 1976 (1991 reprint), pp. 561-570.

Meda, A., *Bianche statue contro il nero abisso. Il teatro dei miti in Pirandello e D'Annunzio*, Ravenna, Longo, 1993.

Milioto, S. (ed.), *Gli atti unici di Pirandello (tra narrativa e teatro)*, Agrigento, Edizioni del Centro Nazionale di Studi Prandelliani, 1978.

Monti, S., *Pirandello*, Palermo, Palumbo, 1980.

Nardelli, F. V., *L'uomo segreto: vita e croci di Luigi Pirandello*, s.l., Mondadori, 1944 (2nd ed.).

Nencioni, G., *Tra grammatica e retorica. Da Dante a Pirandello*, Turin, Einaudi, 1983.

Puppa, P., *Fantasmi contro giganti*, Bologna, Patròn, 1987.

Ragusa, O., *Pirandello: An Approach to his Theatre*, Edinburgh, Edinburgh University Press, 1980.

Raffaelli, S., *Il cinema nella lingua di Pirandello*, Rome, Bulzoni, 1993.

Richards, L., ' "Il buco nel cielo di carta": Pirandello's *Enrico IV* and Sophocles' *Philoctetes*', *The Yearbook of the Society for Pirandello Studies*, 12 (1992), 55-63.

Russo, L., 'Il noviziato letterario di Luigi Pirandello' in *Ritratti e disegni storici*, 4th series, Bari, Laterza, 1953.

Scrivano, R., *La vocazione contesa*, Rome, Bulzoni, 1987.

Sipala, P. M., *Capuana e Pirandello. Storia e testi di una relazione letteraria*, Catania, Bonanno, 1974.

Sogliuzzo, A. R., *Luigi Pirandello, Director: the Playwright in the Theatre*, New Jersey and London, Scarecrow Press, 1982.

Stone, J., 'Cinéastes texts', in *The Yearbook of the British Pirandello Society*, No. 3 (1983), pp. 45-66.

Taviani, F.,'*Sei personaggi*, due interviste in una al primo padre', in *Teatro e storia*, VII, 1992, No. 2, pp. 295-328

Vicentini, C., 'Pirandello and the Problem of Theatre as an Impossible Art', in *The Yearbook of the British Pirandello Society*, No. 4 (1984), pp. 1-20.

Vicentini, C., *L'estetica di Pirandello*, Milan, Mursia, 1985 (2nd ed.)

Vicentini, C., *Pirandello. Il disagio del teatro*, Venice, Marsilio, 1993.

Villa, E., *Dinamica narrativa di Luigi Pirandello*, Padua, Liviana, 1976.

Zappulla Muscarà, S., *Pirandello in guanti gialli*, Caltanissetta-Rome, Sciascia, 1983.

INDEX

This index covers pages 1-284. It does not include the bibliography.

FULVIA AIROLDI NAMER is Professor of Italian at the Université de Paris-Sorbonne, Paris IV. Her numerous publications have included articles and essays on Italian theatre, from Goldoni to the twentieth century. She is the author of *Massimo Bontempelli* (1979).

JOHN C. BARNES is Professor of Italian at University College, Dublin. He has published extensively on Dante, and among his recent publications on Pirandello are his edition of *Il berretto a sonagli* (1990) and *Le due trilogie pirandelliane* (with S. Milioto) (1992).

MARY CASEY is a researcher at University College Dublin, and is a well-known director and translator. She gives a director's view of *Il berretto a sonagli* in the edition of the play prepared by John Barnes (1990).

JULIE DASHWOOD is Head of the Italian Department at the University of Leicester. She has published widely on modern Italian theatre, especially on Futurism and Pirandello. She is co-editor of *Writers and Performers in Italian Drama from the Time of Dante to Pirandello* (1991).

CORRADO DONATI is Professor of Italian Literature at the University of Trento. He is the author of many articles and essays on periodicals and narrative in early twentieth-century Italy. His works on Pirandello include *La solitudine allo specchio* (1980), *Bibliografia della critica pirandelliana (1962-1981)* (1986), *Il sogno e la ragione. Saggi pirandelliani* (1993) and *Pirandello nel linguaggio della scena. Materiali bibliografici dai quotidiani italiani (1962-1990)* (with Anna T. Ossani) (1993)

FELICITY FIRTH was until recently Senior Lecturer in Italian at the University of Bristol. She has published widely on Italian theatre, and her works on Pirandello include her edition of Luigi Pirandello, *Three Plays* (1969) and *Pirandello in Performance* (1990). She is one of the leading translators of Pirandello's plays into English, and is currently Chairperson of the Pirandello Society.

ANN HALLAMORE CAESAR is Lecturer in Italian at the University of Cambridge and a Fellow of Corpus Christi College. Her publications include articles on nineteenth- and twentieth-century Italian literature, from the *Scapigliati* to Francesca Sanvitale. She is currently writing a comparative study of Pirandello and Wedekind.

ANNA LAURA LEPSCHY is Professor of Italian and Head of Department at University College, London. She has edited S. Brasca, *Viaggio in Terrasanta. 1480* (1966) and is the author of *Tintoretto Observed* (1983), *Narrativa e teatro fra due secoli: Verga, Invernizio, Svevo, Pirandello* (1984) and coauthor with G.Lepschẏ of *The Italian Language Today* (1991; new Italian edition 1993).

JENNIFER LORCH is Senior Lecturer in Italian at the University of Warwick. Her publications include articles and essays on Italian theatre from the *commedia dell'arte* to the modern period, and she has recently co-edited (with Susan Bassnett) *Luigi Pirandello in the Theatre* (1993).

ÉANNA P. Ó CEALLACHÁIN lectures in the Department of Italian at the University of Glasgow. His work has been mainly in the modern period, especially on the Nobel Prize winning poet Eugenio Montale, as well as on Pirandello himself.